Contents

(continued over)

FENCING

a practical handbook

Written and illustrated by Elizabeth Agate

Cover illustration by Anne Roper

Fencing is one of a series of conservation handbooks.
Production costs have been grant-aided by the Countryside
Commission, the Carnegie United Kingdom Trust and the
TWIL Group Marketing Ltd. (Sentinel Fencing).

ISBN 0 946752 04 4

First published in 1986

This reprint January 1994

Printed by the Eastern Press Ltd., Read

Acknowledgements

The British Trust for Conservation Volunteers acknowledges with thanks the help it has received in producing this publication from the following individuals and organisations:

Agricultural Training Board

Sean Adcock

Rod Armstrong

Alison Boden

Jo Burgon

Pete Cloke

Countryside Commission for Scotland

G Holland

Terry Howard

Tom Hynes

Christine James

Karl Liebscher

H W Pepper

Jeff Redgrave

Gerry Smith

L A Tee

Tim Turner

William Waddilove

The Publications Committee of the British Trust for Conservation Volunteers, and other volunteers who have contributed their advice and experience.

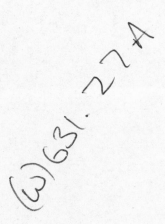

Thanks to Stephen Williams for proofreading.

Typed and prepared for printing by Elizabeth Agate.

Introduction

This is a handbook about the design and construction of fences, and is one of a series of handbooks on practical conservation. Although primarily aimed at readers who are concerned with the management of land for conservation and amenity, many of the materials and techniques described are applicable to fences built purely for agricultural or other purposes.

As with most other projects, the design, materials and workmanship used in fencing are all important in building a functional and long-lasting structure. A fence that is below standard in any of these respects will sooner or later become susceptible to damage by the stock or people it is intended to control. A damaged fence only creates more problems, and soon gets into a downward spiral of damage and disrepair.

The main uses of fencing directly for conservation management are to protect newly planted trees, to enclose established or ageing woodlands where regeneration is needed, and for access control. Another important use is to allow grazing to be established as a tool to manage open land such as grassland and heathland. In many places, the loss of grassland and heathland to coarser vegetation is occurring due to the decline of stock-grazing on marginal land, and the demise of the rabbit population. Fencing can allow controlled grazing to be re-established, to benefit both habitat and stock, and may permit amenity use of the land as well. In other places, fences are needed to exclude stock from over-grazing and damaging delicate vegetation.

It is interesting to note how the changes in techniques to enclose land by fencing have been triggered by the need to develop new lands for agriculture. Barbed wire fencing was first widely used in America for the enclosing of vast areas for cattle ranching, and more recently, the use of electric and high tensile fencing has been developed in New Zealand for more efficient and intensive sheep farming. Britain, with its ancient field boundaries, many hedged or walled, has had less need to develop new methods of fencing. This is possibly still reflected in the fact that, as a general rule, agricultural fencing in lowland Britain involves mainly repairing existing boundaries, or erecting post and wire fences where hedges are no longer stock-proof for cattle. In contrast, fencing in upland areas, and particularly for sheep, is a much more important consideration in the management of the land. In general then, the newer techniques of fencing are being more rapidly adopted in upland Britain.

Much conservation management, such as hedging and walling, involve traditional techniques. The construction of wooden post and rail fences and gates can be included amongst these traditional, and still valuable, skills. However, management for conservation must also look forward, and the recent developments in post and wire fencing are examples of modern craftsmanship, requiring higher levels of skills than those used previously. The results may be non-traditional, and will not have the ecological or aesthetic value of hedges and walls, but are part of a managed, diverse and thriving countryside. A good example of the use of modern techniques is on the Lizard Peninsula, Cornwall, where permanent electric high tensile fencing has been used to allow cattle to re-establish and maintain the specialist short-sward grassland. This type of fence is not only economical, but has lightweight, infrequently-spaced posts of naturally insulating hardwood (see p96), which are very unobtrusive, so the fence does not mar the magnificent coastal landscape. It has also proved to be reliable through three years of full exposure to the Atlantic gales.

The first chapter of this handbook includes 28 different fence designs, illustrated from pages 7-15, with information on the cost and use of each type. Further information on how to build the different fences is given in chapters 4, 5, 6 and 7. Chapter 8 gives more detail on specific ideas and techniques for conservation management.

Throughout the text, sequential operations are ordered 1, 2, 3 etc, and other points a, b, c etc.

Most wire fencing materials are supplied in metric units, and therefore metric measurements are mainly used in this handbook. However, some materials, particularly wooden fencing and gates, are supplied in imperial measurements, and are thus given in these, with metric equivalents.

1 Design and Siting

Fence Types

The main types of fences are described below, with examples of designs given on the following pages.

Strained fencing

Strained wire fencing is the usual type of rural fencing, because of its versatility, ease of erection, and relatively low cost. Wires of various thicknesses and strengths can be chosen to suit the situation and the use, and the fence can be made of single wires or netting, or a combination of both.

All strained wire fences are built on a similar principle, with wire stretched between two or more large posts, called straining posts, and with stakes used to stiffen the fence and keep the wires the correct distance apart. The stakes are driven into the ground, rather than being set in dug holes, making fence erection a quick job for skilled hands.

Strained wire fences are best suited to long fence lines over fairly level or smoothly sloping terrain, where straining posts can be set the maximum distance apart. It is less easy, and more expensive in materials, to build a strong strained fence over uneven terrain, or with many changes of direction.

The life of a strained wire fence will depend on the type of timber and preservative treatment given, the weight of wire and galvanising, and the rate of corrosion, which is higher in coastal and polluted air. As with any fence, the standard to which it is built, and the use it receives, will also affect the life of the fence. A poorly built strained wire fence will rapidly become slack and no longer stockproof, and can be awkward to repair if the straining posts are not satisfactory.

Other types of fencing materials can be strained, such as chestnut paling, and some of the new synthetic webbing materials.

The materials and techniques for strained fencing are described in chapter 4, and the procedure for erecting a fence in chapter 5.

Post and rail fencing

This is used for high quality fences where appearance and durability are important. Post and rail has a traditional rural appearance which makes it acceptable in most situations.

It is more expensive than strained wire fencing, and also takes longer to erect. Posts must be set at carefully measured distances, and for some designs, all posts are set in dug holes.

Post and rail has the advantage of needing no special tools to erect, and can be fitted to any terrain or line of fence. Unlike strained fencing, if one section gets damaged, the whole length does not lose it rigidity. Nailed rails are easy to mend if broken or dislodged. Provided that durable or preserved timber is used, and any damage is repaired as necessary, a post and rail fence can have a very long life.

Post and rail fencing can have wire netting or single line wires added to make it stock proof for sheep, lambs or other stock. The addition of overlapping vertical boards, called pales, makes a strong fence for screening or security.

Panel fencing

This is a fence of prefabricated panels, attached to posts at set intervals. Many different types and sizes of panels are available.

A simple and traditional type of panel fencing are woven hazel hurdles, usually attached to stakes driven into the ground.

Post and rail fencing and panel fencing are described in chapter 6.

Electric fencing

This is a lightweight strained fence, but different in principle to all other types of fences. The electric shock acts as a psychological barrier, thus the fence itself does not have to present such a strong physical barrier. Lighter and cheaper components can therefore be used, as there is less danger of animals leaning on the fence or trying to break through.

The disadvantage is that electric fencing needs frequent supervision and maintenance to keep it in working order, as once the psychological barrier is lost, the fence may become useless as a barrier to stock. Non-electrified temporary netting can be dangerous to animals, as they can become ensnared in it as they push their heads through to graze on the other side.

Types of electric fencing vary from simple temporary fences to complex permanent systems. They are described in chapter 7.

Twenty-eight fence designs are shown on the following pages, with uses and approximate prices per metre of materials. A table comparing the costs, and including labour costs, is on page 19.

1. STOCK NETTING — lightweight

Stakes (round)
1.7m x 63 mm diam.

Straining posts (round)
2.1m x 125 mm diam.

Struts (round)
2.1m x 100 mm diam.

Stock netting
C8/80/30

Wire 4mm mild steel

Staples 40mm

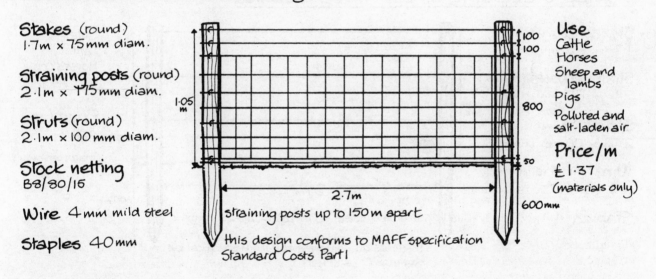

100
100
1.05 m
800
50
2.7m
600mm

straining posts up to 150m apart

this design conforms to MAFF specification
Standard Costs Part 1

Use
Cattle
Horses
Sheep
For lambs use
C8/80/15 netting

Price/m
£1.00
(materials only)

2. STOCK NETTING — heavyweight

Stakes (round)
1.7m x 75 mm diam.

Straining posts (round)
2.1m x 175 mm diam.

Struts (round)
2.1m x 100 mm diam.

Stock netting
B8/80/15

Wire 4mm mild steel

Staples 40mm

100
100
1.05 m
800
50
2.7m
600mm

straining posts up to 150m apart

this design conforms to MAFF specification
Standard Costs Part 1

Use
Cattle
Horses
Sheep and
lambs
Pigs
Polluted and
salt-laden air

Price/m
£1.37
(materials only)

3. STOCK NETTING — high tensile

Stakes (round)
1.7m x 75 mm diam.

Straining posts (round)
2.1m x 175 mm diam.

Struts (round)
2.1m x 100 mm diam.

Stock netting
high tensile HT 8/80/30

Wire 2.64mm spring steel

Staples 40mm

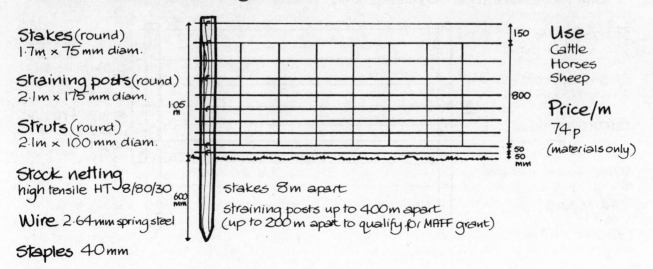

150
800
50
50 mm
1.05 m
600mm

stakes 8m apart

straining posts up to 400m apart
(up to 200 m apart to qualify for MAFF grant)

Use
Cattle
Horses
Sheep

Price/m
74p
(materials only)

4. SPRING STEEL LINE WIRES — with stock netting
based on Forestry Commission specification

Stakes (round)
1.7m × 100mm diam

Straining posts (round)
2.3m × 150mm diam

Struts (round)
2.3m × 100mm diam

Wire
2.64mm spring steel

Netting C8/80/15

Fence connectors
Lashing rods **Staples**

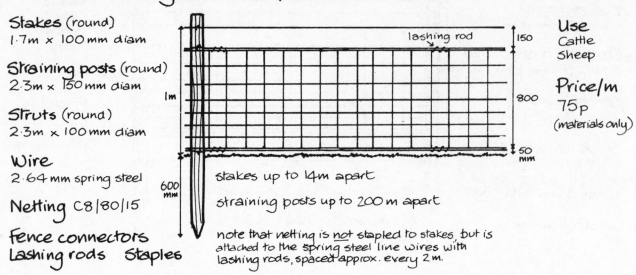

stakes up to 14m apart

straining posts up to 200m apart

note that netting is <u>not</u> stapled to stakes, but is attached to the spring steel line wires with lashing rods, spaced approx. every 2m.

Use
Cattle
Sheep

Price/m
75p
(materials only)

---

5. MILD STEEL LINE WIRES — three line wires

Stakes (round)
1.7m × 63mm diam.

Straining posts (round)
2.1m × 125mm diam.

Struts (round)
2.1m × 100mm diam.

Wire 4mm mild steel
or 2 strand 12½g barbed wire

Staples 40mm

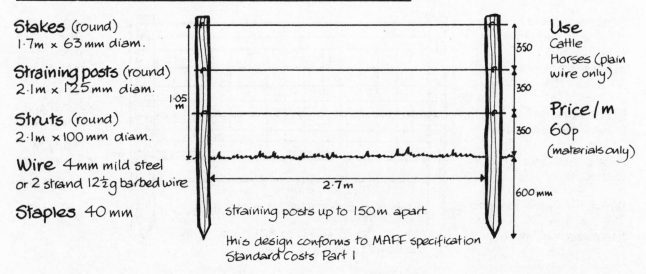

straining posts up to 150m apart

this design conforms to MAFF specification Standard Costs Part 1

Use
Cattle
Horses (plain wire only)

Price/m
60p
(materials only)

---

6. MILD STEEL LINE WIRES — seven line wires
with radisseurs to allow retensioning

Stakes (round)
1.7m × 75mm diam.

Straining posts (round)
2.1m × 175mm diam.

Struts (round)
2.1m × 75mm diam.

Wire 4mm mild steel

Radisseurs
(see p. 58)

Staples 40mm

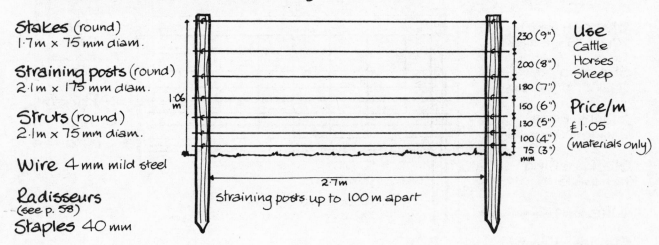

straining posts up to 100m apart

Use
Cattle
Horses
Sheep

Price/m
£1.05
(materials only)

7. HIGH TENSILE LINE WIRES – with wooden droppers

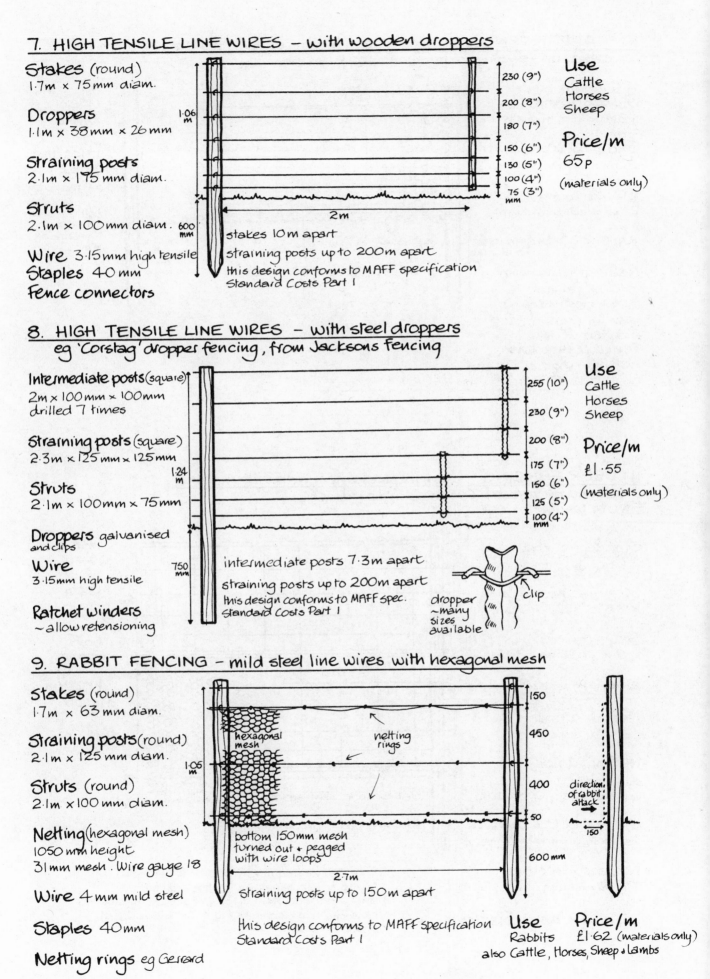

Stakes (round)
1·7m × 75mm diam.

Droppers
1·1m × 38mm × 26mm

Straining posts
2·1m × 175mm diam.

Struts
2·1m × 100mm diam.

Wire 3·15mm high tensile
Staples 40mm
Fence connectors

1·06 m

230 (9")
200 (8")
180 (7")
150 (6")
130 (5")
100 (4")
75 (3")
mm

2m

600 mm

stakes 10m apart
straining posts up to 200m apart
this design conforms to MAFF specification
Standard Costs Part 1

Use
Cattle
Horses
Sheep

Price/m
65p
(materials only)

8. HIGH TENSILE LINE WIRES – with steel droppers
eg 'Corstag' dropper fencing, from Jacksons fencing

Intermediate posts (square)
2m × 100mm × 100mm
drilled 7 times

Straining posts (square)
2·3m × 125mm × 125mm

Struts
2·1m × 100mm × 75mm

Droppers galvanised
and clips

Wire
3·15mm high tensile

Ratchet winders
~ allow retensioning

1·24 m

255 (10")
230 (9")
200 (8")
175 (7")
150 (6")
125 (5")
100 (4")
mm

750 mm

intermediate posts 7·3m apart
straining posts up to 200m apart
this design conforms to MAFF spec.
Standard Costs Part 1

dropper
~ many
sizes
available

clip

Use
Cattle
Horses
Sheep

Price/m
£1·55
(materials only)

9. RABBIT FENCING – mild steel line wires with hexagonal mesh

Stakes (round)
1·7m × 63mm diam.

Straining posts (round)
2·1m × 125mm diam.

Struts (round)
2·1m × 100mm diam.

Netting (hexagonal mesh)
1050mm height
31mm mesh. Wire gauge 18

Wire 4mm mild steel

Staples 40mm

Netting rings eg Gerrard

1·05 m

hexagonal
mesh

netting
rings

150
450
400
50
600 mm

direction
of rabbit
attack

150

bottom 150mm mesh
turned out + pegged
with wire loops

2·7m

straining posts up to 150m apart

this design conforms to MAFF specification
Standard Costs Part 1

Use
Rabbits
also Cattle, Horses, Sheep + Lambs

Price/m
£1·62 (materials only)

9

10. RABBIT FENCING – spring steel line wires with hexagonal mesh
based on Forestry Commission specification

Stakes (round)
1.8m × 75mm diam

Straining posts (round)
2.3m × 125mm. diam

Struts (round)
2.3m × 100mm diam

Wire 2.64mm spring steel

Netting (hexagonal mesh)
1050mm height
31mm mesh 18gauge

Staples 40mm
Fence connectors
Netting rings eg Gerrard

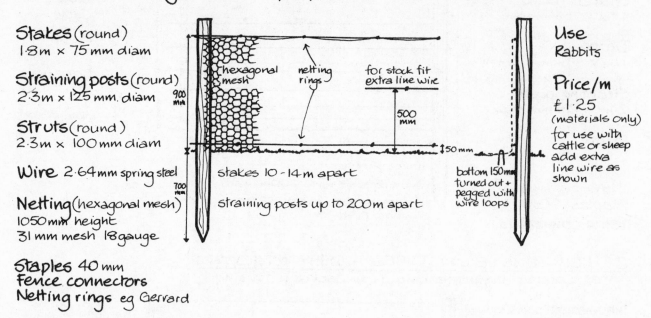

hexagonal mesh

netting rings

for stock fit extra line wire

900 mm

500 mm

150mm

stakes 10-14m apart

straining posts up to 200m apart

700 mm

bottom 150mm turned out + pegged with wire loops

Use
Rabbits

Price/m
£1.25
(materials only)

for use with cattle or sheep add extra line wire as shown

---

11. DEER FENCING – spring steel line wires with netting
based on Forestry Commission specification

Stakes (round)
2.5m × 100mm diam

Straining posts (round)
2.8m × 150mm diam

Struts (round)
2.5m × 125mm diam

Wire 2.64m spring steel

Netting – upper
C6/90/30 stock netting

Netting – lower
a) deer only
or deer + sheep: C6/90/30

b) deer + rabbit: 1050mm wide
hex. mesh, 31mm mesh, 18 gauge

Fence connectors
~ for terminating + joining line wires

Lashing rods   Staples

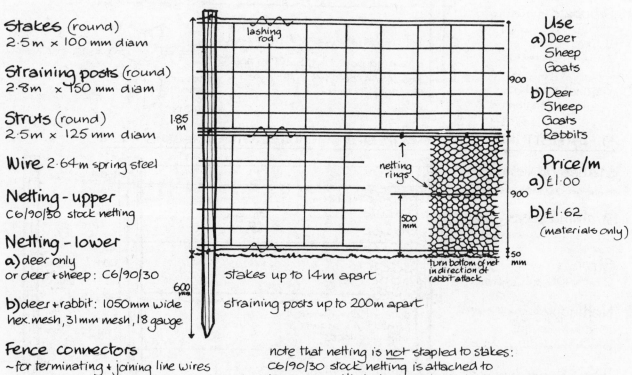

lashing rod

1.85 m

netting rings

500 mm

stakes up to 14m apart

straining posts up to 200m apart

600 mm

turn bottom of net in direction of rabbit attack

900

900

50 mm

Use
a) Deer
Sheep
Goats

b) Deer
Sheep
Goats
Rabbits

Price/m
a) £1.00

b) £1.62
(materials only)

note that netting is <u>not</u> stapled to stakes:
C6/90/30 stock netting is attached to
line wires with lashing rods, at approx. 2m intervals;
hexagonal mesh is attached with netting rings, at
approx. 500mm intervals.

12. DEER FENCING – high tensile netting
eg 'Hurricane', 'Cyclone'

Stakes (round)
2·5 m × 75 mm diam

Straining posts (round)
2·8m × 150 mm diam

Struts (round)
2·5m × 125 mm diam

Netting
high tensile HT 13/190/15

Fence connectors

Staples

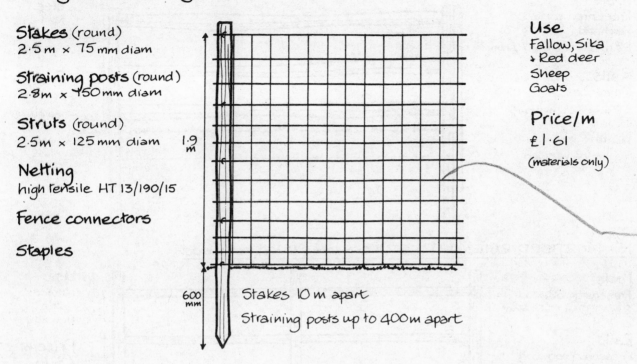

1·9 m

600 mm

Stakes 10 m apart

Straining posts up to 400m apart

Use
Fallow, Sika
+ Red deer
Sheep
Goats

Price/m
£1·61
(materials only)

13. CHESTNUT PALING

Stakes (round)
2·1m × 75 mm diam

Straining posts (round)
2·1m × 180 mm diam

Struts (round)
2·1m × 75 mm diam

Chestnut paling
1·5m high; pales at 75mm
centres. Many other sizes
available

Staples 40mm

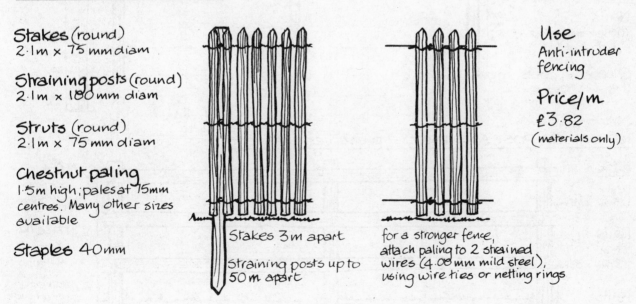

Stakes 3m apart

Straining posts up to
50 m apart

for a stronger fence,
attach paling to 2 strained
wires (4.00 mm mild steel),
using wire ties or netting rings

Use
Anti-intruder
fencing

Price/m
£3·82
(materials only)

14. RIVEN OAK POST AND RAIL

Posts
Preserved softwood,
mortised
1·8 m × 125 mm × 75 mm

Rails
Riven oak
2·8 m × 300 mm girth

Nails
75 mm galvanised

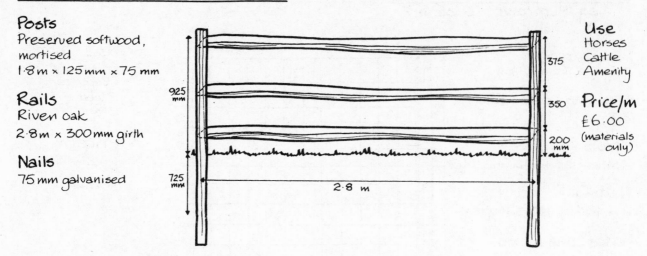

Use
Horses
Cattle
Amenity

Price/m
£6·00
(materials
only)

925 mm   375   350   200 mm   725 mm   2·8 m

15. MORTISED RAILS WITH STUDS – preserved softwood

Posts
Preserved softwood
2m × 150mm × 75mm

Rails
Preserved softwood
2·9m × 90mm × 38mm

Studs
Preserved softwood
1·7m × 90mm × 38mm

Nails
100mm galvanised

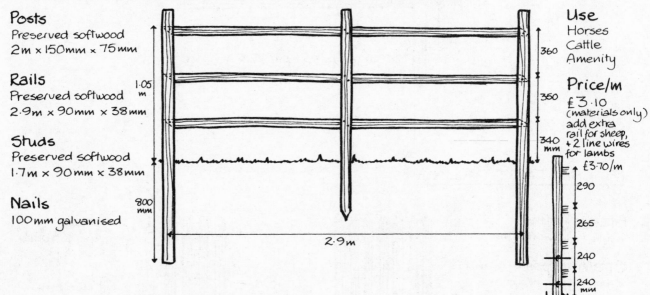

Use
Horses
Cattle
Amenity

Price/m
£3·10
(materials only)
add extra
rail for sheep,
& 2 line wires
for lambs
£3·70/m

1·05 m   800 mm   2·9m   360   350   340 mm   290   265   240   240 mm

16. NAILED POST AND RAIL – preserved softwood

Posts
1·8 m ×
125 mm × 75 mm

Rails
3·6 m ×
100 mm × 38 mm

Nails
100 mm galv.

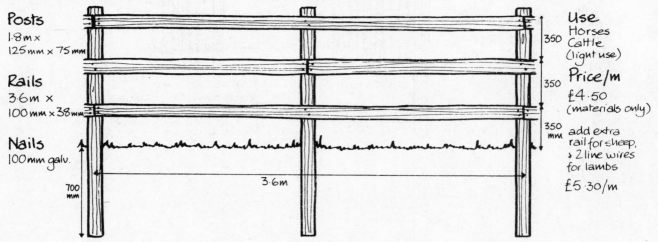

Use
Horses
Cattle
(light use)

Price/m
£4·50
(materials only)

add extra
rail for sheep,
& 2 line wires
for lambs

£5·30/m

350   350   350 mm   700 mm   3·6m

this design conforms to MAFF specification
Standard Costs Part 1

17. HALF-ROUND NAILED POST AND RAIL – preserved softwood

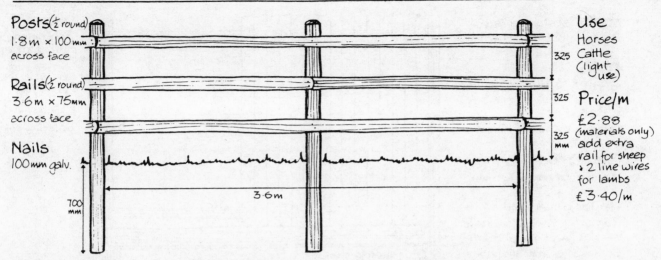

Posts (½ round)
1·8 m × 100 mm
across face

Rails (½ round)
3·6 m × 75 mm
across face

Nails
100 mm galv.

700 mm

3·6 m

325
325
325 mm

Use
Horses
Cattle
(light use)

Price/m
£2·88
(materials only)
add extra
rail for sheep
+ 2 line wires
for lambs
£3·40/m

18. TOP RAIL WITH STOCK NETTING – preserved softwood

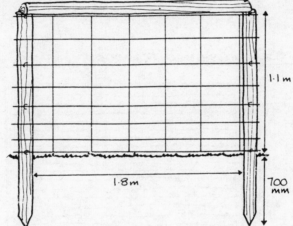

Stakes (round)
1·7 m × 100 mm diam.

Rail (½ round)
1·8 m × 100 mm across face

Netting
C8/11/80

Staples 30 mm

Nails 100 mm galv.

1·1 m

1·8 m

700 mm

Use
Sheep
Horses
Cattle (light use)

Curving fence lines.
No straining posts
needed if netting
only lightly strained.

Price/m
£1·35
(materials only)

19. GUIDE RAIL
~ preserved softwood

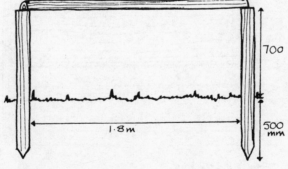

Stakes (round)
1·2 m × 100 mm diam.

Rails (½ round)
1·8 m × 100 mm across face

Nails 100 mm galv.

700

1·8 m

500 mm

Use
Amenity
Car parking
Separation of footpath
+ bridleway use

Price/m
£1·00
(materials only)

20. PALISADE
~ preserved softwood

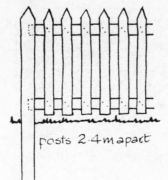

posts 2·4 m apart

Posts (mortised)
1·5 m × 100 mm × 75 mm

Rails
2·4 m × 89 mm × 38 mm

Pales
900 mm × 75 mm × 20 mm

Nails
50 mm galv.

Use
Garden
Amenity

Price/m
£6·80
(materials only)

21. BOARD FENCING – preserved softwood

Posts (rebated for rails)
2·4m × 125mm × 100mm

Rails
2·4m × 89mm × 39mm

Pales
1·68m × 100mm × 10mm

Gravel board
2·4m × 150mm × 25mm

Nails galvanised
75mm – for attaching rails and gravel board
50mm – for attaching pales

Concrete

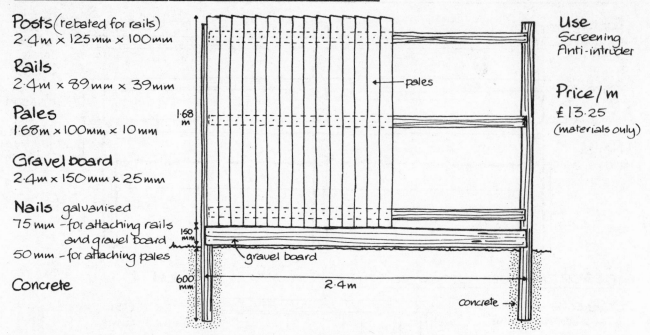

pales

gravel board

1·68 m

150 mm

600 mm

2·4m

concrete →

Use
Screening
Anti-intruder

Price/m
£13·25
(materials only)

22. PANEL FENCING – preserved softwood

Posts
2·4m × 75mm × 75mm

Panel (waney edged)
1·83m × 1·83m

Brackets
for attaching panel to posts

Concrete

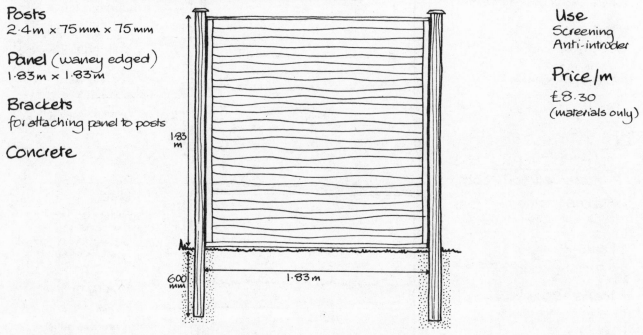

1·83 m

600 mm

1·83 m

Use
Screening
Anti-intruder

Price/m
£8·30
(materials only)

23. WOVEN HURDLES – hazel

Stakes
1·5m × 50mm diam.

Hurdles
1·83m × 920mm

Tying wire
for attaching hurdles to stakes

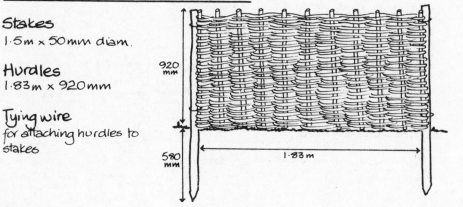

920 mm

580 mm

1·83 m

Use
Screening
Windbreaks
Sheep-pens

Price/m
£3·50
(materials only)

24. PERMANENT ELECTRIC FENCING – five strand

Stakes ('Insultimber')
1·52 m × 38 mm × 38 mm

Straining posts (round)
2·1 m × 150 mm diam

Droppers ('Insultimber')
940 mm × 38 mm × 26 mm

Wire 2·50 mm high tensile
Ties for attaching wires
Insulators for attaching wires to straining posts, & other electrical fittings

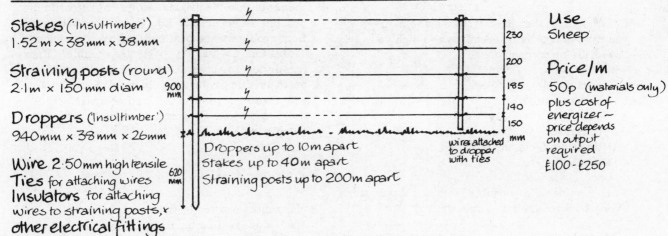

900 mm

620 mm

230
200
185
140
150
mm

Droppers up to 10m apart
Stakes up to 40m apart
Straining posts up to 200m apart

wires attached to dropper with ties

Use
Sheep

Price/m
50p (materials only)
plus cost of energizer –
price depends on output required
£100 - £250

25. SCARE WIRE

Insulated off-set brackets
hold single electric wire, to stockproof existing fences, & prolong fence life by lessening damage from animals

Wire 2·64 mm spring steel or 2·50 mm mild steel

Bracket spacing: 10-12 m
Hgt: $\frac{2}{3}$ hgt of animal

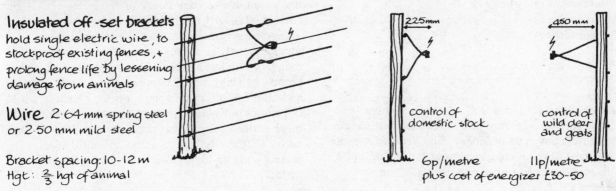

225 mm

control of domestic stock

6p/metre
plus cost of energizer £30-50

450 mm

control of wild deer and goats

11p/metre

26. CATTLE FENCE
~ temporary

Pigtail posts
spaced approx 10m apart

Wire
6 strand polywire

Use cattle
Price/m 13p
plus cost of energizer £30-50

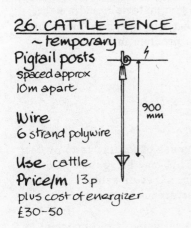

900 mm

27. REEL SYSTEMS – temporary

Reel systems
includes reels, posts + wire

Single reel cattle + horses
200 m system 22p/m
400 m system 18p/m

Three reel sheep + goats
200 m system 43p/m
400 m system 34p/m
plus cost of energizer £30-50

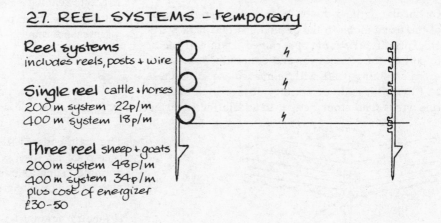

28. ELECTRIC NETTING – temporary

900 mm height (sheep)
46 m length, includes stakes

508 mm height (rabbits)
46 m length, includes stakes

1·1m height (horses + goats)
46 m length, includes stakes

Price/m

65p
plus cost of energizer £30-50

65p
plus energizer

75p
plus energizer

← polywire horizontals

← plastic verticals

Choosing a Fence

Consider first the 'fixed factors' the matters you have to take into account over which you have little or no control.

a   Terrain
b   Access to site
c   Use
d   Boundaries
e   Climatic effects and pollution
f   Snow

Then consider the 'variable factors' the matters over which you do have some control.

a   Cost - labour
         - materials
         - grants
b   Intended life of fence
c   Maintenance
d   Appearance

TERRAIN

In easy terrain, that is flat or gently sloping land with deep, well-drained soil there is no difficulty in erecting any type of fence. The problems come with undulating or steeply sloping land, thin soils with rock exposed or near the surface, or soft marshy soils.

On undulating land the problem is to keep the base of the fence close to the ground, so that it is still stockproof. Any form of strained fence will tend to pull up out of hollows, and either tie-downs and extra straining posts will be needed, or gaps must be filled with rails or netting. It is easier to fit line wires than stock netting to undulating terrrain.

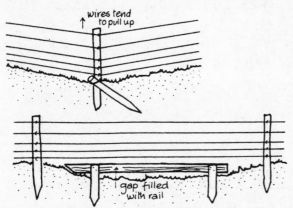

Nailed post and rail fencing is useful in very convoluted land as it can be built to fit the contours. However, such slopes usually mean thin soils, and difficulty in erecting posts. Any form of panel fencing is awkward on slopes, as the panels have to be 'stepped' to fit the slope.

On shallow soils and rock the problem is getting the posts into the ground, while on soft soils the problem is reversed - how to get the posts firm. Both problems are best reduced by choosing a design that uses as few posts as possible. High tensile fencing uses about a fifth of the number of posts used in ordinary (mild steel) wire fencing, with straining posts much further apart. Thus there is obvious advantage in using this type of fencing in difficult soil conditions.

ACCESS TO SITE

Many sites worked on by conservation volunteers are not accessible by ordinary vehicle, and much of the total effort is spent on carrying the materials on site (see also p34 para.d). The fence design chosen should have the minimum number of posts, and avoid single very heavy or bulky items. High tensile wire will reduce the number of posts, and using box strainers instead of conventional strainers will avoid the necessity of carrying massive straining posts. Beware though of high tensile netting, which is supplied in 100m rolls, and although of thinner and therefore lighter wire is considerably heavier than equivalent height and mesh mild steel netting, which is supplied in 50m rolls. High tensile line wires, or mild steel netting hung on high tensile wires may be more suitable.

Electric fencing saves on materials and weight, but distance from power supply and the need for maintenance may be a problem in remote sites.

USE

Conservation

The main conservation use of fencing is to protect tree planting sites. This may be against wild animals, such as deer, hares or rabbits, against stock, or against interference by people.

If fencing against wild animals it is important to try and identify the type of animals and likely amount of damage, as this type of fencing is expensive in materials. There may be cheaper alternatives, such as individual tree protectors, which can be used. See page 108 for further information on fencing to protect trees.

Another important conservation use of fencing is to manage open land, such as downland, grassland or heathland, by the grazing of sheep or cattle. In many cases this is needed to maintain semi-natural habitats, formed in the past by controlled grazing or by rabbits. Cheap forms of fencing, such as permanent or temporary electric fencing may allow grazing to be re-introduced as a means of controlling the spread of rough grasses, scrub and woodland. This may be cheaper than alternative methods such as mowing, and provide some income for reserves, country parks and so on.

A further use of fencing is to try and keep wild animals in conservation sites, and out of adjacent farmland and gardens. This may be necessary for good relations between reserve managers and adjacent landowners. Trouble is caused by deer and rabbits eating crops, foxes attacking poultry and game, and badgers disturbing crops and gardens. It is more difficult however to keep wild animals restricted, than to fence them out, and higher than normal fences will be needed to keep rabbits in for example. Foxes and badgers are almost impossible to restrain by fencing. For further details on fencing against wild animals see pages 103-111.

Stock

There are no hard and fast rules about fence height or wire spacing for different types of stock, although guidelines are given in the table on page 110. The effectiveness of a fence in enclosing or exclosing stock depends a lot on how green the grass appears on the other side. Content animals with sufficient grazing should have no inducement to break through or jump a fence.

Stock may find their way out of an enclosure in the following cases:

a If there is not sufficient grazing or extra feed available for the number of animals.

b If the grazing is better on the other side of the fence. Animals will lean over or push their heads through fences to get at fresh grass on the other side, and to browse on tree leaves. All stock, but especially sheep, enjoy fresh grass that has not been trampled or grazed by another animal.

c Stock will seek shade. If exclosing woodland, try and leave a few trees accessible for stock. There will be extra stock pressure on fences that are shaded by adjacent woodland.

d Mountain breeds and some rare breeds of sheep are more likely to jump than other commercial breeds.

e When being herded by sheepdogs, sheep may jump or break through a weak part of the fence. Corners or narrow lanes where sheep will gather may need slightly higher fences to

prevent them jumping.

f Animals on their own get lonely and bored, particularly horses and ponies used to company and exercise. Getting a sheep or donkey for company may do the trick, and be cheaper than renewing the fence.

Amenity

A whole range of fences may be needed for controlling peoples' use of amenity sites, from simple post and rail barriers for directing people, to substantial safety fences in situations where there is danger to the public.

There are legal aspects to be considered in erecting any safety fencing (see chapter 2), because by erecting such a fence, the landowner is admitting there is a danger. If the fence then fails and someone is hurt, the landowner may be liable.

Barriers and fences to control trampling, and to trap eroding material, are often needed on heavily used sites. These are described in 'Footpaths' (BTCV, 1983). Similarly, the need for sand fencing is usually caused by trampling and destruction of vegetation on popular sand dunes (see p112).

There are occasionally situations on conservation and amenity sites where anti-intruder fencing is needed. Examples may include particular sites for rare or protected wildlife, old quarries and mines, and sites in urban areas where management for conservation also attracts vandalism, and sites need to be closed when not under supervision. Further details are given on page 114.

BOUNDARIES

Boundary fences may be the responsibility of one landowner, or neighbouring landowners may share the responsibility for boundary fences, as is often the case in Scotland. In either situation it may be possible to reach agreement with the adjacent landowner about the type of fence which would suit both parties, and share costs and maintenance accordingly. For example, one landowner may need cattle fencing, whereas the other requires sheep fencing, and the latter could then pay the extra cost required to make the fence sheep proof.

CLIMATIC EFFECTS AND POLLUTION

Wire rusts more quickly in heavily polluted air

and in salt-laden air. In these situations use either wooden post and rail fencing, or heavy gauge wire. Once the layer of galvanising has deteriorated, the life of the wire depends on its gauge or thickness (see p41). The spreading of slurry or lime which comes into contact with fences also lessens wire life.

SNOW

The weight of drifted snow can push a fence over or break parts of the fence. The likelihood of this happening can be lessened by siting the fence away from hollows and breaks of gradient where snow accumulates. However, fences of close mesh are obviously going to offer more resistance and result in a bigger build up of snow than open mesh or line wire fences. The fence also needs to be built extra-strong, or have enough flexibility to recover once the now melts. High tensile spring steel wire has the advantage of more 'springiness' and returns to its original line better than any other type of wire.

Some landowners prefer to use high tensile electric fencing which is the lightest weight fence in terms of wire and posts, and thus least likely to create build up of snow. Good quality electric components should come through any snow covering without damage.

The section below considers the 'variable factors' involved in choosing the type of fence.

COST

Labour

The table opposite shows the estimated cost of labour for various types of fencing operations. Most fall within a third to a half of total costs. The simpler type of fence, for example with three strands of plain or barbed mild steel wire, have about equal labour and material costs. The labour cost per metre remains about the same for a fence with stock netting, but material costs are higher. Labour costs are significantly higher where rabbit netting has to be attached.

Generally, high tensile and permanent electric fencing are relatively low in labour costs. Labour costs are highest for post and rail fencing, but because of higher materials cost, are only about one fifth of the total cost.

Site managers should consider carefully whether to use contractors or volunteers for any fencing work required. BTCV volunteers should only be asked to do fencing work which has a conservation or amenity value. When comparing contractors' rates with the costs involved in using voluntary labour, remember that contractors will be much quicker, especially on straightforward fences. Contractors may therefore be cheaper, in spite of their higher rates. On difficult ground, awkward fence lines and in remote sites, where 'many hands make light work', volunteers should be an economically viable work force, as well as doing a job that may otherwise not be done at all, as contractors are less likely to be interested in this type of work.

The labour cost of checking and maintaining fences should also be taken into account.

Materials

The table opposite shows the approximate costs of materials for different types of fences. These costs are for timber, wire and accessories at average commercial rates for 1985.

For short-term fences costs may be reduced by using home-produced or second-hand timber. For most fences however, it is best to use durable or properly treated timber that will give a max-imum working life (see p36). Wire can always be replaced if necessary, if timber parts of a fence outlast the wire.

Plain wire is sold in coils by weight, and thinner wire is cheaper per unit length. High tensile and spring steel wire, being thinner than mild steel wire, are therefore cheaper, as well as being stronger. Note that special care is needed however in handling and fixing high tensile and spring steel wire (see chapter 4). High tensile stock netting is more expensive than mild steel netting of equivalent height and gauge, but provides greater strength.

Note also the need for extras such as staples nails, fence connectors and other accessories. The cost of these is included in the estimated prices per metre given opposite, and in the designs from pages 6-14.

Grants

Details of grants are given on page 130.

INTENDED LIFE OF FENCE

How long is the fence required to last? There is no point in using top quality materials for a fence only required for a few years. On the other hand, a fence from which one wants the maximum

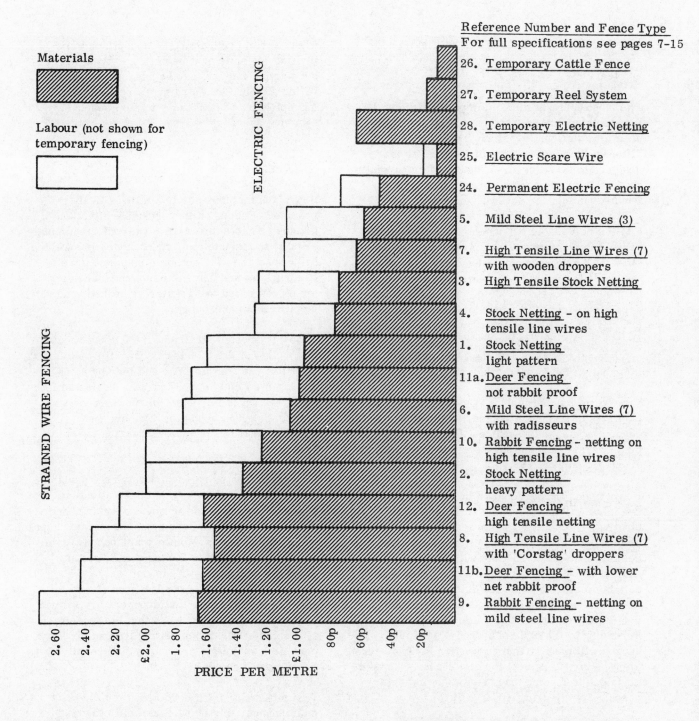

Materials

Labour (not shown for
temporary fencing)

ELECTRIC FENCING

STRAINED WIRE FENCING

Reference Number and Fence Type
For full specifications see pages 7-15

26. Temporary Cattle Fence
27. Temporary Reel System
28. Temporary Electric Netting
25. Electric Scare Wire
24. Permanent Electric Fencing
5. Mild Steel Line Wires (3)
7. High Tensile Line Wires (7) with wooden droppers
3. High Tensile Stock Netting
4. Stock Netting – on high tensile line wires
1. Stock Netting light pattern
11a. Deer Fencing not rabbit proof
6. Mild Steel Line Wires (7) with radisseurs
10. Rabbit Fencing – netting on high tensile line wires
2. Stock Netting heavy pattern
12. Deer Fencing high tensile netting
8. High Tensile Line Wires (7) with 'Corstag' droppers
11b. Deer Fencing – with lower net rabbit proof
9. Rabbit Fencing – netting on mild steel line wires

2.60 2.40 2.20 £2.00 1.80 1.60 1.40 1.20 £1.00 80p 60p 40p 20p

PRICE PER METRE

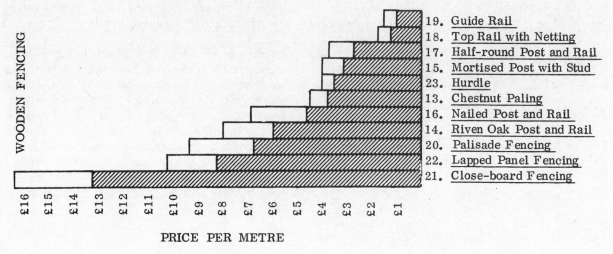

WOODEN FENCING

19. Guide Rail
18. Top Rail with Netting
17. Half-round Post and Rail
15. Mortised Post with Stud
23. Hurdle
13. Chestnut Paling
16. Nailed Post and Rail
14. Riven Oak Post and Rail
20. Palisade Fencing
22. Lapped Panel Fencing
21. Close-board Fencing

£16 £15 £14 £13 £12 £11 £10 £9 £8 £7 £6 £5 £4 £3 £2 £1

PRICE PER METRE

possible life needs to be of the best materials, and of a design to cope with many years of wear and tear.

The most common type of temporary fencing is the electric wire or electrified plastic netting used for rotational grazing. This is rather different from other types of fencing, as it is designed to be re-used. If looked after carefully both while in use and in storage, this type of fencing can last for several years use.

Similar re-useable but non-electric fencing can be used for 'rotational trampling', on popular sites such as archaeological monuments, where one wants to avoid the concentration of trampling on the same lines over a long period. Fences have been successfully used of baler twine or brightly coloured tape, hung on electric fencing stakes or similar. Although these fences form no physical barrier, with the right publicity and information for visitors, they should be respected.

Short term fencing includes those to protect new plantings of trees and hedges, to encourage sand accumulation, and to redirect footpaths and bridleways. Fencing for trees and woodlands is discussed on page 108.

Newly planted hedges should be fenced until they are laid, which is normally ten years after planting. For cattle and horses, a single strand of wire, set about one metre from the hedge, will be sufficient. Stock netting will be required against sheep. Non-durable timber should be suitable for posts if the fence is only required for ten years, although a fence is usually kept indefinitely on at least one side of the hedge. According to the style of hedging, newly laid hedges will need further protection for two years after laying, to protect the new shoots. Temporary electric fencing may be suitable in some cases. See 'Hedging' (BTCV, 1975).

Fencing to prevent erosion of sand dunes is described on page 112. Fences which are designed to trap sand should be of the cheapest possible materials, and certainly need not be of preserved timber, as they should be buried in sand within a few months. The windy, drying conditions on sand dunes are not conducive to rapid timber decay.

Fences and barriers to redirect footpaths are only normally required for as long as it takes to get the new path in established use, and possibly to allow vegetation to disguise the old path. A post and rail fence of non-durable timber would normally be suitable, as it is easy to erect over short distances, and is clearly visible. In places

where the old path is likely to continue to be inviting, in spite of it being 'closed', a more substantial barrier may be needed. Chestnut paling attached to a strained wire fence for example may be necessary to stop people climbing over.

MAINTENANCE

How much maintenance is the fence likely to receive? Fences on innaccessible sites, on islands, remote mountain areas and so on must be built so that minimal maintenance is expected. Although this is the optimum standard for all fencing, you may have to use a cheaper design for fences which are regularly checked, and can be mended as necessary.

Properly erected strained wire fencing should last well, but the effects of snow, flood or falling branches, as well as wear and tear by stock making it no longer stock proof. Advice on fence siting, which is important in ensuring low maintenance, is given opposite. Remove any obvious hazards such as overhanging unsafe branches.

In general, the more sophisticated the design of fence, the more likely it will need attention. Electric fencing needs frequent checking, and any repairs must be done by someone who understands the system. Monitors are now available which are installed in the farm or base, and show any faults along the fence line. Fences of line wires with droppers should be checked to make sure that droppers are still in position, and wires taut, so that the fence is still stockproof. Stock netting fencing requires very little maintenance, and is still usually stock proof even if somewhat slackened.

Post and rail fencing needs possibly the least maintenance, this being one of the reasons it is used for motorway fencing. Any repairs can be quickly done with no special tools required.

Another factor which may affect the need for maintenance is the likelihood of vandalism. Any wire fences which can be easily cut are obviously vulnerable. Wooden fences may attract vandalism and theft for fuel and other uses. A favourite type of location for this is where barbecues are popular, but more organised theft, even using chain saws, is not unknown. Non-wood posts have had to be used in some areas (see p40) and other devices adopted to deter vandalism and theft (see p112).

APPEARANCE

Most well-erected fences look acceptable, but some are particularly associated with urban areas, and thus 'urbanise' if put in a rural setting. Examples are any type of fence with concrete posts, chain-link fencing and chestnut paling.

Post and rail fencing is made of attractive material, and is usually associated with paddocks, stud-farms, farm entrances and so on. Although now widely used for motorway fencing, it remains a high quality 'rural' fence.

Permanent electric fencing of high tensile wire has the advantage of using fewer and smaller posts than other types of wire fencing, and is therefore fairly unobtrusive on open grassland and moorland.

Often though it is the line of the fence, and the landscape which will evolve from the fence's existence, for example the shape of a woodland, which is more important than the actual appearance of the fence.

Factors in Siting the Fence

In some cases the fence must necessarily take a certain exact line. In others, there will be scope for choosing the best route the fence should take.

Terrain

Fences are easiest to erect on flat or evenly sloping land. Considerably more materials are required for all types of fences on undulating land, and strained fences will need extra strainer assemblies, with consequent further expense and effort.

Fences on slopes and uneven ground also tend to be less effective. There may be dips where animals can squeeze underneath the fence, and places where the ground rises sharply near the fence, which allows animals to jump over.

Avoid fencing above, on or beneath unstable slopes, as sooner or later the fence will be destroyed. As animals and people tend to congregate and walk along the edge of fenced areas, site the fence well away from the base or top of the slope, in order to avoid further erosion.

Choose the best soils within the area available, particularly for siting straining posts. Usually avoid rocky and stony areas, where hole digging is difficult. However, in very soft peaty soils, stony deposits or rock outcrops may provide the best place to get a firm anchorage. Avoid permanently or seasonally waterlogged patches, in which posts will not hold firm.

Gullies which become seasonal watercourses are a particular problem, and are not always easy to identify. Look out for any signs of water-flow, including lush grass and other plants of damp ground, water-carved gullies bare of vegetation, and deposits of gravel and silt. Ask local advice. If there is no way of avoiding them, these gullies must be crossed by the fence in such a way that the fence is stock-proof in dry periods, but that water and water borne debris can flow freely down in wet seasons. See page 127 for methods of bridging gullies and constructing water gates.

Snow

In areas where snow is likely to be a problem, site fences out of any dips where snow may accumulate. Try and seek local advice about the places where snow usually drifts, as the weight of snow can break wires and posts.

Also bear in mind that deep or drifted snow can allow animals to walk over fences. In particular, sheep may get into fenced woodlands, and then be unable to get out as the snow melts. If possible, site such fences so that there is a natural means of escape. For example, a rock outcrop, bank or fallen tree may allow animals to jump out of the exclosure. If there is not a suitable natural feature, and the wood is in a remote place which is not frequently visited, it may be worth building a ramp of stones or wood, to allow animals to get out on their own (see p127). Fences around small woodlands should always have a gate of some sort, to allow access for management and in case of fire, as well as getting animals out if necessary.

Boundaries

It may not always be convenient to site a fence exactly along a boundary of ownership. For example, the boundary line may be through very marshy or rocky ground that is difficult to fence, or it may take a very convoluted line. Depending on the purpose of the fence, and the economic value of the land use, it might be better to site the fence along a more convenient line within the boundary. As necessary, the boundary itself can be marked with wooden or concrete markers.

Wildlife

There may be well-established tracks made by

wild animals which cross the proposed fence line. Badgers will use the same tracks, possibly for years, and are almost impossible to fence out. They are strong enough to push under tightly strained stock netting, and will soon make a hollowed run through which a lamb can escape. Badgers will also dig under a solid fence to get at their watering or feeding areas.

Either site the fence so that it avoids their tracks, or install badger gates to allow their access, while keeping the fence lamb or rabbit proof (see p107).

Problems also occur with red deer, which will attempt to break through any fences that bar their way to traditional rutting grounds.

Appearance

The line of the fence may be important in its visual effect on the landscape, both in itself, and in any future change it may bring about - the patterns made by the different uses of the enclosures it creates.

The natural boundary line, along a stream, break of slope or soil type is likely to be the most pleasing in appearance. This should also allow for the best economic use of the land, so that the capability of each piece of land, taking into account its soil, water and aspect, is fully utilised. For example, an area of land which is partly south facing and well drained, and partly north facing and damp, will not grow a uniform crop. A division along the natural boundary may allow a better land use.

An exception is where a fence along the natural boundary also follows the skyline, for example along a ridge. If such a fence would be intrusive in appearance, consider siting it just below the skyline. However, as such sharp divides in the landscape are often also boundaries of ownership, this may not be feasible.

The basic problem with fences in the landscape is that the easiest and most economical line to fence is a straight one, but this does not necess- arily blend well with the undulating British landscape. Straight fences up and down hillsides are amongst the most obtrusive because they can be seen from long distances, and because they introduce straight lines into landscapes which are often uncultivated or semi-natural. An oblique straight line, such as that taken by a gently sloping track, would possibly blend better, and would also lessen the problem of erosion that follows from clearing vegetation and encouraging animals and people to walk up and down the

fence line.

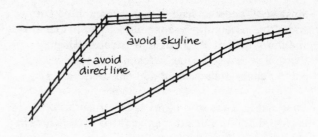

Straight lines for fencing new woodlands can be 'disguised' by not planting right up to the fence all along its line. Leave a few areas unplanted, if possible keeping them clear by cutting. The effect can be enhanced by planting a few individual trees or small clumps outside the fence, and protecting them separately. Although the fence line will still be visible as the trees grow, the mature effect will be of a semi-natural woodland.

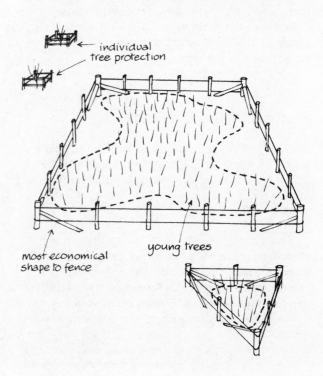

2 Fences and the Law

FENCE OWNERSHIP

a Ownership of boundary fences may be shown on the deeds of a property. The 'T' symbol, shown below, indicates the side to which the fence belongs. Occasionally a double 'T' may be shown, which indicates the boundary is jointly owned by the two properties.

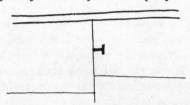

b The normal rule with garden fences, such as palisade fencing, is that the fence belongs to the side on which the fence posts stand. This is because the more attractive side, that has the fence posts hidden, usually faces outwards from the property it encloses.

RESIDENTIAL and URBAN PROPERTY

likely that fence belongs this side

AGRICULTURAL PROPERTY

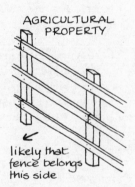

likely that fence belongs this side

With agricultural fencing, the reverse is more likely to apply. Posts are usually put on the non-stock side of the fence, that is the side away from the owner's land. This makes the fence more secure, as stock are less likely to loosen the fixings of the rails or wires by leaning on the fence.

c If the fence replaces the visible remnants of a hedge and ditch this may indicate the fence ownership. The hedge and ditch normally belong to the property adjacent to the hedge, and thus a fence on the hedge side will also belong to that property. A fence on the non-hedged side of the ditch is more likely to belong to the other owner. Because the presumption is that the owner dug the ditch to make the hedge bank, this rule does not apply to natural ditches.

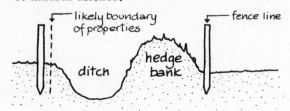

likely boundary of properties — fence line

ditch — hedge bank

MAINTENANCE

a An owner is under no obligation to maintain a fence except where:

i the deeds contain covenants or conditions that the owner maintain fences in good condition
ii local Acts or regulations require it. These apply to house owners in the London area and a few other urban areas.

However, an owner may be liable for damage resulting from a fence being in a dangerous condition. If a fence adjoining a highway becomes dilapidated, and a person using the highway is injured as a result, the owner of the fence may be liable. Action can also be taken for 'nuisance', where for example, there is detriment to a neighbour's enjoyment of his land.

b The responsibility of a tenant to maintain fences will be set out in the lease.

c Where a fence is jointly owned, each owner must not dismantle or do anything to his half which could cause his neighbour's half to collapse.

d There is no general right to enter a neighbouring property to repair a boundary fence, even if that is the most convenient or even the only practicable way of doing it. An owner who enters land to repair a fence without authority can be restrained by injunction.

CONTROL OF LIVESTOCK

a The onus is always on the owner of livestock to control it by fencing or other means so that it does not stray onto other people's land, or onto public highways. Livestock includes cattle, horses, mules, sheep, pigs, poultry, and captive deer, pheasants, partridge and grouse. Dogs and cats are not included, nor are 'exotic' animals. Control of the latter may be included under Acts governing the ownership of dangerous animals.

b If livestock stray onto a public highway, the owner is liable for any damage or injury caused, if he was negligent in allowing the livestock to escape there. For example, if the fence was found to be defective, the owner would be liable, but if it was found that a gate had been left open by someone else, that person may be liable.

An owner can be fined for livestock found straying or lying at the side of the highway, and not necessarily causing damage or injury. However, an owner is not liable if animals are on a highway adjoining common land or a village green, or where fencing is not customary. Here the onus is on the road user to take special care.

c If livestock stray onto someone else's land, the owner of the livestock is liable for damage to property, even though he may not have been to blame for the animals escaping. The owner of the livestock has the following defences:

i the victim was either wholly or partly to blame (but the lack of a fence enclosing the victim's land is not sufficient to apportion blame on the victim).

ii the livestock were lawfully on a public highway, and strayed from there. The victim's land does not have to directly adjoin the highway. However, the victim may be able to prove that the owner was negligent by not keeping control of the animals on the highway.

iii the victim was responsible under a covenant or condition in the deeds of his property to maintain a fence around his land.

d If a boundary fence belonging to a neighbour is dilapidated, you must erect additional fencing as necessary to control your own stock. This fence must be on your own land.

TRESPASS BY WILD ANIMALS

A landowner is not liable for damage caused by wild animals from his land 'trespassing' on and causing damage to another's land, unless he brings onto his land a greater quantity of wild animals than can reasonably and properly be kept on it. A landowner is not liable for failing to keep existing stock within reasonable limits, for example the natural increase of a rabbit population on a nature reserve surrounded by agricultural land.

DAMAGE

An owner or rent-paying tenant can claim for damage done to fences by any trespasser, including a hunt.

BARBED WIRE

a The law states that barbed wire should not be used on land adjoining a public highway (which includes public rights of way) where it may cause injury to people or livestock legally using the highway. However, there is no rule on the minimum distance of the barbed wire from the edge of the highway, and each situation must be judged for itself. Barbed wire on fences immediately adjacent to narrow footpaths or bridleways would be likely to be considered dangerous, whereas barbed wire at a few metres distance from the edge of the path would probably not.

b Barbed wire must not be electrified, nor be included in any fence of which part is electrified.

ELECTRIC FENCING

a Electric fencing must be insulated at stiles and gates on public rights of way.

b There should be warning signs every 80-100 metres on electric fences on or adjacent to land to which the public legally have access. The signs should display the words ELECTRIC FENCE, with letters at least 50mm high.

COMMONS

Fencing of common land by owners or commoners is only allowed if consent is given by the Secretary of State for the Environment (or Secretary of State for Wales). The person wishing to build the fence must advertise his application in a local paper, and the Secretary of State must allow 28 days for members of the public to make representations. Consent can only be given if the work would be 'for the benefit of the neighbourhood', for example, to stops commoners' animals straying into nearby gardens. The consent may include safeguards, such as a certain number of gates and stiles for access. External fencing, along a road for example, is more likely to be given consent than fencing which divides the common into parcels of land.

SAFETY FENCING

a The occupier of land used for dangerous operations or for the storage of dangerous objects must prevent the entry of people likely to be harmed there, as well as the escape or removal of dangerous items.

b The Occupiers Liability Act 1957 imposes on an occupier the duty to take care that a visitor (but not necessarily a trespasser) will be reasonably safe using the premises for the purpose for which he has been invited or permitted to be there.

c Under the Mines and Quarries Act 1954, the owner of an abandoned mine, or one that has not been worked for 12 months, must fence it to prevent injury to persons or animals falling down the shaft.

d The Local Authority has power to require fencing to remove danger from an excavation on land accessible to the public from a highway, or on a place of public resort.

e If natural dangers, such as cliff edges, are fenced, the owner or occupier may then be liable if accident or injury results from failure of the fence. Thus the need for fencing of natural features must be carefully considered before any work is undertaken.

f The Highways Act 1980 imposes an obligation upon the owner of land adjoining a public highway (which includes public rights of way), to adequately fence anything which is a source of danger to people using the highway, for example a building being demolished. However, where the source of danger is a drop in level, the owner cannot be compelled to fence, because the danger does not exist in or on his land. A fence which is part of the highway, and protects the users of the highway from a dangerous drop, is the responsibility of the Highway Authority. The Highway Authority may also be liable if damage occurs following the removal of such a fence.

RAILWAYS

When the railways were constructed, they were required to fence their land 'in perpetuity'. However, they were empowered to pay compensation to adjacent landowners in return for a release from any obligation to fence. The responsibility for maintaining fences bordering railway land may be given in the deeds of the adjacent property, or if not, should be checked with British Rail.

PLANNING PERMISSION

The Town and Country Planning General Development Order 1977 gives general permission for erection of gates, fences, walls and other means of enclosure that do not exceed one metre in height when abutting upon a road used by vehicles, or two metres elsewhere.

The formation or laying out of means of access to highways requires planning permission. This applies to access, whether private or public, for vehicles or pedestrians. The General Development Order gives an automatic consent for access onto unclassified roads where:

i   the work is required in connection with development for which permission has been given or
ii access is required, but not in connection with any development.

Check with the District Council if there is any doubt over the status of the road in question, or whether any intended work will constitute development.

No gate may open out onto a street, except in the case of a public building, and with the consent of the Highway Authority.

3 Safety, Equipment and Organisation

Most fencing work requires a wide selection of tools, as the job may entail clearing vegetation, digging holes, carpentry as well as handling and straining wire. Non-strained fencing, such as wooden post and rail, is usually the simplest type of fencing job, requiring no specialist tools and with no particular safety risks. At the other extreme, high tensile wire fencing requires specialist tools, and the job can be dangerous if not done properly.

When working with a group of volunteers, careful organisation is needed to get the work done in proper sequence, to use all the labour effectively, and to keep a close eye on progress along a length of fence. Complex or long fencing tasks should not be attempted with only one experienced fencer.

Safety Precautions

GENERAL

a Have a first aid kit to hand. A suitable kit is listed below.

b All volunteers should have had a tetanus injection within the last 10 years.

c Do not work in soaking rain. Once gloves, tools and materials are sodden, the danger of accident increases, and slopes become hazardous.

LIFTING AND CARRYING

a Avoid this as much as possible, by getting the materials delivered right to the fence site. Lifting and carrying materials is tiring, time-consuming work, and may not be the best use of volunteer labour.

b When lifting always bend the knees and not the back. Make full use of the stronger leg muscles rather than the weaker back muscles. Keep the back straight, though not necessarily vertical, as in the diagram below.

c Always place the feet apart in such a way that the body is balanced. Lifting tends to pull the body off balance, and if this is counteracted by the lower back muscles instead of the legs and feet, damage to the back can occur. When lifting or putting down, place one foot in front of the other as shown, to help one's balance.

Look up as you lift, as this helps to get the spine into the best position. Never lift anything while reaching away from the body, with your feet at a distance from the object. If you can't get right up to the object because of some immoveable obstruction, don't attempt the lift. Find someone to assist you or use a lever to move the obstruction.

d Don't attempt to carry more than you're capable of! Just because the person in front of you wants to be a hero doesn't mean you have to try. Back injury can be caused literally in a moment, and can give years of trouble. It is not worth risking it.

e Carry with your arms held fairly straight to avoid strain to the muscles of the upper arm and chest. Grip with the palms of the hands, not the fingers. If you slip let go of the item so that it falls away from you.

f Large straining posts are best carried on the shoulders of two people, who should be of about equal height and strength, and ideally walk at a similar pace. Both of them lift one end, and rest it on the shoulder of one person.

The other person then lifts the other end onto his own shoulder, bending the knees and keeping the back straight as described above. If you're not wearing a thick jacket, one folded across the shoulder helps prevent any chafing. Remember that when carrying up or down a slope, the person on the lower side carries much more of the weight. When traversing a slope, carry the post on the lower side, so it will fall safely out of the way if either person slips. Straining posts for deer fences may need to be carried by three people, though it is not easy to fairly distribute the weight.

g Rolls of barbed wire should be carried on a stake or crowbar, one person holding either end and wearing a leather glove. Beware of the roll slipping on the crowbar when being carried on a slope.

h Rolls of stock netting can be carried by one person on the shoulder, or by two people, one holding at either end. Rolls of deer netting can have two crowbars pushed through, to allow four people to carry. Pushing a roll down a convenient slope may seem an easy way, but can be dangerous if the roll gets out of control. The wire galvanising will also be damaged by any stones in the way.

i Large tools should be carried at the side of the body, with the blade or point facing forwards and downwards. If the carrier then slips, the tools can be safely dropped to the side. Carry small tools in a bucket or belt (see p34).

HANDLING MATERIALS

a Beware of recently creosoted wood, and of any creosoted wood in hot weather. Delivery of recently treated timber should not really be accepted (see p39), but sometimes this may be unavoidable. Wear industrial rubber gloves and take special care not to rub your eyes with a creosote-stained finger. If you do bathe the eye immediately. The person holding a post while it is being melled into the ground is particularly vulnerable to creosote spurting out and safety glasses are advisable. Also take care while hammering staples into the post.

b Timber treated with a copper/chrome/arsenic preservative (see p38) should also be delivered dry, but likewise, this is not always the case. Wear gloves, and wash your hands before eating.

c Take care when unrolling stock netting, and extreme care with high tensile netting. It has been known for a person handling the roll to be knocked over when the roll suddenly uncoils from the centre. Also keep your fingers out of the mesh, or they may get trapped as the roll uncoils.

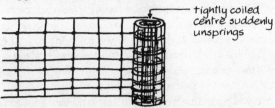

tightly coiled centre suddenly unsprings

d Always anchor the free ends of unrolled netting, plain or barbed wire, as it will recoil. The ends of plain or barbed wire can be anchored by poking them into the ground. High tensile wire should be held secure on both sides of any cut being made, and then the ends fastened or pushed into the ground (see p53).

e When removing or repairing old fences, take care while releasing any tensioned wire, as it may spring back. Hold the wire while cutting and then loosely secure the free end, before removing staples and rewinding the wire.

f Always wear gloves when handling barbed wire. Wind up disused barbed wire onto an old stake and fasten the end securely.

TIDYING THE SITE

a Collect up any pieces of timber treated with copper/chrome/arsenic or creosote. Such timber gives off noxious fumes when burnt, and should either be buried or disposed of at a dump.

b Collect up every piece of unused wire, including all staples, as they can be a danger to animals. Small pieces of wire can be buried on site, but any rolls of disused barbed wire or netting that cannot be salvaged should be taken to a dump. Don't leave it piled up somewhere in the expectation that someone else will soon be clearing it up, because the chances are that in no time at all it will be half grown over with vegetation and a hazard to man and animal.

Clothing

a Wear overalls, a boiler suit or close-fitting
   clothing. Loose clothing and scarves are
   dangerous when working with tools or
   moving heavy objects.

b Heavy leather work boots with vibram or
   nailed soles and steel toe-caps give good grip
   and protect the feet. If wellingtons need be
   worn, preferably wear the type with steel
   toe-caps.

c Wear gloves when handling timber treated
   with creosote or copper/chrome/arsenic.
   Heavy duty industrial rubber gloves are best,
   particularly if the preservative is still wet,
   as leather gloves absorb the preservative and
   become unpleasant to wear. Special gloves
   with protection across the knuckles are
   available for handling barbed wire, but in
   practice it is the inside wrists which are most
   at risk. Gloves with a long gauntlet give
   better protection. Another type of glove which
   is useful for barbed wire has 'staples' all
   over the palm to give protection.

d Wool trousers or breeches are useful in wet
   or cold weather, particularly in the uplands,
   as they retain warmth even when wet.

Tools and Accessories

Many of the tools listed below are included in the
BTCV Tool Catalogue, which is issued to all
BTCV and affiliated groups. Addresses of
manufacturers or distributors of specialist tools
or brands that are particularly recommended are
given in Appendix E (p133). Groups buying other
than through the BTCV will find the best selection
in the ranges of agricultural and contractors tools.

Tools are listed under the various stages of
fencing work, and requirements will vary for
different types of fencing. A suggested list is
given on page 34 of the numbers of tools
required for groups of 12 doing post and wire
or post and rail fencing.

It is possible to put up a fence with only a few of
the tools listed, but a full range of tools allows
fencing to be done more quickly and effectively.
A major consideration is often the distance that
tools have to be carried to the site. For this
reason, multi-use tools are recommended, such
as the crowbar with the rammer head. However,
one must still bear in mind the need to have
enough tools to keep everyone busy.

FOR ALL TASKS

First aid kit. Keep this with you at all times.
The BTCV can supply standard first aid kits
which comply with the 1981 Health and Safety
Regulations (First Aid). For six to ten people,
the contents are:

1 guidance card
20 individual sterile adhesive dressings
2 sterile eye pads with attachments
2 triangular bandages
2 sterile coverings for serious wounds
6 safety pins
6 medium size sterile unmedicated dressings
2 large size sterile unmedicated dressings
2 extra large size sterile unmedicated dressings

From experience on tasks, the following are
also found to be useful: 100mm crepe bandage,
tweezers (round-nosed), scissors (round-nosed),
insect repellant, antihistamine cream for insect
bites, sunscreen cream, mild antiseptic cream,
eye lotion and eye bath.

A list of local hospitals with casualty departments
should also be to hand.

CLEARANCE

In some cases there is no need for any clearance
of vegetation or other obstructions, but in dense
woodland or scrub this will amount to a considerable part of the whole task, and the following
tools will be needed.

a Slasher. A long-handled tool for use on
   brambles, nettles and light scrub.

b Billhook. Used for trimming branches and
   for clearing scrub and small trees.

c Pickaxe. This has a very hard blade, and is
   used for breaking up rocky ground, stones,
   concrete and tarmac.

d Mattock. This has softer blades, of which the
   wide one is used for breaking up clay and hard
   soil. The pick ended mattock has a pick end
   for breaking up stony ground, but is not hard
   enough for breaking up rocks. The grubbing
   mattock has a short cutting blade for chopping
   through tree roots.

pick-ended mattock   grubbing mattock

e Bowsaw. The 21" (530mm) bowsaw is useful in scrub or coppice, and can also be used for any carpentry required when putting up the fence. Larger saws will be needed if there are trees or logs to clear.

f Chain saw. For major clearance. Chain saws must only be used by trained operators, and if possible, any such clearance should be done before, and if not, well away from, other clearing and fencing operations.

HOLE DIGGING AND POST ERECTION

a Crowbar. Various sizes and weights are available. Usual lengths are 5ft or 6ft (1.5m or 1.8m). A crowbar should be about the height of the user, so choose lengths accordingly. A very useful modification is a small punner head on one end of the crowbar (see below).

A strong but light crowbar can be made from a length of hexagonal jumper steel, available from scrap merchants or steel stockholders (see local 'Yellow Pages'). Cut to length and have one end forged to a point. The hexagonal shape also allows better grip.

Unless your hands are hardened to it wear gloves when using a crowbar, or you'll quickly get blisters. Stand well-balanced, with the feet apart, and use the weight of the bar, loosening the grip slightly on impact. When accusomed to it, more force can be used with the arms and shoulders. If you have to crouch or kneel to use a crowbar in a deep hole, take care not to hit your head with the upper end. If the bar gets stuck, pull up to one side of the body, so that if it suddenly comes free it won't hit you.

b Spade. The most suitable type will depend on the ground being encountered. A strong garden garden spade is sufficient in deep loamy or clay soils. Those with metal 'YD' handles are recommended for durability.

Trenching spades, listed in the BTCV Tool Catalogue are very useful tools. They are reasonably light and easy for anyone to use and have a slightly pointed and curved blade which is strong enough for digging in stony ground. They are also effective shovels.

Specialist spades are available for digging holes. These include the 'GPO rabbiting tool (Hunter Wilson) which is recommended by the Forestry Commission for fencing work. It

has a small curved blade and long steel handle. The Forestry Commission recommend welding a rammer head to the handle end, as described below for crowbars, to make a dual-purpose tool. Other types with long narrow blades include the draining spade (Spear and Jackson) and the trenching spade (Bulldog Tools).

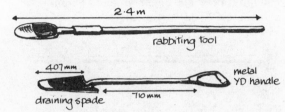

2.4m
rabbiting tool

407mm
metal YD handle
draining spade
710mm

c Shuv-holer. This is a large implement, consisting of two pointed and long-handled spades hinged together. It is used like large tongs to make holes in sand or very soft soil or for lifting debris from holes that are being dug with spades and crowbars. It should not be used for driving holes in hard or stony ground, as the blades become bent and damaged. The shuv-holer is indispensable for quickly making a deep narrow hole in most types of soil and does away with the discomfort of grovelling with your hands in deep muddy holes (see p70). It is however, a fairly heavy and cumbersome implement and takes up space in a vehicle. The shuv-holer is available in the standard or heavy-duty model (Drivall). The standard model weighs 6kg, and can dig at 250mm diameter hole to a depth of 1.4m.

A new development is the mini shuv-holer (Drivall), which has blades of spade thickness for use in heavy ground, and can dig a 150mm diameter hole to a depth of 1.4m. It weighs 5kg.

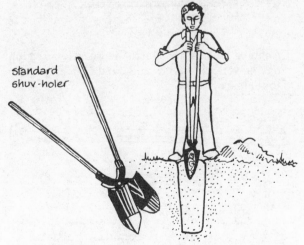

standard shuv-holer

The 'shuv-breaker' (Drivall) has a hardened steel point, and is designed to be used in conjunction with the shuv-holer for breaking up hard and stony ground.

d Auger. Manual augers are useful in loam and clay soils. in which you can quickly make a deep cylindrical hole. A large hole for a strainer or gate post can be made by making two or more holes immediately next to one another. An auger is no use in stony soil. Various diameters are available, including 150mm (Spear and Jackson) and 150mm 230mm and 300mm (Drivall).

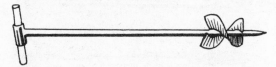

e Punner. This is used for firming the soil back around the post, and must be narrow enough to fit down between the post and the side of the hole. The nearer the diameter of the hole is to that of the post, the firmer the post will be. Most earth punners are 100mm or more in diameter, and are made of cast iron, which will shatter if used on rock.

A much more useful tool is one with a narrow mild steel head, of about 75mm diameter. Agricultural merchants may stock a crowbar with a rammer head, commonly called a 'mushroom-headed' crowbar. Another commercially available tool is the tapered square punch (Hunter Wilson), which has a punch at one end for making holes, and a rammer at the other. If these tools are not easily obtainable, a rammer can be made by welding a suitable piece of mild steel to the chisel end of a crowbar (the chisel end being normally less useful than the pointed end).

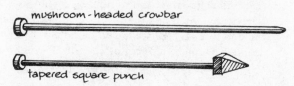

mushroom-headed crowbar

tapered square punch

Another idea is the design shown below. which has been well tried by the Cardiff Conservation Volunteers.

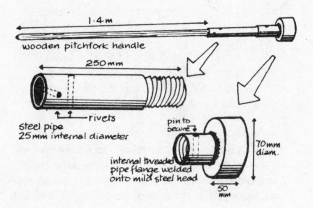

1·4 m

wooden pitchfork handle

250 mm

steel pipe
25 mm internal diameter

rivets

pin to secure

internal threaded pipe flange welded onto mild steel head

70mm diam.

50 mm

Some fencers favour using a wooden rammer, which at its simplest is merely a stout piece of unsawn hardwood, such as a birch bough, and is the type of tool which becomes irreplaceable to its owner. It is not recommended to use a softwood stake up-ended, as you will rapidly get blisters, and the earth will not firm as well as when a steel rammer is used.

f Mell. This is a long-handled tool with a cast iron head. used for driving wooden posts into the ground. Some strength and experience is needed to use a mell effectively, and it should be swung so the head hits the post squarely on the top. If it hits the edge. the post will not go in straight. and post top will be damaged. The post should be held steady by another person preferably using a stob holder (see below), in order to keep a safe distance from the mell. Do not use a mell on metal, as the cast iron head will shatter.

g Rubber mell. This type of mell has a large cylindrical head of hard, solid rubber. and in the right hands. is an extremely effective and quick tool for knocking wooden posts into the ground. However, some people find the 'rebound' awkward. and because of the larger head, it has to be held higher than a cast iron mell in order to hit the post squarely.

h Maul. This is a traditional tool, with a large wooden mallet head, bound with metal straps. The head tends to get worn, especially if not hit 'squarely' to the post, and needs replacing from time to time. They are similar in use to a rubber mell, the large driving face being advantageous. but the longer head requiring the tool to be held high. Mauls and replacement heads are available from agricultural merchants.

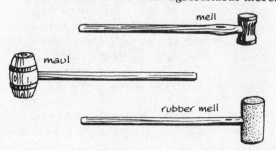

mell

maul

rubber mell

i Stob holder/twister. These can be made out of any suitable piece of solid square-section mild steel bar, available from scrap merchants, or steel stockholders.

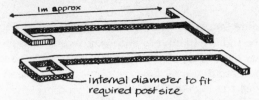

1m approx

internal diameter to fit required post size

j Drivall. This tool is designed especially for driving posts into the ground, and is preferred by many people to the mell. If used properly, it is a safer and less tiring method than using a mell, but if used wrongly it can be dangerous. The post driver should only be lifted by a small amount, and dropped down with a regular, easy movement. If heaved up very high it can come off the post and hit the user on the head as it topples over. It is recommended that volunteers should wear safety helmets when using drivalls.

Various sizes are available, as listed below, the smaller sizes having two handles for use by one or two people, and the large sizes having four handles for use by up to four people. Those sizes marked * on the list below can be supplied with safety view vents cut in the side, which allow the user to see the top of the post, and thus avoid lifting the drivall higher than necessary.

SIZES OF DRIVALL

Size	Weight (kg)	Max. post diameter (mm)	
		Square	Round
1	2.5	19	19
2	9.0	35	45
3	13.5	52	70
3A	18.5	50 x 50 angle iron	
4*	16.5	67	95
5*	19.5	89	120
6A*	25.5	108	146
6*	31.0	as 6A but with 4 handles	
7	39.0	124	171
8	45.5	140	197

* can be supplied with safety view vents

Sizes 4,5,6A and 6 are the most popular sizes.

Drivalls are heavy tools, and you need to be fairly strong even to lift one up and onto a 1.6m stake. However two less strong people can manage to lift and effectively use a small drivall probably with more success than using a mell. Take care always on slopes or slippery ground when lifting a drivall on or off a post. When using it stand erect with legs apart to give balance and use the arms and bend the legs if neccessary not the back.

The drivall does avoid any damage to the post top, thus lengthening post life, as any splits will hasten rotting. However, if too large a size drivall is used for the size of the post, the movement of the drivall does tend to damage and chafe the post at the point shown below. A disadvantage of the drivall is that it can only be used effectively on the correct sized post and not at all on a post that is too big, or bent. Guides are available from the manufacturer (Drivall), designed to convert a round drivall for use with square posts, and to stop the chafing problem described above.

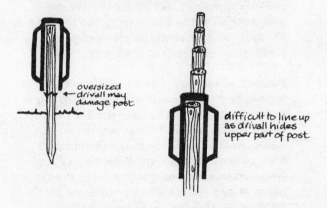

oversized drivall may damage post

difficult to line up as drivall hides upper part of post

It is also not easy to exactly line up fence posts when using a drivall particularly if it is over-sized, as you cannot see the upper part of the post. Even a few millimetres can make the fence line wobbly, which apart from appearance, is less strong than a perfectly straight fence.

The drivall can be useful in confined spaces where you cannot swing a mell, but conversely it cannot be used, for example where a post needs to be driven flush with a wall or tree.

The manufacturers sell extension handles to enable the drivall to be used on tall posts for deer fencing etc. However some fencers find it easier to lay the post on the ground, slide the drivall on and then hoist the post upright into the pilot hole. You can then reach up to use the drivall, and should be able to lift it off safely from the finished height of 1.8 - 2m.

Similar types of post drivers can be custom made for square or any other shape post, including those with weathered (sloping) tops. These are used by fencing contractors who may be putting up miles of fences with identical size sawn posts.

In conclusion, the correct size drivall is a very useful tool especially for those people who find mells difficult to use, but it is a heavy tool, and may not be worth carrying to a work site innaccessible by vehicle. Most people find though that ease of use outweighs any disadvantages.

SECURING THE FENCE

a Hammer. Ball pein hammers have the advan-tage of not suffering the abuse that claw hammers receive. in being used for extracting large nails. This is the usual cause of broken hafts. steel hafts included. A ball pein hammer with a wooden haft will probably have the longest life and can be rehafted as necessary. A 16oz head (the weight is stamped on the side) is suitable for most volunteer use.

b Fencing pliers. This is a multi-purpose tool for bending cutting and straining wire and removing staples. The hammer head is not heavy enough to knock large staples in but can be used as shown to knock the tool with a hammer in behind a stubborn staple. Some fencers claim that this does weaken the hinge of the pliers and it is better to use a proper staple extractor (see below), if available.

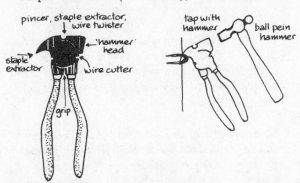

Always choose good quality fencing pliers such as those made by CeKa. Fencing pliers are not suitable for cutting high tensile wire for which special cutters are needed (see below).

c Wire strainers. These are essential for straining plain wire barbed wire and stock netting either of mild steel or high tensile steel. Monkey strainers manufactured by Trewhella Bros., are probably the best and most widely used. They can be used on mild or high tensile steel wire and the grip does not scratch or bend the wire excessively either of which can damage and weaken the wire. They can also be used with a wire strop, which keeps the strainer out of the way of the

wire fixings. The Monkey strainer has a chain guide which helps prevent the chain getting twisted as the strain is taken up. Spares are available as necessary.

Some fencers favour Hayes strainers, which are lighter to carry, and equally effective. However they do not have a chain guide, and the grip distorts the wire slightly more than does the Monkey strainer.

Further information on the use of strainers is given on page 55.

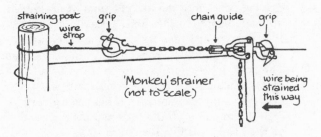

d Wire strop. This is not essential but makes the job of securing the wires easier as the strainer is well out of the way. The strop needs to be strong enough to withstand repeated straining to high loads. Hunter Wilson market one of galvanised plaited wire 1.2m long, which can withstand a load of one ton.

e Straining boards or clamps. These are used for straining stock netting, particularly high tensile netting and make it easier to achieve an even tension. Clamps are available in wood or steel (Drivall), or they can be home-made. A suitable design is shown below, for use on 8/90/30 or 8/80/30 netting (see p46) Hardwood should be used, as this gives a better grip on the wires than does softwood.

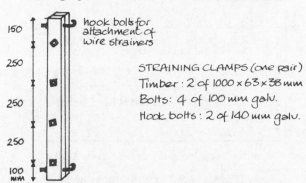

Clamps are used either as one pair attached to the straining post with normal Hayes or Monkey strainers, or alternatively two pairs are used, with specially adapted strainers (see p56). Clamps take some time to attach and are heavy to carry, and are probably only worth obtaining if a lot of fencing is to be done.

OTHER TOOLS

a Wire dispenser. This is essential when
   handling high tensile or spring steel wire, to
   prevent any kinks being made while the wire is
   being unrolled. An all-steel model is available
   from Hunter Wilson, or a wooden one can be
   made at home.

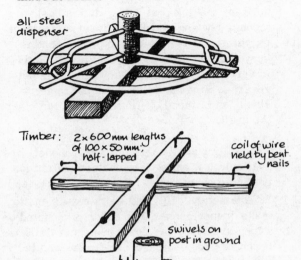

b Wire cutters. High tensile steel wire cannot
   be cut with ordinary fencing pliers, and is best
   cut with special cutters such as the Felco C7
   (available from Felco, Hunter Wilson).
   Alternatively bolt-croppers or a junior hack-
   saw can be used. Either of these are also
   useful for cutting mild steel wire of 3.15mm
   diameter or more, which is hard work to cut
   with fencing pliers.

c Ring fastener gun. This is used for fastening
   wire rings to attach netting to line wires
   (Gerrard). A cheaper tool which can also be
   used for attaching netting is the wire tying
   tool designed for securing sacks (Drivall).

d Wire twister. This is a very simple small
   tool easily made from a suitable piece of
   metal, through which a hole is drilled. The
   dimensions are not critical but the bar should
   not be longer than 100mm. in order to use with
   stock netting. The loose end of the wire is put
   through the hole. and the twister is wound
   around to make a neat finish.

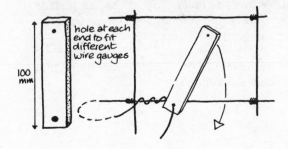

e Wire bending tool. This neat but rather costly
   tool bends wire without causing any damage to
   the galvanising. It is recommended by the
   Forestry Commission for use on high tensile
   spring steel wire (Pullmaflex).

f Staple extractor. This effectively removes
   staples or nails from timber, even if embedded.
   To use, position the jaws over the staple or
   nail head, and then drop the sliding handle
   which drives in the jaws and closes them. Then
   push against the lever to pull the staple out.

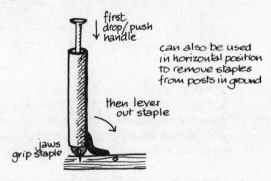

g Swan neck or wrecking bar. For removing
   large nails and staples.

h Tension meter. It is useful to be able to check
   the tension on a strained wire, so it can be
   strained to the most effective tension. A tension
   gauge which attaches to Monkey or Hayes
   strainers is available (Drivall), or one can
   be made at home using a spring balance. For
   further details see page 44.

i Anchor disc tool. This is used on high tensile
   fencing to screw anchor discs into the ground.
   These hold down the fence where it crosses
   a dip (see p80).

j Lump hammer. For breaking up large stones
   or knocking them to shape for use in wedging
   strainer posts firmly into the ground.

k Spirit level. For checking horizontal and
   vertical components, particularly in post and
   rail fencing.

l Builder's line. For laying out fence lines,
   siting holes and posts, especially in post and
   rail fencing.

m Tape. 50 or 100m tapes are useful for
   measuring the fence line to estimate materials,
   to lay out post and rail fences and to measure
   distances between straining posts. A 5m tape
   is also handy, especially for post and rail.

n Measuring stick or measuring blocks. These
   are home-made, to suit the dimensions of the

fence. Make sure there are sufficient for each working group to have one. A measuring stick for post and wire fencing is best made with slots cut at the wire heights, so it can be 'hung' on the fence while other wires are measured and attached. Measuring blocks are used between the rails of post and rail fencing.

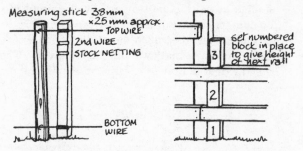

o Fencing belts. Various types are available, either as complete belts, or pouches which fit onto ordinary belts. They are useful for anyone doing a lot of fencing or other construction work out of doors (Curnow).

p Canvas buckets. These are useful for carrying nails, staples and small tools, and can be carried comfortably at your side.

The following tools are suggested for groups of twelve people doing fencing work.

Post and wire fencing

2 crowbars	2 wire twisters
2 wrecking bars	1 staple extractor
4 spades	1 pair wire cutters
2 shuv-holers	3 wire strainers
2 punners	1 wire dispenser
1 drivall	1 tension gauge
2 mells or mauls	2 measuring sticks
1 stob holder	1 spirit level
1 lumphammer	1 50m tape
2 bowsaws (530mm)	creosote
2 mallets	clearing tools, as needed
2 chisels (25mm)	2 safety helmets
3 pairs fencing pliers	goggles
4 hammers	first aid kit

Post and rail fencing - posts set in dug holes

2 crowbars
5 spades
2 shuv-holers
1 auger/post hole borer (use instead of spades and
    shuv-holers in suitable ground)

3 punners	builders line
2 bowsaws (530mm)	1 spirit level
2 mallets	1 50m tape
2 chisels	1 5m tape
2 surforms	creosote
4 hammers	first aid kit

Machines

These are mainly used by farmers and fencing contractors, but hire of a machine may make feasible a job which otherwise volunteer groups could not undertake.

a Power auger. This is a hand-held machine used for making post holes. and is basically a chain saw engine with an auger attachment (eg Stihl). It is held by two people. and is very quick in loam or clay soils. but no use in very stony soils. As the auger does not reverse. care has to be taken not to get it stuck. and it needs lifting frequently to clear the spoil.

b Tractor-mounted auger. Several models are available. Fleming manufacture hydraulic post hole borers in 4". 6 9 . 12 , 18 and 24" diameters, 30" long, with extensions to make deeper holes. The auger is mounted on a long arm, and has great manoeuvrability so it can be used over hedges, ditches and in awkward corners. The auger reverses to un-jam.

Opico market the Arps K23 for use with mini tractors, which can be fitted with a 9", 12" or 18" auger. The Arps 103S, recommended for farm use, makes holes 40" deep and up to 18" diameter.

c Tractor-mounted post driver. This is the quickest way of erecting posts, and also gives the firmest results (see p62). The best known make is the Parmiter.

d Transport. Transporting materials to the site is often a very important factor. especially on upland sites, and voluntary bodies should beware of getting involved in tasks which are basically just carrying materials, and which could be done more effectively by machine. Any of the following could be used:

i Four wheel drive vehicle.

ii Tractor and trailer.

iii All terrain vehicles. These are vehicles with with low ground pressure for use on soft ground and steep slopes. Makes include 'Snowback', 'Bombi', 'Highland Garron' and 'Argocat'.

iv Helicopter. For lifting heavy items into innaccessible sites.

Organising the Job

a Fencing is a skilled job. If voluntary groups are doing the work, try and ensure that at least three experienced people are included for tasks involving twelve or so volunteers. Because of its linear nature, fencing is not easy to supervise, and if only the leader is skilled he or she is likely to have an exhausting time chasing up and down the fenceline, and work will progress only slowly.

b Site managers and voluntary groups should consult carefully before agreements are made about undertaking fencing work. For the site manager, volunteers may not be the most cost effective method of getting the work done. In spite of their higher labour charge, contractors may be able to do the job for a similar or cheaper price, because they have the skills and the equipment to do the job much more quickly. This is likely to apply particularly on long and fairly straightforward stretches of fencing. On very difficult terrain and stony ground where the job of post-hole digging is a major factor, the speed difference between contractors and volunteers is likely to be less.

On the other hand, organisers of voluntary groups should be wary of work which perhaps contractors have for good reason not been keen to undertake. These include fencing on sites where there is no vehicle access, and a lot of time and energy must be spent in moving materials. This may be acceptable , depending on the conservation value of the work, but it may also put some volunteers off good works for life!

c Fencing is quicker and easier with sufficient numbers of the correct tools, some of which are quite expensive and used exclusively or mainly for fencing. Local groups should perhaps decide whether fencing is going to be a useful skill for them to offer in their particular area, and equip themselves accordingly with tools and training.

d The leader of any group should if possible be involved in the planning and siting of the fence, in the ordering of materials and in deciding where materials should be off-loaded if delivery is being made to the site. The leader should not be expected to cope with a poorly planned job or inadequate materials. If such involvement is not possible, the leader should at least try to visit the site ahead of the group, so that details can be planned out carefully for work to start without delay when the group arrives.

e Materials should be ordered as early as possible, to lessen the chance of having to make do with inadequate materials through lack of time. This particularly applies to wooden posts, as if these have to be purchased in a hurry you increase the likelihood of getting improperly dried and preserved timber.

f Consider whether it should be safe to leave materials on site overnight, or whether you will need to only take sufficient for each day's work, leaving the rest in a secure place.

g Fencing is not only geographically linear, but also chronologically, ie the basic pattern of work involves starting at one end and proceedin through an ordered sequence of operations to the other! This is not the easiest type of task for effectively using a large group of volunteers. Consider the following approaches:

i Divide the fence line up into lengths, for example between straining posts for a strained wire fence, or from the corners of a post and rail fence. Divide the group into twos or threes, preferably with one skilled person in each. Each pair then does the same sequence of jobs on a different section of fence. This system is limited by the number of tools and skilled volunteers available.

ii Another approach is to phase the work so that pairs or threes are doing entirely different jobs, for example carrying materials, clearing vegetation, lining out the fence, digging post holes etc. This is usually the more efficient method, especially if the stronger and more skilled volunteers are used effectively, but it means that volunteers don't necessarily get the chance to see all the phases of the task, even if the leader is conscientious about rotating jobs.

iii It is useful to have some other work arranged in case there are spare hands at any stage. Coppicing, scrub clearance, weeding young trees, rubbish removal or any other fairly straightforward job might be suitable. There are also the jobs ancillary to fencing such as stile building, gate hanging and footpath work.

4 Strained Fencing – Materials and Techniques

Fencing Timber

Consider what timber is available, as it may be possible to use other than the normal commercial supplies. Areas with woodland may be self-sufficient in timber for fencing, such timber usually being referred to as 'estate timber'. The need for fencing timber may usefully combine with woodland management work in nature reserves. Oak, sweet chestnut, larch, yew and western red cedar are the only native or introduced species with naturally durable heartwood. As shown in the table opposite, all other home grown timber is either 'perishable' or 'non-durable', but most can be effectively treated.

Second-hand materials may be available. The most commonly used are railway sleepers and telegraph poles, which if still in good condition should give many years useful life as gate posts or straining posts. A simple method of testing such timbers is to knock them at intervals along their length with a hammer. A 'ringing' noise indicates sound timber, whereas a dull thud indicates rotting timber.

Other second-hand material may include posts or rails from dis-used fences, and demolition materials. Provided it is free from decay, recovered timber is as good as new, and can be given preservative treatment if long outdoor life is required.

See page 18 for notes concerning the intended life of the fence. There is no point in using naturally durable or preserved timber in a fence which is only going to be needed for a few years.

TIMBER DECAY

Wetting and ageing do not in themselves cause timber decay. Decay is caused by fungi which feed on the timber. As described below, these fungi also require moisture, oxygen and warmth in order to live.

Wood is also attacked by insects, but in exterior use, timber treated against fungal attack will also be proof against insects.

a Food. Timber which is naturally durable against fungal attack contains substances produced by the tree, which are harmful or toxic to fungi. Treatment of non-durable timber with preservative produces the same effect.

b Moisture. Freshly felled timber may contain as much water as actual wood, and is then described as having a moisture content of 100%. Once dried to below 20%, timber will not decay as there is not sufficient moisture for the fungi to live. Timber dried to 20% will not re-absorb water from damp air only, but direct rainfall, splashing or the presence of any 'trapped' water, for example at timber joints, will cause the moisture content to rise above 20%. Thus all fencing in Britain of non-durable non-preserved timber is subject to fungal attack, although the degree will vary with the location and the site. A fence in damp woodland, for example, will rot more quickly than a fence in an open windy site. Timber in contact with the ground will rot much more quickly than timber out of ground contact.

c Oxygen. Fungi only require minute amounts of oxygen in order to live, and it is not possible to exclude oxygen from the wood by any form of surface coating such as paint or varnish. Timber totally immersed in water, or in an impermeable, heavy soil may avoid fungal attack due to the lack of oxygen.

d Warmth. Fungal growth and timber decay is most active at around 20 degrees centigrade. Below 5 degrees it becomes dormant, so although the rate of timber decay is reduced in cold winters, the British climate is not cold enough to control it.

HEARTWOOD AND SAPWOOD

Bark is the external corky layer of the trunk. It is impermeable, and must be removed before the timber is dried or treated.

Sapwood is the outer layer of wood. Its pale colour makes it easily recognisable in species which have a dark heartwood, but difficult to distinguish in pale timbers such as spruce. The presence of bark can be a useful indication of sapwood. Sapwood of all species has a low resistance to decay, but on the other hand it is permeable and relatively easy to treat with preservative.

Heartwood is the central part of the trunk, and is very variable between different species. Some have naturally durable heartwood, while others are perishable, and likewise their permeability to preservative treatment varies from high to low (see table opposite).

Round timber, with a protective layer of sapwood that can be deeply penetrated with preservative is generally considered to be the best material for fence posts. Square posts of treated softwood are also suitable, but those containing a proportion of non-durable heartwood are more difficult to treat effectively. Round timber also has advantages in the construction of strained wire fences (see p74).

Cleft timber is split along the grain, and the cleft surface sheds water better, and therefore rots less quickly, than the same timber sawn.

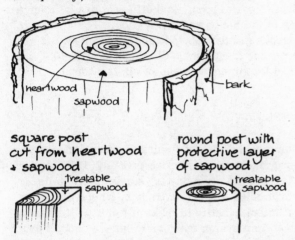

heartwood
sapwood
bark

square post cut from heartwood + sapwood
treatable sapwood

round post with protective layer of sapwood
treatable sapwood

Natural durability

The table below shows the natural durability of the heartwood of British native and introduced species. The assessment is made by testing standard size posts 50 x 50mm square, partly buried in the ground, and tested over many years. In practice, durability will vary according to the site and weather conditions. Durability is also proportional to the size of the timber, and for example, a post of cross section 100 x 100mm would have twice the life of one 100 x 50mm.

Ease of preservation

The table shows the permeability to preservative of different heartwoods. All sapwoods are in the categories of either moderately resistant or permeable, and can therefore be effectively treated.

Timber must be dried to 25-30% moisture content before treatment. This is done either in the open air (see p40), or in a kiln, which is a very much quicker and more accurate operation.

Table 4a: BRITISH TIMBERS (heartwood)

	NATURAL DURABILITY				EASE OF PRESERVATION			
	Durable 15 - 25 yrs	Moderately durable 10 - 15 yrs	Non-durable 5 - 10 yrs	Perishable Less than 5 yrs	Extremely resistant	Resistant	Moderately resistant	Permeable
Alder				*				*
Ash			*				*	
Beech				*				*
Birch				*				*
Cedar, Western Red		*					*	
Douglas Fir			*				*	
Elm, Wych			*				*	
Fir, Grand			*				*	
Hemlock, Western			*				*	
Hornbeam				*				*
Horse chestnut				*				*
Larch, European		*					*	
Larch, Japanese		*					*	
Lime				*				*
Oak, European	*					*		
Pine, Lodgepole			*				*	
Pine, Maritime		*					*	
Pine, Scots			*				*	
Poplar, Grey			*				*	
Spruce, European			*				*	
Spruce, Sitka			*				*	
Sweet chestnut	*					*		
Sycamore			*					*
Willow, white			*				*	
Willow, crack			*				*	
Yew	*						*	

PRESERVATIVE TREATMENTS

Properly preserved timber of a perishable species will outlast untreated timber of a durable species. The following section describes the various types of preservative and methods of application.

Organic solvents

These contain various chemicals dissolved in an organic solvent similar to white spirit. The solvent, which is flammable, carries the preservative into the wood, and as it evaporates, leaves the preservative behind. Once evaporated, the flammability of the wood is not increased. Organic solvents do not contain water, and their use does not cause the wood to swell or distort. They are not suitable for wood in contact with the ground, but can be used for fencing panels and rails. They are best applied by double vaccuum, but can also be applied by immersion or by brush or spray. Products available include various types of Cuprinol (Cuprinol Ltd), Vacsol (Hickson's Timber Products Ltd) and Rentokil preservative (Rentokil Ltd). All are non-corrosive and non-staining.

Waterborne copper chrome arsenate (CCA)

The wetting of the timber during treatment with this preservative can cause it to swell or distort, but this does not affect their use for fencing. Within about a week of treatment the preservative becomes chemically bonded to the timber and is resistant to leaching. Timber should never be supplied still wet from treatment. The treated and dried timber has a clean finish of a pale greenish-grey colour, and the surface can be treated with a stain or other coating. CCA preservatives can only be applied by vaccuum pressure impregnation.

Products include Tanalith C (Hickson s Timber Products Ltd) which is the preservative used in 'tanalised' timber and Celcure A (Rentokil Ltd) which gives 'celcurised' timber also called SupaTimba.

Tanabrun is a tanalith preservative containing a wood stain, which preserves and colours the timber in one process. The colour is only effective on sawn timber and this treatment is designed for panel fencing post and rail fencing and so on. Celbronze is a similar type of product from Rentokil Ltd.

Creosote

This is a tar-oil in use for many years for heavy exterior timbers. It is very resistant to leaching,

and gives the wood a degree of water repellancy, but treated wood is unpleasant to handle, particularly in hot weather when it becomes sticky. It does not seriously corrode metals, so staples, gate fittings etc are not damaged. Treated timber cannot be given any form of surface coating. Once thoroughly dried, creosoted timber is slightly more fire resistant than untreated timber.

Creosote is available in various shades from light to dark brown, and different grades, according to the method of application. The heavy viscous grades (BS 144) are only suitable for pressure treatment. Fluid grades (BS 3051) are used for immersion and brush treatment.

APPLICATION METHODS

Commercial methods using pressure and heat are very much more effective than any 'DIY' method of treatment. The latter is only likely to be worth doing for estate timber, where there is sufficient quantity to make it worth while setting up an immersion tank, and where a shorter life expectancy than commercially treated timber is acceptable.

Vaccuum pressure

Under this system timber is put into a sealed cylinder, and then a vaccuum is used to draw air out of the timber. The cylinder is then filled with preservative, and pressure applied to force it into the wood. This method is suitable for CCA and creosote preservatives, and gives the highest standard of protection.

Double vaccuum treatment

This method is similar to that described above, except that a second vaccuum is drawn to remove excess solvent and speed drying. The pressure used is not as high as in the previous method, and the dimensions of the timber are not affected. It is therefore mainly used on accurately cut timbers for building work. Of the preservatives described above, this method is only used with organic solvents, and is the best method for this type of preservative.

Hot and cold open tank

This process is only used for applying creosote. The timber is immersed in an open tank of creosote, which is then heated to 90 degrees C, and kept at this temperature for one to three hours. The heat causes expansion of the air in the timber. The tank is then left to cool, and as the timber cools it draws in the creosote. This gives a good level of protection.

Immersion

This simple treatment is done by totally immersing the timber in the preservative for a period of not less than 3 minutes. Suitable preservatives are the organic solvents, or the fluid grades of creosote. This does not give as good protection as the other methods described above, but may be suitable for short to medium life fencing, or for timber not in contact with the ground.

Standards for commercial timber preservation

Timber treatment is strictly governed by British Standards, British Wood Preserving Association Specifications, and 'special purpose standards such as those of the Ministry of Transport for motorway fencing. Rentokil Ltd (SupaTimba) and Hickson's Timber Products Ltd (Tanalised timber) both have authorised processors throughout Great Britain, and Tanalised timber is also available from many builders' merchants and agricultural suppliers. Jacksons Fencing Ltd have CCA treatment plants at four sites in England, and distribute 'Jakcured timber' direct to customers in Great Britain and Ireland.

Rentokil Ltd have a 'specifiers code' which applies to timber treated by any of their authorised processors. These codes are aimed to simplify the job of specifying timber so that both purchaser and supplier know what is wanted. The relevant codes for fencing timber are as follows:

ST15 Timber for motorway or by-pass fencing
ST16 Timbers in ground contact (specify 20 or 40 year service life)
ST17 Rails and other timbers out of ground contact (specify 20 or 40 year service life)
ST18 Panels

Hickson's Timber Products Ltd operate a similar scheme via their authorised processors.

There is no easy method of checking the standard of preservation treatment, so it is worth buying from a reputable source. Each individual in a batch of similar size timbers, such as stakes, should weigh roughly the same. Any heavy ones may not have been properly dried or re-dried, although the weight difference may also be due to a difference in the type of timber. CCA and organic-solvent treated timber should always be dried at the processors after treatment, before being supplied to the customer. Organic-solvent treated timber is usually re-dried as part of the double vaccuum process. CCA timber should be left to dry for at least 48 hours after treatment, and seven days should elapse after treatment

before the timber is put anywhere where animals could come in contact with it. Always order treated timber well in advance of the time it is required, so that there is no risk of being supplied timber that has not been sufficiently dried.

Both CCA and organic solvent treated wood is safe to handle once the re-drying period has elapsed. Creosoted wood retains an oily surface for some time after treatment. Always wear gloves and protective clothing when handling it.

End-sealing

Don't cut pressure treated timber unless necessary for the construction of the fence. Even under pressure, the preservative only penetrates the outer layer of wood, and any cut across the grain will expose untreated timber. Don't finish off the fence by cutting the tops of the stakes just to give a neat and even appearance. Where cuts are unavoidable, such as in fitting struts to strainers, treat the cut area by brush application.

Special products are available for the end treatment of the various types of pre-treated timber. For example, 'Ensele' for use on tanalised timber, and 'Celcure B' for use on celcurised timber. These should be obtained from the timber processors who supply the timber. If not available, creosote or cuprinol can be used. When applying it, flood the area of the cut with preservative, and as soon as the first coat has started to dry on the surface, apply a second coat, to keep the preservative moving into the wood. Keep animals away for at least seven days.

DIY treatment

Of the methods described above, hot and cold open tank or immersion are the only two possible for use on estate timber. Hot and cold open tank treatment is not recommended, because of the danger involved in heating creosote to the required temperature.

The most suitable estate timber is likely to be round timber of 100-200mm diameter, which can be used un-split. As it is the sapwood which is treatable, it is best to use this as an outer protective layer. Larger timbers which need splitting are probably only worth using if they are of species with naturally durable heartwood. Non durable heartwood is difficult to impregnate without pressure treatment, and timber of this size is better converted and treated commercially.

To treat estate timber, first de-bark the timber, using a bark peeling spade, draw knife or sharpened garden spade. It is easier to peel the bark immediately after felling, before the sap dries. If using a peeling spade, brace the end of the timber against a support to keep it steady. If a draw knife is being used, it is worth constructing a 'shaving brake', to hold the timber at an easy working height.

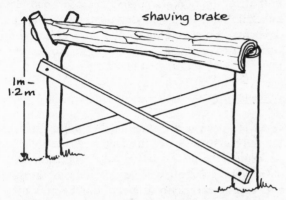

shaving brake

1m – 1.2m

The timber should then be stacked for drying on a level, dry site, in alternating layers as shown. Cover the top against the rain with a sheet of corrugated iron or similar, well weighted down.

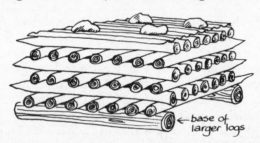

← base of larger logs

Drying time will vary according to the size of the timber, the weather and the time of year. As a guide, 150mm diameter softwood poles, stacked in autumn or winter, should dry in about 6 months. Wood felled in spring should season in 2-4 months in a dry summer.

The moisture content of the wood can be checked with a special meter that measures the electrical resistance across two steel pins which are pushed into the timber (Verus Instruments, p135). Alternatively, an estimate can be made by weighing a few sample pieces before and after seasoning. The timber should lose $\frac{1}{4}-\frac{1}{3}$ of its original weight.

Immersion treatment can be done using either creosote or an organic solvent preservative. Any suitable tank can be used, according to the length of the timbers. These could include old baths, galvanised tanks or oil drums. Arrange it so that the timber is not directly handled, but is lifted in and out of the tank by a hoist, which can transfer the timber to a stand for drying. Alternatively, use slings as shown below, to move the timber. A simple economy method for stakes is to merely treat the base ends by standing them in a partly filled drum. Treat to 250-300mm above ground level.

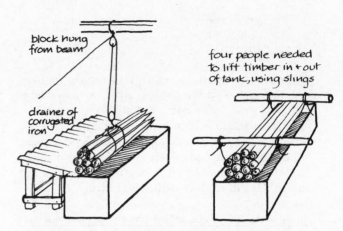

block hung from beam

drainer of corrugated iron

four people needed to lift timber in + out of tank, using slings

Timber should be immersed for at least three minutes. Don't bundle the timber tightly or this will inhibit the flow of the preservative. Timbers in a large tank may need pushing down and turning to ensure even coverage. Immersion only results in slight penetration of the wood, and is only suitable for permeable timber. Resistant timbers absorb little even after long periods of immersion.

Penetration of the timber can be increased by using heat. Because direct heating of the preservative is dangerous, the method recommended (MAFF, 1977, Fixed Equipment of the Farm 17) is to heat the timber in a tank of water over a fire, to a temperature of 82-93 degrees C. Keep it at this temperature for 1-2 hours, and do not allow it to cool or water will be absorbed. Then quickly remove the timber to a tank of cold preservative, where it remains another 1-2 hours.

Although giving improved penetration, this will not be to the standard of pressure treatment, and the time and expense of immersion treatment and its shorter life expectancy must be weighed against the costs and benefits of purchases pre-treated timber.

Brush or high pressure spray

These methods only give limited protection against decay, and should only be used where no other method is possible. The fluid grades of creosote and organic solvents can be applied using a pressure sprayer, of the type usually sold for garden use. This is cleaner and quicker than using a brush, but gives similar surface covering only. Protect hands and eyes when spraying, and do not use a spray on a windy day.

Non-timber Posts

Concrete posts

These are used mainly for chain link security fencing. Slotted posts are also available for use with concrete or wooden panel fencing. Concrete posts have the advantage of durability, but are heavy to transport and erect, and do not look appropriate in countryside settings. They may be useful however in places where vandalism is a problem, or timber posts are stolen for use as firewood.

Posts for chain link fencing are produced in the following heights and sizes. Others are available with a bent arm at the top to take barbed wire. The strained wires of the chain link are attached to the posts by stirrup wires, threaded through holes in the post. Galvanised 2.5mm or PVC coated 3.15 or 2.24mm wires are supplied in 5kg bundles, cut to length for stirrup wires.

Chain link Height	Intermediate posts taper to 3"x 3"section		Straining and gate posts	
	Length	Base section	Length	Section
3' (900mm)	5'3"	4½" x 4½"	5'3"	5" x 5"
4' (1.2m)	6'3"	5" x 5"	6'3"	5" x 5"
4½' (1.4m)	6'9"	5" x 5"	6'9"	5" x 5"
5' (1.5m)	7'3"	5" x 5"	7'3"	5" x 5"
6' (1.8m)	8'9"	5" x 5"	8'9"	5" x 5"

Slotted posts for panels are available in heights of 5, 6, 7, 8, 9 and 10ft, to be set in the ground 2ft. Corner posts are also available, and concrete gravel boards to protect the base of wooden panels from rot.

Other materials

For some years posts have been available which are made out of waste plastics. These have the advantage of durability with no maintenance, and are less attractive to vandals than timber posts. They also 'recycle' an otherwise wasted material. Posts can be cut with a saw, driven into the ground, accept nails and screws in the same way as hardwood, and can be used for electric fencing as they are non-conductive. They are more expensive than equivalent size pressure treated softwood.

'Duraposts' are available in the following sizes. See page 135 for supplier.

Section	Max. length
50 x 50mm	2m
75 x 75mm	3m
100 x 100mm	3.35m
24mm diam	1m
35mm diam	2m
50mm diam	2m
75mm diam	2.45m
100mm diam	3.35m
150mm diam	2m

Metal posts

The most widely available metal posts are of angle iron, designed for use with chain link fencing. They are supplied with holes drilled for the line wire positions appropriate to the height of the fence. Straining posts are supplied with the necessary fittings for stays, and normally have a base plate. Posts are usually supplied painted with one coat of oxide paint.

Although usually used with chain link, the posts can be used for other types of fencing which can be supported on strained wires. This could include hexagonal mesh, chestnut paling or other materials.

The following sizes are available. The size given is the angle, by the thickness of the metal. Taller sizes are also available, for fences up to 3.6m high.

Chain link height	900mm	1.2m	1.4m	1.8m
Post height	1.5m	1.8m	2.0m	2.6m
Line wires (no)	2	3	3	3
Intermediates	all 40 x 40 x 5mm			
End posts	all 50 x 50 x 6mm			
Corner posts	all 50 x 50 x 6mm			
2-way strainers	all 50 x 50 x 6mm			
Stays	all 40 x 40 x 5mm			

Wire

GALVANISING

Galvanising is a process which coats the surface of the steel with a layer of zinc, to lessen the rate of corrosion. Steel wire is coated by running it through a bath of zinc. In clean air zinc corrodes 15 to 20 times slower than steel. It also has the useful property of corroding preferentially to steel in localized areas, so at cut ends or scratches where the steel is exposed, the zinc corrodes to cover the exposed steel.

The length of life of any wire product depends on the effectiveness of the zinc coating, and the atmosphere in which the wire is used.

The effectiveness of the zinc coating is determined by:

a The weight or thickness of the zinc coat. A minimum coatweight of 260 grammes per square metre is required by the British Standard for galvanising of agricultural fencing (BS 443:1982). This is known as heavy galvanising .

b The adherence of the zinc to the steel. This depends on the quality of the steel and the process used.

c The concentricity of the coating. Corrosion starts at the point where the coating is thinnest.

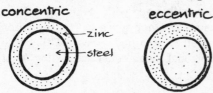

Any deficiencies in the zinc coating cannot be recognized by the customer, and will only become obvious when the wire rusts and breaks after a relatively short time. It is important to always use wire that is manufactured to BS 443, and bears the label of a reputable manufacturer.

The atmosphere in which the wire is to be used should be taken into consideration. Zinc corrodes more quickly in air polluted with sulphur dioxide, and also on coasts, where the air is heavily salt laden. Polluted coasts give the worst situation for wire life.

The following figure and table show the expected wire life for three weights of galvanising in different situations. This information is from the Sentinel Fencing Advisory Service.

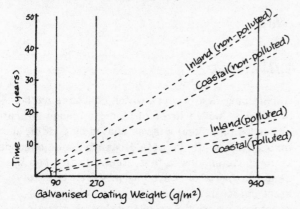

Expected lives of galvanised coatings in different situations

Coat wgt (g/m^2)	Expected life (years) Inland non-polluted	Coastal polluted
Commercial (wiped galvanising)	90	4.5	1
BS 443:1982 (heavy galvanising)	270	13.5	4
Triple galvanising	940	47.5	14

Another important factor in the reduction of corrosion is in the storage and handling of the wire.

a Wire stored in damp conditions, on concrete floors or in contact with fertilizers, chemicals or other corrosive materials may be damaged.

b Sharp kinks due to careless unwinding, or rough handling with fencing pliers or other equipment with serrated jaws will damage the zinc coating and increase corrosion. In addition, kinking weakens the wire, possibly causing it to snap.

c Loose fastening with staples on intermediate posts will allow the wire to rattle in the wind, which will damage the galvanising. Grommets can be used (p57) to prevent this damage.

d Frequent wetting and drying, such as occurs at ground level, will increase corrosion. Foot wires (see p65) should preferably be of stainless steel wire to avoid this problem. All other wires should be clear of the ground.

e There is some evidence that contact with timber recently treated with CCA preservative can increase the rate of corrosion.

Galfan

A recent introduction for fencing is wire coated with Galfan, which is a long lasting zinc and aluminium alloy. Although more expensive, it has three times the life of heavily galvanised wire. Stockfencing, barbed wire, plain wire and staples are all available coated with Galfan, and are marketed under the name of Triple Life, from Estate Wire Ltd. Triple Life is eligible for MAFF grant.

TENSILE STRENGTH

Tensile strength is the maximum load that a material can support when being stretched divided by the original cross sectional area of the material. It is measured in force per unit area. Tensile strength is given here in Newtons per mm^2 (N/mm^2) and tons per inch^2 (t/in^2). The tensile strength depends on the constituents of the wire and the method by which it is drawn. Thus tensile strength can vary for wires of the same thickness.

The table below shows the tensile strengths and other characteristics of the most commonly used fencing wires.

Mild steel wire, when pulled, stretches in two

FENCING WIRES: Tensile strengths and other characteristics

	Gauge	Diam (mm)	Tensile strength t/in^2	Tensile strength N/mm^2	Breaking strain N	Breaking strain kg	Recommended tension N min-max	Recommended tension kg min-max	Length m/25 kg
High tensile spring steel	12½	2.50	120	1850	8900	916	2450-3922	250-400	651
	12	2.65	100	1550	8000	810	2450-3432	250-350	581
High tensile steel	12½	2.50*	70	1080	5560	567	980-1470	100-150	651
	10	3.15	70	1080	8900	916	2450-3922	250-400	410
Mild steel	10	3.15	30	450	3500	355	735-980	75-100	410
	8	4.00	30	450	5650	576	980-1470	100-150	254

* this wire is only suitable for electric fencing, where high tensions are not required.

High tensile wires with a tensile strength greater than 1550N/mm^2 are called high tensile spring steel wires, or spring steel for short.

If using knots to join wires, rather than fence connectors (see p60), only strain to the minimum tensions shown.

1 ton force sq in = 15.444 N/mm^2 1 kg force = 9.806 N

distinct stages. The first is the elastic stage. when if the load is removed, the wire springs back to its original length. If pulled further, into the second or plastic stage, the wire elongates but does not spring back when the load is removed. The wire elongates considerably in the plastic stage before it breaks. The change from the elastic to the plastic stage is called the 'yield point'.

In contrast. high tensile and spring steel wires have no yield point but stretch elastically under high loads.

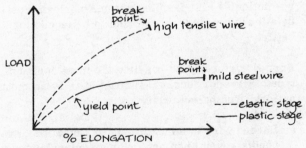

Because high tensile wire has greater elasticity than mild steel wire. it is able to retain tension under impact and varying atmospheric conditions. In cold weather wire contracts and the tension increases. In hot weather the wire expands. decreasing the tension. The change in length is similar for all types of wire, but the resultant increase or decrease in tension depends on the wire elasticity. If the contraction of mild steel wire in cold temperatures takes it beyond the yield

point, the wire will lose all springiness as temperatures rise.

For example:
4.00mm mild steel
Tension of 135 kg at 15 degrees C
Tension of 185 kg at -1 degrees C

2.5mm high tensile steel
Tension of 135 kg at 15 degrees C
Tension of 155 kg at -1 degrees C

For practical purposes, the effect of temperature can be ignored for high tensile wires. but can cause permanent loss of tension in mild steel wires.

The diameter of the wire also affects its elasticity, as the thinner the wire. the greater its ability to return to its original length after being stretched. Thin wire also has the advantage that it is lighter in weight per unit length than thicker wire, and is thus easier for handling. As wire is sold by weight. it is also cheaper. However, selection for thin diameter should not be made at the expense of strength. As shown in the table. the high tensile (non spring steel) wire has a tensile strength of 1080 N/mm^2, which for a 2.50mm diameter wire, does not give sufficient strength for general fencing. It is suitable for electric fencing, where animals keep clear of the wire. and which therefore does not need to be highly tensioned. The best type of wire is the high tensile spring steel. which has the greatest tensile strength. and thus even at the small diameter of 2.50mm can withstand high tension.

Measuring wire tension

The tension put on any wire should fall between the minimum and maximum given in the table. Maximum tension should only be used where the wire is terminated at the straining posts by spiral fence connectors, radisseurs or ratchet winders (see p58). If staples are used instead to fasten the wire, the minimum tension should be used. Similarly, if wires are joined by knots, rather than by spiral fence connectors or torpedo connectors, minimum tension only should be used.

Maximum tension can only be achieved if strainer assemblies are built to the best possible standard and if any tie-downs. turning posts and other parts of the fence are equally strongly made.

If ratchet winders or radisseurs are being used, which are adjustable. wire can be strained to a lower tension within the range given, and then tightened as necessary at a later date. Mild steel wire slackens in use, and usually needs tightening after a few months.

Always check exactly which type of wire you are handling, and in particular do not confuse 2.50mm high tensile wire with 2.50 or 2.65mm high tensile spring steel wires. The former is not so strong as spring steel, and should not be tensioned above 150 kg. If high tensile wires are over-tensioned they are likely to snap, possibly causing injury.

Wire tension can be measured by a gauge, or it can be estimated by measuring the elongation of the wire.

a Hayes Tension Indicator. This device can be used with any type of chain wire strainer (eg Hayes, Monkey). and gives a direct reading as the strainer is operated. It is designed mainly for use with 4.00mm mild steel and 2.50mm high tensile wire, giving a maximum reading of 180kg. It is therefore not suitable for use with spring steel wires, which are normally strained to a higher tension. The Hayes Tension Indicator is available from Drivall Ltd.

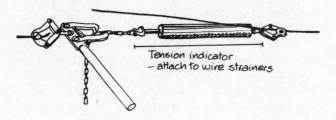

Tension indicator
– attach to wire strainers

b A tension gauge can be made as shown below. To use, hold the screws against the wire, and then pull with the spring balance until the wire reaches the 12mm deflection mark. Then take the reading on the balance. and multiply it by 20 to give the wire tension in kg.

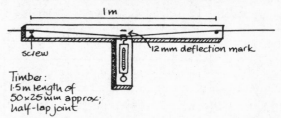

For testing tensions up to 400kg, use a spring balance which reads up to 20kg. For lower tensions, a smaller balance of up to 12 or 15kg would be suitable. Spring balances are available from agricultural merchants. angling shops and so on.

c Measuring the elongation of the wire is used to achieve correct tension on high tensile stock netting. This should stretch by 1.5m for every 100m of netting. and is measured by the amount of chain taken up by the wire strainer. Monkey strainers have 1.5m of chain. Straining boards have 6m or more of chain, allowing at least 400m of netting to be strained in one pull (see p56).

BARBED WIRE

Prior to the invention of barbed wire in the 1860s. post and rail fencing was the only type of fencing available to most farmers. Following the mechanisation of the manufacture of barbed wire in 1874, this cheap and quick method of fencing spread rapidly in America and later Europe. It revolutionised the farming of the American West. by allowing large tracts of land to be fenced for cattle.

Barbed wire remains possibly the most common type of wire for fencing, although it is by no means an ideal fencing material.

a Barbed wire is an unpleasant material to handle, even when new. Removing and disposing of old barbed wire is a job so unpopular that it is often never done, and the old wire is just left in place and more wire or another fence put up next to it.

b As well as the distress caused to wild and farm animals which get injured by barbed wire, considerable damage is caused to animal skins, reducing their value. The Hide and Allied Trades Improvement Society have been cam-

paigning for some years for the greater use
of alternative stock fencing, including high
tensile and permanent electric systems. In
1984, a survey by the British Leather Confed-
eration showed only 20% of hides without any
barbed wire damage, and the average loss in
value per hide from barbed wire damage was
£5.90.

c Barbed wire does not deter animals from
   jumping fences, but merely injures them when
   they do. Nor does it deter animals from leaning on or putting their heads through fences in
   order to forage on the other side. Cattle will
   even sometimes rub themselves against barbed
   wire, apparently for pleasure!

   Electric wires provide a more effective and
   less damaging way of discouraging animals
   from leaning on fences. Scare wires (p98)
   can be positioned to deter jumping animals.

   A more positive approach to lessen fence
   damage is to provide a strong rubbing post,
   separate from the fence line. This is useful in
   small paddocks which have no trees or other
   objects on which the animals can rub.

d Barbed wire has not found to be entirely
   satisfactory with high tensile fencing systems.
   High tensile twin strand barbed wire is available, but some users find the barbs not long
   enough to be any deterrent. An electric wire
   is usually preferable.

e Barbed wire can be effectively used at the
   base of a fence, to stop pigs and sheep rooting
   and pawing at the base of the fence. This may
   also be some discouragement to badgers.

Advice from experienced fencers is to avoid the
use of barbed wire wherever possible. Always
consider carefully the purpose of the fence, and
don't merely put up a top line of barbed wire
because it is the tradition to do so.

Types of barbed wire

a 2 ply mild steel. This should be galvanised to
   BS 443, and both line wire and barb should be
   of minimum tensile strength 350 N/mm^2, as
   specified in BS 4102. Each strand of the 2 ply
   wire is 2.5mm (12½ gauge) wire, with 4 point
   barbs, spaced at approximately 85mm intervals.
   Normally supplied in 200m reels.

b 2 ply high tensile steel. This should be galvanised to BS 443, and the line wire should be
   or minimum tensile strength of 1050 N/mm^2,
   and the barbs of minimum 350 N/mm^2. Each
   strand of the 2 ply wire is 1.7mm (15½ gauge)
   wire, with 4 point barbs, spaced at approximately 85mm intervals. Supplied in 200m
   or 500m reels. Motto barbed wire (Sentinel
   Fencing) has a reverse twist in the ply. This
   is a safety feature, so that if the wire is over-
   strained, it will untwist, rather than break.

reverse twist ply

c Single strand. This is a high tensile 2.36mm
   steel wire with a flattened section, crimped
   to hold the barbs in place. 'Rybarb', from
   Sentinel Fencing has a breaking strain of
   between 900 and 1200lbs. This wire is
   difficult to handle, and is not recommended.

d Concertina barbed wire. This type of wire
   is used mainly by the Ministry of Defence,
   and for security at airfield, prisons, mines
   and quarries etc. However, the use of razor
   wire as a short-term measure at Stonehenge
   has become a rather notorious example of its
   use in the management of a conservation site.
   Concertina wires should only be handled by
   specialists, and their use must conform to
   local byelaws and/or public safety restrictions.
   Available from Sentinel Fencing.

STOCK NETTING

This type of fencing material is also known as
sheep netting, pig netting, 'Rylock' (Sentinel
Fencing) and field fencing. There are many
different grades and sizes available, as listed in
the following table. All wire should be galvanised
to BS 443. All sizes of netting are supplied in
rolls of 50m, except for for high tensile netting
which is supplied in rolls of 100m.

The following two types are available, which differ
in their method of manufacture:

a Hinged joint fencing. The continuous horizontal
   wires are joined by lengths of vertical wires,
   which are wound around the horizontal wires
   to form strong hinged joints. An example is
   'Rylock' fencing. All high tensile netting is
   made in this way, because high tensile wire
   cannot be joined by welding, as in the type
   described below. The hinged joints give some

flexibility over undulating ground, but the fence is liable to 'concertina' if put up badly.

b Welded netting. The horizontal and vertical wires are joined by welds, which have 90% strength compared to the wire strength. In spite of appearing less flexible than hinged joint netting on undulating ground, it is possible to get the net very taut. The welded netting is slightly lighter in total weight than the equivalent grade and size of hinged joint netting. This is the type of netting used by the Forestry Commission. An example is 'Weldfence', manufactured by BRC.

The hinged joint netting sizes are coded as follows. Equivalent sizes of 'Weldfence' are given in the table below.

The first letter refers to the grade of netting, which is determined by the diameter and tensile strength of the wire. The first number refers to the number of horizontal wires. The second number refers to the height of the netting in centimetres. The third number refers to the spacing of the vertical wires in centimetres.

eg B8/80/30

heavy grade — 8 horizontal wires — 80 cms height — vertical wires 30cm apart

Grades

B = Heavy grade. For areas of industrial pollution, coastal areas, high stocking rates, or for any use where a heavy weight fence is required. More difficult to handle than other grades.

C = Medium grade. For normal use.

L = Light grade. For temporary fencing. Universal Fencing (Sentinel) is similar in weight to light grade.

HT= High tensile. Requires fewer posts but stronger straining posts. Very strong.

Wire sizes and tensile strength

	Top and bottom horizontals		Intermediate horizontals		Verticals	
	Nominal wire diameter	Minimum tensile	Nominal wire diameter	Minimum tensile	Nominal wire diameter	Minimum tensile
Light	2.50mm	$695N/mm^2$	1.90mm	$770N/mm^2$	1.90mm	$415N/mm^2$
Medium	3.15 "	600 "	2.50 "	600 "	2.50 "	350 "
Heavy	4.00 "	550 "	3.00 "	600 "	3.00 "	350 "
High tensile	2.50 "	1050 "	2.50 "	1050 "	2.50 "	695 "

WIRE NETTING

This familiar fencing material is also known as chicken wire, or hexagonal wire mesh. It should not be strained, as it will pull out of shape. For permanent fencing, it is hung on line wires of mild or high tensile wire, attached with netting rings (see p61). For temporary fencing, the

Wire netting

Mesh size	Wire gauge	Height in mm									Use
		300	450	600	750	900	1050	1200	1500	1800	
13mm	22 (.71mm)	*	*	**	*	**p		**		**	Aviaries
	19 (1.00mm)					*					
19mm	22 (.71mm)			*		*		*			Vermin control
	20 (.90mm)	*	*	*		*		*		*	
25mm	20 (.90mm)	**	**	**	**	**p	*	**		**	Small animal cages
	19 (1.00mm)			*		*		*		*	
	16 (1.60mm)					*		*			
31mm	19 (1.00mm)			*		**	*	*		*	Rabbit fencing
	18 (1.25mm)			*		*	*	*			
38mm	19 (1.00mm)		*	**	*	**	*	**		*	
50mm	19 (1.00mm)	*	**	**	**	**p		**	**	**	Poultry
	17 (1.42mm)					*				*	
75mm	19 (1.00mm)			*		*		*		*	Sheep
100mm	16 (1.60mm)		*	*	*	*					

* supplied in rolls of 50m   ** supplied in rolls of 50m and 25m   p green PVC coated, in rolls of 6m

SIZES AND USES OF STOCK NETTING

Grade	Hinged joint	Weldfence	No. of line wires	Height (mm)	Spacing of verticals (mm)	Roll length (m)	Roll wgt (kg)	Use	Brand name/manufacturer
Light	L8/80/15	FF13	8	800	150	50	20	temporary	Rylock/TWIL Weldfence/BRC
Universal	15/120	–	15	1200	150	50		general purposes, goats	Rylock/TWIL
Universal	10/90	–	10	900	150	50		general purposes	Rylock/TWIL
Universal	8/75	–	8	750	150	50		sheep	Rylock/TWIL
Universal	7/65	–	7	650	150	50		hedge gaps, wall tops, temporary	Rylock/TWIL
Universal	6/50	–	6	500	150	50		hedge gaps, wall tops, temporary	Rylock/TWIL
Medium	C8/11/30	FF7	8	1150	300	50	27	cattle, horses, goats	Rylock/TWIL Weldfence/BRC
Medium	C6/90/30	FF3	6	900	300	50	50	cattle, sheep	Rylock/TWIL Weldfence/BRC
Medium	C8/80/30	FF5	8	800	300	50	25	cattle, sheep, lambs	Rylock/TWIL Weldfence/BRC
Medium	C8/80/15	FF1	8	800	150	50	32	cattle, sheep, lambs, pigs	Rylock/TWIL Weldfence/BRC
									Triple Life/Estate Wire Ltd
Medium	–	FF9	5	750	300	50		sheep, lambs	Weldfence/BRC
Medium	–	FF650	7	650	150	50		hedge gaps, wall tops	Weldfence/BRC
Medium	C4/60/15	–	4	600	150	50	19	hedge gaps, wall tops	Rylock/TWIL
Medium	–	FF510	6	510	150	50		wall tops	Weldfence/BRC
Heavy	–	FF8	8	1145	300	50		cattle, horses, goats	Weldfence/BRC
Heavy	B6/90/30	FF4	6	900	300	50	31	cattle, horses, sheep	Rylock/TWIL Weldfence/BRC
Heavy	B8/80/30	FF6	8	800	300	50	37	cattle, sheep, lambs	Rylock/TWIL Weldfence/BRC
Heavy	B8/80/15	FF2	8	800	150	50	48	cattle, sheep, lambs, pigs	Rylock/TWIL Weldfence/BRC
High	HT13/190/15	–	13	1900	300	100		deer, internal fence	Hurricane/Balfour Westlar
Tensile	HT13/190/30	–	13	1900	150	100		deer, boundary fence	Hurricane/Balfour Westlar
''	HT8/90/30	–	8	900	300	100		cattle, horses, sheep	Hurricane/Balfour Westlar
''	HT8/90/15	–	8	900	150	100		cattle, horses, sheep, lambs	Hurricane/Balfour Westlar
''	HT8/80/30	–	8	800	300	100	50	cattle, sheep, lambs	Hurricane/Balfour Westlar Rylock/TWIL
''	HT8/80/15	–	8	800	150	100	63	cattle, sheep, lambs, pigs	Hurricane/Balfour Westlar
''	HT5/52/30	–	5	520	300	100		wall tops	Rylock/TWIL Hurricane/Balfour Westlar

Balfour Westlar will manufacture any height or specification netting to order; minimum length 1000m.

netting is simply stapled to stakes.

Wire netting is woven from mild steel wire. Sheep netting is made of heavily galvanised wire whereas the smaller mesh sizes are galvanised after being woven. All wire netting should be manufactured to BS 1485:1971.

Sheep netting has a 3 ply selvedge at the top and bottom. The taller sizes also have a centre strand for extra strength. All sizes are supplied in rolls of 50m.

Sheep netting

Height (mm)	Mesh (mm)	Wire gauge
600	100	16 (1.6mm)
600	100	14 (2.0mm)
900*	75	16 (1.6mm)
900	100	16 (1.6mm)
900*	100	16 (1.6mm)
900*	100	14 (2.0mm)
1050*	75	16 (1.6mm)
1050*	100	16 (1.6mm)
1050*	100	14 (2.0mm)
1200*	100	16 (1.6mm)

* with centre strand

OTHER WIRE PRODUCTS

Chain link

Chain link fencing is produced in a very wide range of wire size, mesh size and height. It is available either galvanised, PVC coated over a bright (ie non-galvanised) core, and PVC coated a galvanised core. The PVC coat is available in green or black.

Usually chain link is erected on metal or concrete posts, but wooden posts can also be used. For details of posts see page 40.

Chain link is widely used for safety and security fencing though it can be quickly cut with wire cutters to force a breakthrough. Chain link is not generally recommended by this handbook for use on conservation and amenity sites, because of its association with mainly urban use, such as roadsides, railways and industrial premises. In places where people need to be excluded for safety or security, welded mesh or close-board panel fencing are possible alternatives.

Some of the types of chain link available are listed below, together with the manufacturer's recommended uses. Full details of all sizes can be obtained from manufacturers of chain link, such as Sentinel Fencing, or from fencing suppliers. Most sizes are supplied in 25m rolls and include the required length of line wire.

| Use | Height (mm) | Mesh (mm) | Pattern | Wire size in mm | | | No of line wires |
				Bright core	Galvanised core	Galvanised	
Residential property	900	50	Light	1.70	2.00		2
	900	50	Medium	2.24	2.24	2.50	2
	900	50	Heavy	2.50	2.50	3.00	2
Playgrounds	1200	50	Heavy	2.50	2.50	3.00	3
	1200	50	Extra heavy	3.00	3.00	3.55	3
Highways	1400	50	Medium	2.24	2.24	2.50	3
	1400	50	Heavy	2.50	2.50	3.00	3
	1400	50	Extra heavy	3.00	3.00	3.55	3
	1400	40	Medium		2.24	2.50	3
	1400	40	Heavy		2.50	3.00	3
Recreation grounds	1400	50	Extra heavy	3.00	3.00	3.55	3
Security	1800	50	Heavy	2.50	2.50	3.00	3
	1800	50	Extra heavy	3.00	3.00	3.55	3
	1800	50	Super weight			3.55	3
Railway and general safety	1800	40	Heavy		2.50	3.00	3

Twilweld

This material is welded from mild steel, and then either galvanised or galvanised and plastic coated. As well as fencing it can be used for animal cages fruit cages shelving etc. It is available in several different wire sizes and mesh classed as either light or heavy. The heavy grades are suitable for sheep pens gate panels, dividing screens and hay racks. Twilweld can be fixed by stapling, bolting or welding according to its use. It can also be attached to strained line wires. It is manufactured by Twil as part of their Sentinel Fencing range.

Galvanised and plastic coated Light Twilweld	Supplied in rolls of 6m and 30m	Height in mm			
Mesh (mm)	Wire diam (mm)	450	600	750	900
13 x 13	1.00				*
25 x 25	1.60				*
25 x 38	2.75	*	*	*	*
50 x 50	1.60	*			*

Galvanised Light Twilweld	Supplied in rolls of 6m and 30m	Height in mm							
Mesh (mm)	Wire diam (mm)	300	375	450	600	750	900	1200	1800
13 x 13	1.00						*		
	1.60						*	*	*
13 x 25	1.00						*		
	1.60						*	*	
19 x 19	1.60				*		*		
	2.00						*	*	
25 x 25	1.00						*		
	1.60	*			*		*	*	
	2.00						*		
25 x 38	2.00		*	*	*	*	*		
50 x 50	1.60						*		

Heavy Twilweld is supplied in 18.28m lengths, and in heights of 1220mm, 1830mm and 2130mm. These are available in all the following mesh and wire sizes.

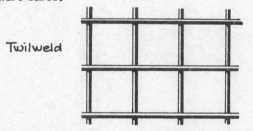

Twilweld

Heavy Twilweld Mesh (mm)	Wire diam (mm) 2.50	3.15	4.00	5.00
25 x 25	*	*		
25 x 50	*	*	*	
50 x 50	*	*	*	*
25 x 76	*	*		
13 x 76	*			
76 x 76		*	*	*

Twilweld security fencing is manufactured from heavily galvanised wire. The following sizes are supplied in 25m rolls, except where otherwise marked.

Mesh (mm)	Wire diam (mm)	Height in mm						
		900	1200	1400	1500	1800	2150	2400
50 x 50	2.50	*	*	*		*	*b	
	3.00	*	*	*	*	*a	*b	*b

a 20m roll
b 12.5m roll

49

OTHER FENCING PRODUCTS

Tensar

Tensar is the trade name for a range of cladding, windbreak and fencing materials made by Netlon Ltd. They are made of high density perforated sheet polyethylene or polypropylene, stretched to form a mesh. This makes a very durable fabric, with none of the frictional problems of woven materials. The following products are available:

Fencing. This is a high tensile lightweight mesh, used on its own for access control, and with high tensile steel line wires for stock proof fencing. An advantage for handling and erection is its light weight, a 50m x 1.2m roll weighing only $12\frac{1}{2}$ kilos. High fences are impossible to climb, but are easy to cut.

Shelter Shading. This is designed for erection in exposed areas to give protection to new-born lambs. It is also used for sand and snow fencing, as the reduction caused in the wind-speed results in the load of sand or snow being deposited behind the fence.

Cladding. This is used to clad the sides of farm buildings used for housing and rearing of stock. The cladding gives protection from draughts, rain and snow whilst allowing sufficient ventilation for a healthy environment. It is eligible for MAFF grant aid on designated applications.

Windbreak. This is designed for giving protection to stock in unroofed areas such as cattle collection and feeding yards. It is eligible for MAFF grant on designated applications. Note that it is supplied in 2m width rolls only.

To aid tensioning of permanent structures, Netlon market a slit mild steel galvanised tube, which is slid onto the end of the material and tensioned using special hook bolts, also available from Netlon. Tubes are supplied in 1m lengths (cladding tubes) for use with cladding or shelter shading, and in 0.9, 1.2, 1.8 and 2.75m lengths (fencing tubes) for use with Tensar fencing.

Tensar Fencing, Cladding and Shelter Shading can also be mechanically tensioned using monkey strainers, attached with a wire strop to a slit tube, or to a steel bar threaded through the netting. Only light tension should be used however. Windbreak should be tensioned by hand only.

All Tensar products can be cut with secateurs or snips.

The manufacturers recommend the following method to erect Tensar Fencing, using slit tubes and hook bolts. This method is only suitable for access control or boundary fences. Fences for stock control should include line wires (see below).

1   Drill holes in the end support posts at the heights shown. All posts should be 75mm square or diameter round posts, spaced 3m apart.

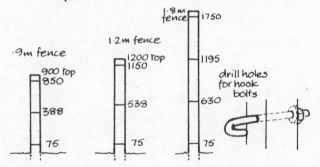

Product specification

	Fencing	Shelter Shading	Cladding	Windbreak
Roll sizes and prices (approx)	50 x .9m £70 50 x 1.2m £92 50 x 1.8m £135 40 x 2.75m £161	10 x 1m £23 30 x 1m £65	10 x 1m £26 30 x 1m £77	30 x 2m £140
Weight	210 g/m^2	360 g/m^2	433 g/m^2	388 g/m^2
Open area	-	42% (58% protection)	37% (63% protection)	45% (55% protection)
Material	Polypropylene	High Density Polyethylene	High Density Polyethylene	High Density Polyethylene
Max. tensionable load	-	2.4 tonnes per metre width	3.1 tonnes per metre width	0.5 tonnes per metre width
Mesh aperture	35 x 35mm	104 x 27mm	23 x 5mm	30 x 6mm
Thickness	-	1.5mm	1.5mm	1.5mm

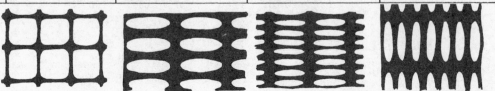

2 Slide a slit tube onto the end of the roll, and attach with the hook bolts to the posts. The base of the tube should rest on the ground.

3 Tighten the bolts with a spanner, to leave a gap of 50mm as shown.

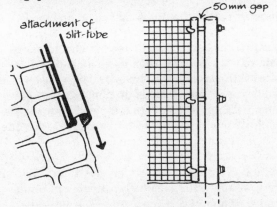

attachment of slit-tube

50mm gap

4 Roll out the netting, and either cut as necessary, or position end post so that it is approximately 50mm beyond the end of the netting. Attach with slit tube as above.

5 Return to first post and tighten bolts to give an even finish. Do not over-tighten.

6 Staple every 100m from top to bottom on each intermediate post.

7 Check one week after installation and tighten as necessary.

Alternatively, the netting can be erected by simply stapling to the first post, and then unrolling it and manually tensioning it, stapling it to each intermediate post as you go.

Tensar Fencing should be joined by overlapping it at posts, or between posts, by overlapping and threading a 20mm mild steel bar or similar through the overlapped mesh.

For control of sheep or deer, erect a traditional fence using high tensile or spring steel wire (design 4, page 8 and design 11, page 10). Wires should be spaced as shown below to fit the Tensar neatly.

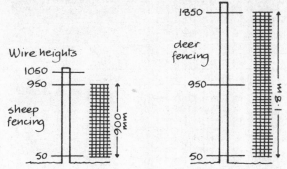

Wire heights

1050
950

sheep fencing

50

900mm

1850

deer fencing

950

50

1.8m

Having erected the posts and wire, attach the Tensar Fencing as follows:

1 Staple the netting to the first straining post.

2 Unroll to next straining post, joining lengths as necessary. Attach to the straining post using monkey strainers and wire strops around a steel bar threaded through the mesh. Strain lightly; sufficient merely to hold the net taut and in position for easy attachment to the wires.

3 Attach the netting to the wires, using gordian rings every 300mm.

4 Staple to second straining post.

Tensar Cladding and Shelter Shading should be erected as follows:

1 For permanent fixing, batten the end of the roll to the first support post.

2 Unroll and attach monkey strainers as described above. Note that the strainers must be attached to a sufficiently strong support. The extra post system shown on page 56 is suitable, as this allows the last piece to be strained properly. Only use light tension on the monkey strainers.

3 Attach to each post using battens, nailed every 200mm from base to top.

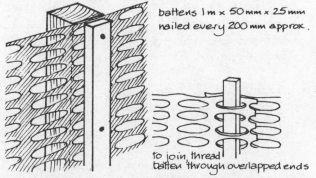

battens 1m x 50mm x 25mm nailed every 200mm approx.

to join, thread batten through overlapped ends

4 Join lengths by overlapping, and then threading a wooden batten through the overlap.

For Shelter Shading, use support posts of 100mm square or diameter round, spaced every 3m. Cladding can be stretched across spans of up to 6m without any horizontal support.

For temporary erection of shelter shading use 50mm posts threaded through and knocked into the ground.

For further details on Tensar see the manufacturer's literature.

Paraweb

This material is designed for windbreak construction, but can be used for many of the purposes given above for Tensar. Paraweb is made from continuous terylene filaments, encased in polyethylene, and is widely used for crop protection and plant establishment in difficult environments in many parts of the world. It has also been used for sand fencing (see p112).

Height (mm)	No of horizontal webs	Wgt per 30m roll (kg)
1000	10	14
1400	14	20
1800	18	25
2000	20	28
2200	22	31

The horizontal webs are 50mm wide, spaced 50mm apart, and joined by vertical webs. The following heights are available, supplied in 30m rolls. Special staples are available to fix the paraweb to wooden support posts. Paraweb is manufactured by ICI Linear Composites Ltd, from whom further details are obtainable.

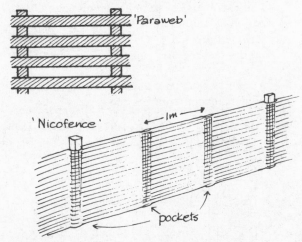

'Paraweb'

'Nicofence'

1m

pockets

Nicofence

This is a range of windbreak materials for crop protection. The styles given below have 150mm pockets woven into the material at 1000mm spacings, through which the posts can be threaded. This eliminates the need for any staples or other fastenings together with the damage these cause to fabric and posts. Both styles have a windbreak value of 50%. Nicofence is available from Clovis Lande Associates.

Style	Height	Roll length
27/15	1400mm	50m
41/15	1500mm	100m

Chestnut paling

This well known fencing material has been used for many years in gardens and playgrounds, at roadsides, for temporary and anti-intruder fencing.

Chestnut paling should be manufactured to BS 1722:Part 4:1972. The pales of half-round or roughly triangular sweet chestnut should have a girth of not less than 100mm. The pales are bound with two or three lines of wires, each line consisting of four strands of 2mm wire. The lines are fixed 150mm from top and bottom with the third line mid-way on taller sizes. One line of wire is stapled to every pale.

The following sizes are widely available. All sizes are available with gaps between pales of either 50mm, 75mm or 100mm.

An example showing post sizes and spacing for a 1500mm height fence is given on page 11.

Height (mm)	2 line	3 line	roll length
750	*		9.1m
900	*	*	9.1m
1100	*	*	9.1m
1200	*	*	9.1m
1400		*	4.5m
1500		*	4.5m
1800		*	4.5m

Chestnut paling is a relatively expensive fencing material, and should be handled with care.

For short lengths or for temporary fencing, the paling can be used on its own, and stapled directly to posts. For permanent or longer lengths of fencing, first erect an ordinary strained wire fence, with horizontal wires coinciding with the wires of the paling. Then attach the paling to the wires using gordian rings or netting rings (as used for chain-link fencing). This not only gives rigidity to the fence, but avoids having to attach the paling using staples, which damage the wire.

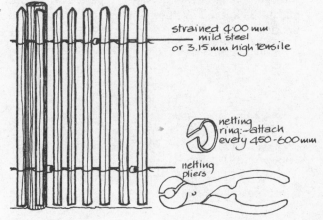

strained 4.00 mm mild steel or 3.15 mm high tensile

netting ring:- attach every 450-600mm

netting pliers

Note the following:

a The wire on chestnut paling is easily damaged
by hammering staples in too far, which can
result in the wire breaking. If the paling has
to be attached using staples, they should only
be driven in so far as to just grip the wire.

An alternative method is to use stirrup wires
(see p41 and 102) to attach the paling to the posts.

b Chestnut paling should not be over-strained,
as the only method of attaching it at high
tension is to hammer home the staples at
each post, which merely damages the wire.

c Lengths of paling should be joined by neatly
twisting the free ends of wire around the
first pale of the next length, in the same
way as the wire is twisted between the pales.
Do not twist the wire back on itself or bend
it more than necessary, as this weakens it.

Strain the paling in one of the two following ways:

a Strain by hand at each post. This can either
be done by simply pulling it, or by using
a spade, crowbar or piece of wood to <u>lightly</u>
lever behind the post, as shown. If this is
done too enthusiastically the pale will break
or the post move. As described above, this
will be tighter than it can satisfactorily be
attached.

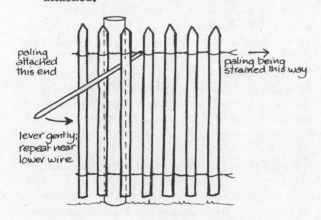

b Monkey strainers can be used by removing
the last pale and inserting a crowbar, and
attaching the strainers using wire strops
(see p32). Only light tension should be
put on the strainers, just sufficient to hold
the paling taut. This method is useful if
only one or two people are working on the
fence, as it holds the paling in position and
leaves hands free to attach the paling. Note
that this method can only be used where the
end post is strong enough to attach the
strainers.

Handling, Straining, Fixing and Joining Wire

Always treat wire with care, both to prevent
damage to the wire and to ensure there is no
risk to the handler or any bystanders.

HANDLING PLAIN WIRE

Plain wire is supplied in coils weighing 25 10,
5 or $\frac{1}{2}$ kg. The start of a new coil should be
marked with a label. After use, always mark
the start end of a partly used coil by bending it
back on itself to make it easy to find. If you are
unlucky enough to have to use an un-marked
partly-used coil, stand the coil on its side and
carefully separate the loops until an end is found.
It is possibly to unwind from either end but it is
easier to continue from the start end.

Methods of unwinding wire are as follows:

a The simplest method is to anchor the 'start'
end, and then walk backwards, unrolling the
coil along the ground. This is satisfactory on
reasonably level grassland, but difficult in
rough terrain or grassland. It is also fairly
slow.

b The quickest and safest method of unwinding
wire is to use a wire dispenser, as described
on page 33. The coil is put on the dispenser
so that the wire feeds off the top of the coil.

The actual sequence of operations will depend on
the situation but a suggested method is as follows:

1 Put the dispenser at the second straining post
from the start of the fence.

2 Pull out the wire to the first straining post and
fasten off.

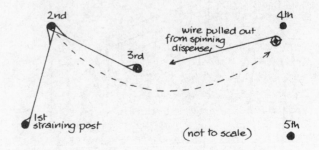

3 Attach the wire strainers to the second straining post, strain the wire, then cut it and
fasten off. Repeat stage 2 and 3 as necessary,
depending on the number of line wires
required.

4 Without moving the dispenser, pull the wire

out to the third straining post, fasten off and strain back to the second straining post and fasten off as before. Repeat as necessary.

5 Then move the dispenser, strainers and other tools to the fourth straining post, and repeat the procedure onto the third and fifth straining post. Following this procedure saves moving the dispenser and other tools more than is necessary. Remember always to cut the wire from the dispenser after it has been strained. This saves having a 'free' end of wire which will recoil if you don't anchor it, and also means there is no wastage of wire and no odd pieces which have to be collected up and disposed of.

HANDLING BARBED WIRE

a Always wear thick gloves, preferably of leather, with gauntlets to protect the wrists.

b Take care when transporting reels of barbed wire inside vehicles. If possible, place the reels inside tool boxes or separate compartments. Failing this, make sure the reels are securely wedged or tied in so they can't move if the vehicle stops suddenly.

c To unroll barbed wire, slide a short crowbar or stout piece of wood through the reel, so it can safely be carried by two people. Place the reel so the wire feeds off the bottom. A useful tool for carrying barbed wire can be made from 20mm diameter mild steel, with a piece welded as shown. This stops the reel sliding onto the hands.

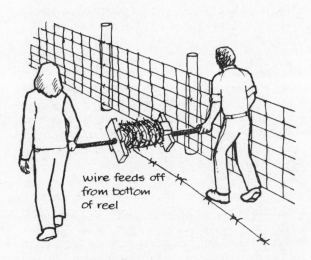

wire feeds off from bottom of reel

d Always put up any barbed wire as the last job, to avoid the chance of people damaging themselves on it while the fence is being erected.

HANDLING STOCK NETTING

a On short grassland and fairly level ground, netting can be unrolled by laying the roll on the ground, and then walking backwards along the fence line, unrolling the netting as you go. Don't stick your fingers down between the wires, because every so often the middle part of the roll suddenly unwinds, and can trap the fingers. Use the 'heel' of the hand, and don't let go towards the end or the whole lot will roll back up again.

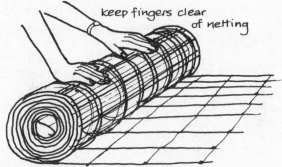

keep fingers clear of netting

b On difficult ground you will have to keep the roll of netting upright, lifting and turning it to unroll the netting. This is easier with Rylock netting, which is usually wound in such a way that the centre of the roll forms a handle.

STRAINING WIRE

Many different methods have been devised for straining wire, some of which are described below. The function of the straining post is not only to hold the strained wire in position, but also to act as the anchor point to which the straining device is attached while the wire is being strained. An exception to this is the method of straining together two rolls of netting midway between two straining posts. This method is mainly used on high tensile netting (see p56).

With the normal method of attaching the wire strainers to the straining post, you are then left with the problem of straining the last short length of wire or netting between the wire strainer and the straining post. This has to be done by hand, and usually results in some loss of tension.

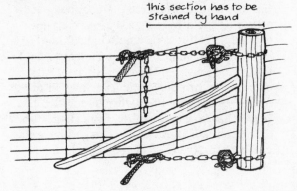

this section has to be strained by hand

To avoid this problem, other methods of attaching the wire strainers have been devised, but not all are suitable for all types of fencing, and not all are recommended. They are described further below.

When using the wire strainer, always make sure before you start operating the lever that the grips are securely holding the wire and that the chain is not twisted. If the chain is twisted, it will quickly jam as the strain is taken up.

Back-straining

The strainers are attached as shown, with the wire passed around the post. Make sure the wire is at the correct height around the post, because it will not be possible to slide it up or down once the strain is on it. Loosely tack a guide staple. Strain the wire to the required tension, and then secure it by one of the methods shown on p58-60.

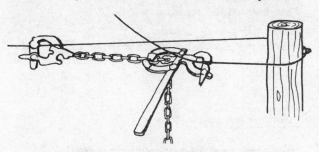

Back-straining is the best method for straining plain wire around a round straining post. It is less easy with a square straining post, as the wire digs into the corners of the post as it is pulled around. Straining barbed wire or stock netting by this method is not normally recommended, as the barbs and joins catch on the post as the strain is taken up.

Normal straining

The strainers are attached as shown, with the chain looped around the post. Make sure that the chain is just out of the way of the line of the wire. If it is on the same line it will be in the way when you come to fasten the wire, and if too far above or below it will be pulling the wire out of line.

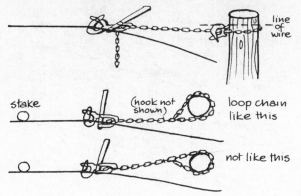

Loop the chain as shown, so that it runs out on the same side of the post as the wire, to keep the line of strain straight.

Pull the wire reasonably taut by hand before you attach it to the grip, or you will run out of chain before the wire is fully tensioned, and then have to release the strainers from the wire and start again. This is especially important on long strains. As the total length of strain increases, so does the amount of 'stretch' which you need to take up with the strainers.

It requires some practice and dexterity to attach wire strainers quickly and efficiently, particularly on awkwardly-placed wire such as the bottom wire on a roll of stock netting. It is easier done with someone else to help, either holding the wire or netting in position, or forcing the wire down into the grip of the strainers.

Once the strainer is attached, one person should easily be able to operate it. Never add a longer handle to give extra leverage, as the strainers are designed to allow a person of average strength to put sufficient tension on the wire.

It is advisable for other people to stand out of the way while the wire is being strained, in case the wire slips and springs back, or breaks. Stop when the wire reaches the required tension (see p43). For most types of wire this will be at the point when the lever becomes very hard to move, but it is preferable to test the tension with a meter (see p44), until one gets to know the feel of the correctly tensioned wire.

The last short section between the wire strainer and the straining post must then be tensioned by hand. One person should use a pair of fencing pliers to pull the wire around the post, while another fastens it by one of the recommended methods (see p58).

To allow for the small overall loss of tension resulting from doing this by hand, slightly more tension can be put on the wire strainer to compensate. This shouldn't need to be as much as one link in the chain, but it should be sufficient if the operator of the strainers can hold the lever at the 'half-way' stage for a few moments while the wire is fastened off. This may seem rather a fine point to worry about, but especially on strains less than 50m, the difference can be significant.

A variation of this method is to use a wire strop, attached as shown to the straining post. This can be used with either Monkey or Hayes strainers. The advantage of using a strop is that it keeps the chain well away from the straining post, so that it does not interfere with the operation of fastening the wire to the post. It also allows the full length of chain to be used, so that a longer length of wire can be strained.

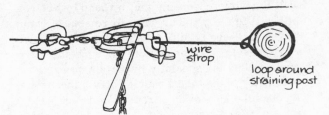

Fixed object

In order to avoid the problem of straining the last piece by hand, it is possible to attach the strainers to a convenient object such as a tree, or a stationary vehicle. However, this method is not recommended, for the reasons given below.

a   The straining post must be allowed to gradually take up the strain as tension is put on the wire. If you strain to another object, fasten off to the straining post and then release the strainers, the tension is suddenly transferred to the straining post, which is thus much more likely to move and possibly pull out of the ground.

b   With the strainers in the position shown, there is no satisfactory way of securely fastening the wire to the straining post so that the wire does not slip when the strainers are removed. In order to get a staple to hold the wire securely, the staple has to be knocked in so far that the wire is kinked and the galvanising damaged.

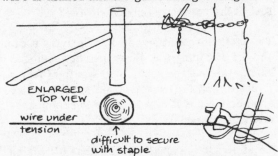

Other methods of straining allow either the wire to be taken around the post, or the free end to be bent into a gentle 'U', giving increased friction between wire and staple (see p58). Don't be tempted to try and use a stationary object placed at an angle to the straining post, in order to give a longer length of contact between the wire and the post. Strainers so placed will then be pulling the straining post in a direction which it is not designed to withstand.

Extra post

Some fencers favour using an extra post, temporarily braced against the straining post, in order to avoid straining the last piece by hand. However this does have the same disadvantage described above (b), although it does allow the straining post to gradually take up the strain.

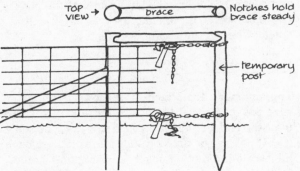

Mid-strain

This is used for mending wires.

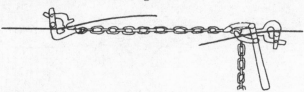

Straining boards

These are used for straining stock netting. Boards are available commercially or can be home-made (see p32). There are two methods of using straining boards.

One method is to attach a pair of boards to the straining post, using strops and standard Hayes or Monkey strainers arranged in either of the two ways shown. The last section of netting must be strained by hand. Monkey strainers have 1.5m of chain which means that only 100m of high tensile netting can be strained as this stretches 1.5m in every 100m. If you try to strain a longer length of netting you will run out of chain before the netting is fully strained.

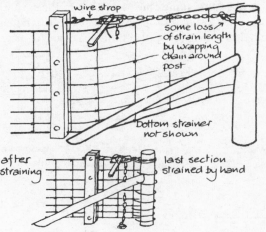

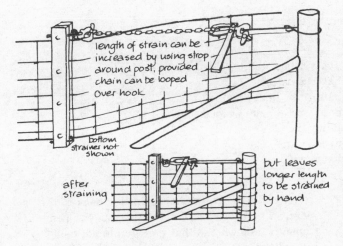

length of strain can be increased by using strop around post, provided chain can be looped over hook

bottom strainers not shown

after straining

but leaves longer length to be strained by hand

Another method of using straining boards is to attach two pairs of boards to join the ends of two lengths of netting part way between straining posts. This avoids doing any straining by hand, as the ends are attached to the straining posts before straining, and a very even tension can be achieved along the whole length. The wires are joined by knotting fence connectors or torpedo connectors (see p60). A disadvantage is that the effective strength of the wire is weakened by knotting, and using connectors makes additional cost.

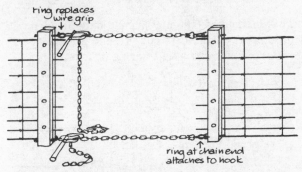

ring replaces wire grip

ring at chain end attaches to hook

Commercial straining boards include adapted Hayes strainers, with a chain attachment instead of a grip. The two pairs of boards must be 1.5m apart for every 100m of high tensile netting. The adapted strainers have over 6m of chain, to allow 400m of netting to be strained. Pairs of straining boards can be used on mild steel netting, but because of the shorter lengths involved, there is less benefit to be gained.

FIXING WIRE

Stapling

Staples are the traditional method of fixing wire to straining posts and intermediate posts. Staples are easy to use. and are available everywhere. They are still probably the best method to use on intermediate posts, but there are disadvantages in their use on straining posts.

On intermediate stakes staples are always fastened to a 'running fit'. This means they are knocked in far enough to hold the wire against the post, but not so far as to grip the wire. This allows an even tension to be made between the two straining posts. The wire can also later be tightened as necessary, without having to loosen the staples on the intermediates. Any extra strain imposed on the wire by a weight leaning against it is taken up along the whole length of wire. The intermediates are in effect only stiffening the fence, and holding the horizontal wires at the correct distance apart.

Don't leave a large gap between staple and wire, or the wire will rattle in the wind and the galvanising will be damaged. Staples should always be angled as shown. If the staple is aligned vertically with both points entering the same grain, the wood is likely to split. When stapling netting or barbed wire onto intermediates before the wire is fully strained, ensure the staple is so placed that it will allow the wire to be tightened.

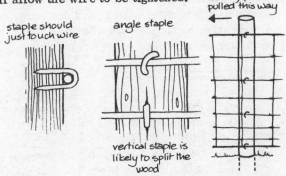

staple should just touch wire

angle staple

netting free to be pulled this way

vertical staple is likely to split the wood

'Grommets', made from heavy gauge split plastic can be used to protect the wire from any wind damage (available from Hunter Wilson).

Use two staples on dips or rises, to reduce the kink of the wire, and increase holding strength. This also allows the wire to feed through more easily.

On turning posts staples should be knocked to a 'running fit', but in order to prevent the wire cutting into the post, it is a good idea to place an extra staple, as shown.

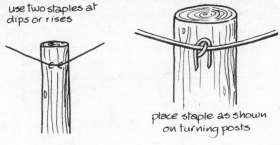

use two staples at dips or rises

place staple as shown on turning posts

Galvanised staples : approximate weights and quantities

metric	imperial	approx. no. per kg	use
15 x 1.60mm	$\frac{1}{2}$ x 16 gauge	2060	wire netting, light welded mesh
20 x 2.00mm	$\frac{3}{4}$ x 14 gauge	931	chestnut paling
25 x 2.65mm	1 x 12 gauge	488	chain link, heavy welded mesh
25 x 3.15mm	1 x 10 gauge	358	chain link, heavy welded mesh
30 x 3.55mm	$1\frac{1}{4}$ x 9 gauge	221	plain wire
40 x 4.00mm	$1\frac{1}{2}$' x 8 gauge	134	barbed wire
50 x 5.00mm	2'' x 6 gauge	73	strand wire

If staples are used to fasten off wire at straining posts, the staples have to be knocked in so that they securely grip the wire. This should not be done by knocking the staples in so far that they kink the wire and damage the galvanising.
It should instead be done by sharply angling the staple so that it pinches the wire. In order to make a secure fixing, the wire must be bent into a 'U' curve. Avoid making a sharp 'V' which damages the galvanising. Use either of the following methods, on mild steel wire only. High tensile or spring steel wire should not be fastened off with staples, but with a knot or one of the devices listed below.

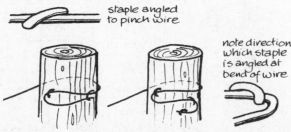

staple angled to pinch wire

note direction which staple is angled at bend of wire

However, even these methods shown have several disadvantages. The bending inevitably causes some damage to the wire galvanising, and on stock netting or multi-strand wire fencing the number of staples used can be considerable. For example, a straining post part way along a run of eight strand stock netting with a top and bottom strand of plain wire might have over 40 staples knocked into it. Staples can also work loose in time, from frost causing expansion and contraction of the wood. For these reasons, the other methods described below are recommended to be used instead of stapling at straining posts.

Knotting

This method of knotting wire was developed for use with high tensile wire, but it can also be used on mild steel wire.

This only requires one staple, not driven home,

to locate the wire in position at the back of the post. The knot should not pull tight, but remain 'open' as shown, so that the wire is not bent more than necessary. This method can be used on barbed wire if a few barbs are removed, and similarly on stock netting if at least one vertical wire is removed to give sufficient length for knotting.

This is a cheap and simple method of fastening wire, and does not damage either the wire or the post. It does have the disadvantage that it can be easily vandalised.

Twisting

This method of fastening should only be used on mild steel wire. It is not suitable for high tensile wire, which will spring undone.

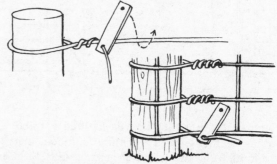

The neatest finish is achieved by using a small tool called a wire twister (see p33). This method is useful on stock netting, where many staples would otherwise be needed, and the cost of wire connectors (see below) is not really justified. Make sure the wire twister is short enough to pass through the smallest 'window' in the netting. The disadvantages of this are that the wire twister can scratch the galvanising, and the twisted wire is difficult to re-attach if the fence has to be restrained.

FIXING AND TIGHTENING DEVICES

Radisseur

The radisseur or butterfly tightener is a galvanised

steel device used on mild steel and high tensile steel line wires. They are not suitable for stock netting.

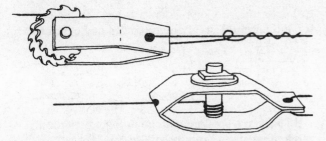

The radisseur can be used to adjust tension at any time, both while the fence is being erected, or if the wires subsequently lose tension due to temperature change or movement of posts. Mild steel wire, however well tensioned initially, normally requires re-tensioning after a few months. A spanner is needed to adjust the radisseur.

Radisseurs can be fastened in a number of different ways as shown below.

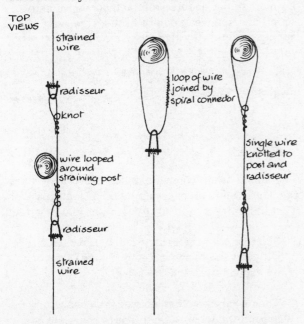

Ratchet winder

This is similar in principle to the radisseur, but is a stronger device. It avoids having to use the tying loops shown above, but does require drilling a hole through the post.

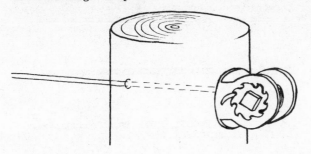

Eyebolts

These are mainly used on metal and concrete posts, but they can also be used on wooden posts. Many sizes are available.

If not pre-drilled, a hole must first be drilled through the post. As the eyebolt has a relatively small adjustment, the wire must be almost fully tensioned using wire strainers. The eyebolt is then pushed through the hole, the wire attached by knotting or twisting it through the eye, and the wire strained to full tension by tightening the nut and washer. Further adjustments to the wire tension can be made as necessary.

Eyebolts are available either $\frac{2}{3}$ threaded for use at ends of fence lines, or fully threaded for use on straining posts part way along fence lines. Loop adaptors are used on the latter type to form the second eye for attaching the wire.

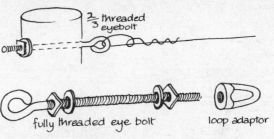

Fence connectors

These are used both for joining wires and for fastening off at straining posts.

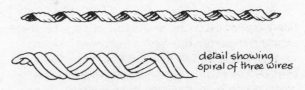

The spiral design was originally developed for use in the telecommunications industry. This principle has been extended for use on strained wire structures for hop, vine and fruit growing as well as for fencing. For cost effectiveness, connectors are best used on high tensile wire, although they can also be used on mild steel wire. Connectors can be taken off and re-used if the wire needs retensioning, but after two or three times they lose their grip. Therefore, they are better not used for securing mild steel wires which may need re-tensioning at intervals. By comparison, high tensile fences should not need any re-tensioning and can therefore be strained 'once and for all' using fence connectors.

Two sizes are available, for use on 2.64 mm (12 gauge) or 3.25mm (10 gauge) wire. The gripping capacity of the connector exceeds the breaking strain of the wire it holds.

Connectors are attached as follows:

1 To fix a wire that is not under strain; ie at the start of a strained section, pass the wire around the post, locating it at the back with a staple.

2 Allow at least 500mm from the start of the wire to the post. With the centre mark on the connector level with the end of the wire, wrap that half around the wire, starting from the centre point.

3 Then wrap the other half of the connector around the wire, checking that the end of the connector is snapped into place.

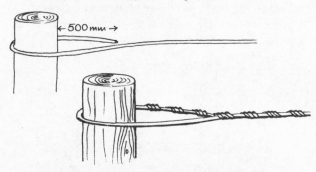

4 Strain as normal to the next straining post using the back-straining method. Leave enough tail end of the wire free for attaching the connector. Strain to the required tension, and then attach the connector as described above.

Some fencers like to leave a tail of wire protruding to make it easier to remove the connector, if re-tensioning is necessary. This tail of wire can then be 'unwound', rather than trying to prise the connector free and unwind it off the wire.

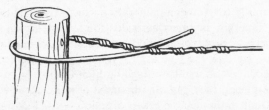

However, this is not generally recommended, as it makes the connector easier to vandalise, and also leaves the temptation to undo the wire while it is under tension, which is dangerous. If re-tensioning is likely to be required, it would be better to fit radisseurs or ratchet winders.

Spiral fence connectors are manufactured by Preformed Line Products Ltd and are available throughout the UK from specialist fencing suppliers (see p133).

JOINING WIRE

Knotting

Either of the two knots shown below can be used for joining mild steel high tensile and barbed wire.

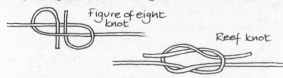

All knots are weaker than an unjoined length of wire, therefore the strength of the knot will determine the effective strength of the wire. In the table below, the knot strength is expressed as a percentage of the breaking load of the wire.

Knot	Wire type	
	4.00mm mild steel	2.50mm high tensile
Figure of 8	80%	76%
Reef knot	78%	71%
Double loop	69%	47%

Do not use the double loop method shown below, which creates weak points in the wire, and will spring undone with high tensile or spring steel wire.

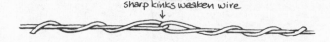

Connectors

The spiral fence connectors described above are the neatest and strongest method of joining wires. Two units are required to form the join or splice.

1 Starting with the centre mark of one unit level with the end of the wire, wrap half the connector around the wire.

2 Then wrap the other half of the connector around the wire to be joined.

3 Repeat with the second unit winding it into the spaces in the first unit. Ensure all ends are snapped into place.

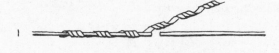

The torpedo connector is a simple push-fit device for joining wires. The wire ends are pushed into the connector where they are held by spring loaded jaws. The join cannot be taken apart nor can the connector be re-used.

Twisting

This method is usually used on mild steel netting, where it is not cost effective to use spiral or torpedo connectors.

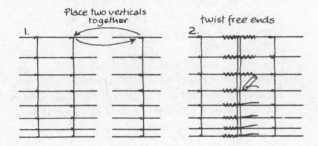

Joining netting to line wires

One of the basic fencing techniques is to suspend a netting fence on line wires, preferably of high tensile spring steel (see designs 4, 10 and 11 in Chapter 1). The netting is only lightly strained, and the tension is kept in the fence by the line wires.

The netting can be joined to the line wires either by rings or lashing rods. Wire rings are applied using a ring fastener gun, which is quick and easy to use. The gun closes the ring, which should stay closed unless put under strain by the weight of drifting snow or animals leaning or rubbing on the netting.

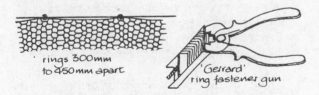

rings 300mm to 450mm apart

'Gerrard' ring fastener gun

A stronger join is made by using lashing rods, which were developed by the same firm (Preformed Line Products Ltd) that manufacturers the spiral fence connectors. Lashing rods are available in two sizes:

5.74mm For securing B or C grade stock netting to 2.65mm line wire
7.26mm For securing B grade stock netting to 3.15mm line wire, or two C grade nets to 2.65mm line wire, as used for deer fencing.

Lashing rods are supplied in boxes of 500, and should be supplied neatly packed. Once tangled, they are awkward to disentangle for use. The easiest way to wind on the lashing rod is to use a short piece of wire as shown. They should be spaced at about 2m intervals. Lashing rods are not suitable for use on hexagonal mesh, as the mesh is too small to easily attach them.

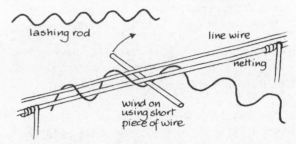

lashing rod   line wire

netting

wind on using short piece of wire

Fence Mechanics

GENERAL PRINCIPLES

1 The most important factor in the strength of a strained fence is the straining posts. They take all the load of the strained wires, and the intermediate posts are only there to stiffen the fence, and to hold the wires at the correct height from the ground.

2 Wires should be attached to a 'running fit' at the intermediate posts so that any extra load, for example from an animal leaning on the fence, is transferred along the length of that strain.

TOP VIEW   extra load on wire   movement of wire

intermediate stake

3 Always build the fence so that the wire can be re-tensioned. This means either fitting tensioning devices (see p58), or fastening off at the straining post in such a way that the wire can be released, re-tensioned and re-attached. This is more easily done if the the wire is fastened by knotting (see p58), rather than by excessive use of staples.

4 At any hollows in the fence line, the wire will require a 'tie-down' in order to keep it stock proof at ground level. The strength of the tie-down must increase for steeper hollows and greater wire tension (see p80).

5 Although mature living trees can make very strong straining posts, they should never be used for this purpose, because the staples and

61

wire become embedded in the bark and eventually in the wood of the tree as the girth expands. This damages the tree, and reduces its commercial value if it is felled for timber. Damage to chainsaws from embedded metal is so frequent that some operators will only fell trees above fence height if they think the tree may previously have been used as a fence post. It is not recommended to use stumps of dead trees, such as elm, as they are often rotten.

Load

The load on the straining post comprises:

a the number of horizontal wires
b the tension put on the wires by the monkey strainers or tensioning device
c any extra load such as leaning animals, fallen trees, wind, drifted snow.

The total strain taken by the straining posts will therefore be greater for a fence of six line wires, each strained to 100kg, than for a fence of three line wires, each strained to 100kg.

The top wire has to bear the most strain from leaning animals, fallen trees and wind. In theory the top wire should be of a heavier gauge and/or greater tensile strength than the lower wires. In practice, the top wire needs re-tensioning more often. The 2 ply mild steel barbed wire, which is often used as the top wire, has a low tensile strength, and although of heavy gauge, can usually bear less strain than the lower wires.

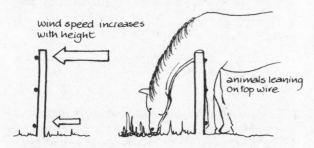

The length of strain is only significant in dealing with any extra load on the wires, such as leaning animals. The longer the length, the more this extra load is spread, and the less likely that the wire will break or the straining posts move.

Posts

The holding ability of a fence post depends on:

a the type of ground
b the amount of ground disturbance caused as the post is put in
c the length and diameter of the post
d the presence and size of the foot.

a the type of ground
   The following table gives an indication of the strength of various soils.

Boulders and rocks	Strongest
Gravels and gravelly soil	
Sands and sandy soil	
Silts and fine sands	
Medium clays	
Fine silts and soft clays	
Peat	Weakest

In weaker soils, anchorage should be increased by using larger and longer posts, and on straining posts, larger feet and thrust plates, or even the type of underground structure shown on page 72. Box strainers are useful in difficult soils.

b the amount of ground disturbance.
   This is important, as it is not possible to back-fill the hole in such a way that it is as firm as the undisturbed soil.

The best method of erecting a post firmly is to drive it directly into the ground, using a mell or similar tool on smaller stakes, and a tractor mounted post driver for large posts. Posts driven into the ground are 150% firmer than posts rammed into holes dug oversize, measured by a sideways force. They also withstand greater lifting forces. Tests by New Zealand Wire Industries Ltd showed that to lift posts out, the following forces were needed:

dug and rammed   90kg force
pilot hole and hand driven 900kg force
machine driven   1260kg force

There is thus obvious advantage is using machinery where possible, as posts are not only erected much more quickly, but are firmer than dug posts. The lack of ground disturbance compensates for the fact that a foot cannot be fitted to straining posts.

Theoretically, posts should be driven with the smaller end down, so that the post tightens as it goes down. In practice, posts are often supplied with the larger end pointed, but if you are making your own stakes, sharpen the smaller end.

For the same reasons, keep pilot holes as narrow as possible. If made wide, the post will loosen at ground level and the gap may fill with water, which hastens rot.

Posts set in dug holes and rammed should be put with the larger end downward, to give the maximum surface area against the soil.

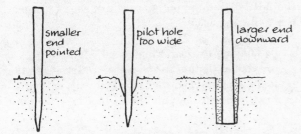

c the height and diameter of the post.
The depth the post is put into the ground is very
important. The average rule is that straining
posts are embedded to about half their total
height and intermediate posts to about one third.

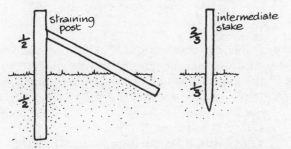

Tests have shown that increasing the depth by
one third will double the resistance to the post
pulling out. For example, if a stake is
normally knocked in 600mm, an addition of
200mm will double its holding ability. Extra
long posts may be worth obtaining for fences in
weak soils (New Zealand MAFF, Aglink FPP 114).

In strong soils, long posts are more likely to
fail under extra strain by breaking, rather
than pulling over. Tests have indicated a
relationship between the diameter of the post,
and the depth to which it is embedded. A post
embedded to a depth of over ten times its
diameter, in medium clay, will break rather
than move. The same post must be embedded
up to fifteen times its diameter in soft soils
before it fails by breaking.

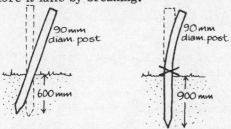

An average size for a fencing stake is 1.7m x
75mm diameter, embedded 600mm. Although
a 1.85m x 75mm diameter posts, allowing
a depth of 750mm in the ground (ie ten times
the diameter), would be stronger in medium
strength soils, there is no advantage in having
one longer that this, except in weak soils.
There is also little advantage in having a
wider post, unless it is correspondingly longer.

Slopes

In theory, fences which run up and down slopes
should have straining and intermediate posts set
at right angles to the slope, and not vertically.
The posts then have the maximum depth in the
ground, whilst holding the wires at the correct
height. The parts of the strainer assembly; ie
posts, struts, wire and ground stay in the same
relationship to oneanother as on level ground.

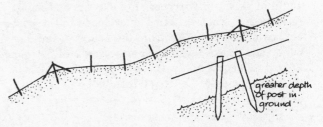

Problems with this are:

a It looks 'wrong' to most people, and may
therefore not be acceptable.

b It is awkward to dig post holes at an angle to
the vertical, and difficult to drive in posts
using a drivall.

c The straining post must be vertical at a
corner or on a three-way assembly, where a
fence line is being taken off across the slope.

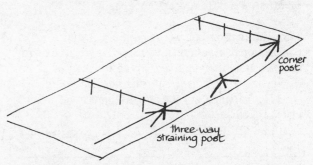

Fences across slopes should be set vertically,
as shown. If set at right angles to the slope,
there is increased gravitational pull on the fence.
This, combined with the force of leaning animals,
wind or snow acting on the upper side may push
the fence over.

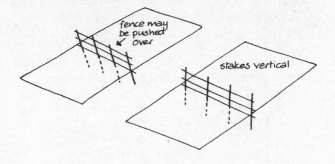

STRAINER ASSEMBLIES

Conventional

This pattern of strainer is seen on most fences throughout Britain. However, one major difference in the design shown here compared to to that normally seen is in the length and angle of the strut. Usually the strut is attached nearly at the top of the post, and meets the ground at an angle of about 45 degrees. In fact, the assembly in strongest when the strut is attached to the post at a point about $\frac{1}{3}$ down from the height of the top wire, and meets the ground at an angle of between 25 and 30 degrees. In order to make this angle, the strut needs to be longer than those normally supplied.

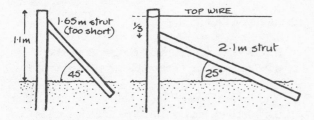

The strut transfers some of the force from the wire downwards to the ground, making a pivot. This produces an upward force on the straining post. The recommended angle to minimise this pivoting action is 25 to 30 degrees.

The illustration below shows the parts of a conventional strainer. Post and strut sizes for various fence designs are given in Chapter 1. However, the general rule for normal height (ie 1.1m) fences is that the post and strut are of equal length.

Post	Strut	Use
2.1m x 125mm diam	2.1m x 75mm diam	Mild steel fencing
2.3m x 175mm diam	2.3m x 100mm diam	Heavy pattern mild steel and high tensile

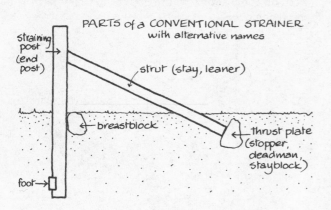

PARTS of a CONVENTIONAL STRAINER with alternative names

Strainers fail. that is either move or break when the full tension is applied to the wires, by one of the following ways:

a by pushing through the ground. This is prevented by the thrust plate, which takes the force transferred through the strut, and to a lesser extent, by the breast block.

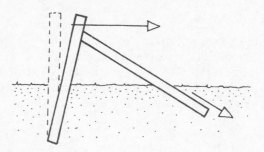

b by twisting to one side. This is prevented by ensuring that the strut is fitted in line with the wires, that the joint of the strut and post is well made, and that the strut cannot slip off the thrust plate. Twisting is also less likely if the wires pull off from the centre of the post, rather than from the edge (see p75), and if the post has a foot.

c by jacking out of the ground. This is prevented by the foot, and by having sufficient length of post in the ground, with the backfill carefully tamped.

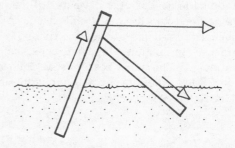

d by breaking. Use a sound post of sufficient diameter.

Details of construction are given on page 72.

Variations on the conventional strainer

A technique developed in New Zealand is to fit a 'swinging foot'. The foot is attached to a piece of wire, and pushed down to the base of the post after the post is put in position. The wire is then strained and attached at ground level. The strained wire resists the upward pivoting action of the strut on the straining post.

The foot is made of a piece of wood, of the size shown. Hardwood is best, but if of softwood this does not need to be preserved. as rot should not be a problem deep in the soil. Use stainless steel wire if possible, to resist corrosion at the ground surface. If not available, use 4.00mm (8 gauge) galvanised mild steel wire. Staple as shown so that the wire pulls from the centre of the foot.

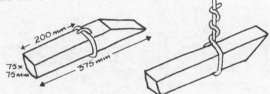

Procedure for fitting is as follows.

1 Place the foot as shown.

2 Tap down with rammer until the foot is about 100mm from the base of the hole. Staple home, using one staple as shown.

3 Continue using the rammer, which tightens the wire, and then finish off as shown. Make sure the stapling is done towards the strut side of the post, on a post with one strut only. If done towards the back, the post will tend to lean backwards.

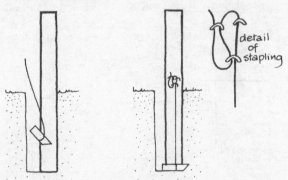

detail of stapling

Another alternative is to fit two feet, attached separately and each making a half spiral around the post. These counteract the rotating force which acts on the straining post when the fence is strained to full tension. The wires of the swinging feet spiral up in the same direction as the anticipated movement of the straining post.

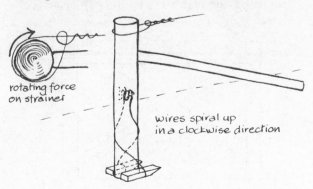

rotating force on strainer

wires spiral up in a clockwise direction

Sloping ground

The advice of the Ministry of Agriculture and Fisheries of New Zealand is to build straining posts on sloping ground as shown below. In practice, this is not easy, because of having to dig a deep hole at an angle to the vertical. Normal vertical posts are suggested, with a box strut (see p60) if necessary on the lower side, where the ground drops steeply away.

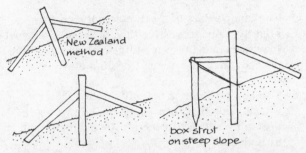

New Zealand method

box strut on steep slope

Another method sometimes seen is to build the fence from the top of the slope, and apart from the initial strainer only erect struts on the upward side.

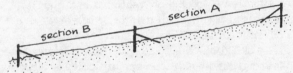

section B

section A

The section of the fence already strained then provides the anchorage for the next section. The disadvantage of this is that the strain of each section is not being fully taken by each straining post. If for example, section A on the above diagram fails due to a tree falling on it, post 2 may then be pulled towards post 3, because it has no supporting strut. Section B will then go slack. For good, permanent fencing it is recommended to always include a strut on the lower side.

Box strainers

Like many fencing techniques, the use of box strainers was developed in New Zealand. As in a conventional strainer, the box strainer relies on the principle of the triangulation of forces, but in the case of the box strainer, the force is taken by the strained wire.

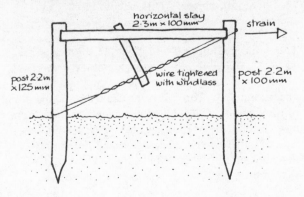

horizontal stay 2.3m x 100mm

strain

post 2.2m x 125mm

wire tightened with windlass

post 2.2m x 100mm

a The box strainer is as strong as a conventional strainer in firm soil. In weak or very shallow soils the box strainer performs better than the conventional strainer.

b The posts in a box strainer do not need feet, and where possible, are best driven into the ground. The fitting of the horizontal stay and the tensioned wire takes longer than fitting a conventional strut.

c The components of a box strainer are only slightly more expensive than those of a conventional strainer, because although two posts are needed, they are of smaller diameter.

d The box strainer is not suitable for areas where vandalism is a problem, as the whole assembly will fail if the strained wire is cut or undone.

In conclusion, the box strainer is a more complex structure than a conventional strainer, with more to go wrong, and its use is probably best restricted to situations where a conventional strainer is difficult to build. Full details of box strainers, conventional and other strainer assemblies are given in Aglinks FPP 818-821 (New Zealand MAFF). Where ground conditions are difficult, or very high strains have to be held, a double box strainer can be constructed. This has over twice the strength of a single box strainer. Although the optimum depth is 1m, it is possible to construct one in only 300mm of soil, for example over bedrock.

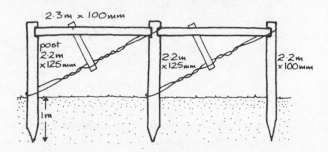

In emergencies, or where there are not sufficient large posts for conventional strainers, a double box strainer can be made of normal size stakes, 75-100mm diameter. This should be strong enough for short strains of mild steel fencing.

The same principle is employed in the box strut which is a very useful device for fence corners, slopes, and for repairing and strengthening posts and strainers. The following diagrams show some of these uses. An incidental advantage, for farm use, is that the horizontal stay provides an easy way of getting over fences, without damaging yourself or the fence. This may, in turn, be a disadvantage if it provides unwanted access.

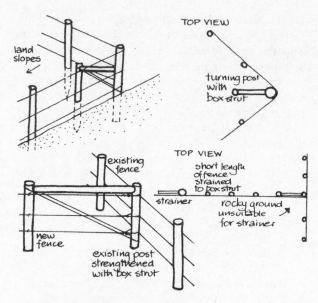

Construction of box strainer

1 Knock the two posts into the ground, the distance apart of the horizontal stay.

2 Cut recesses of about 15mm near the top of each post. Place the stay in position.

3 Drill a hole through the post into the stay, and then hammer in a 200mm length of 12mm mild steel bar. Repeat at the other end of the stay.

4 Using 4.00mm mild steel wire, make a loop as shown.

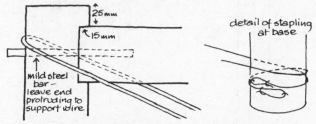

5 Preferably using a piece of hardwood, about 50 x 50 x 450mm, insert the wood between the wires. Hold it at an angle as shown, so it will pass underneath the horizontal stay, and twist it round until taut. Then lock the wood behind the stay, and fasten it with wire if stock can reach it.

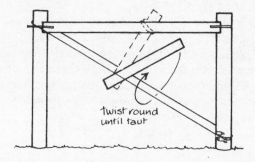

Designing the Fence Line

The simplest strained wire fence is a straight fence stretched between two straining posts, with intermediates between. Complex layouts around fields or following boundaries are made up in one of the following ways:

a A series of straight lines between a series of straining posts. As the fence is built, Monkey strainers are attached to each straining post in turn and the wire is strained and fastened off, and may be cut and restarted.

b A single strain of wire, taken around turning posts as necessary. Turning posts are slightly smaller than straining posts, and do not always need struts. Monkey strainers are not used on them, but only on the end straining post. The wire is pulled from there in one go, with the wire running freely around the turning posts. This method has the advantage of being quicker, and saving on materials for fastening off and joining wire, as well as on straining post construction. However, there is less margin for error, and straining posts must be really well constructed. Also if the fence is broken at one point, the entire fence may be affected, instead of just the section between adjacent straining posts.

Which of these two basic methods is used will depend on:

a The type of wire being used. The recommended maximum strain length for mild steel wire is 150m. There is no theoretical maximum strain for high tensile wire, so this is normally determined by the length of the wire. High tensile wire can thus be strained around a longer and more complex route.

b The length of the wire. Mild steel stock netting is supplied in 50m lengths, and thus distances between strainers of 50, 100 or 150m are ideal, as these avoid having to cut or waste any netting. High tensile netting is supplied in 100m rolls, therefore multiples of 100m are ideal.

c The terrain. It is more difficult to strain netting over dips and hollows, as it distorts. In this case it may be necessary to place a straining post at high and low points, and cut and restrain the netting. Line wires can be strained up or down as necessary, but there is extra strain at the low points, which need increased anchorage.

d Other features. Gateways, junctions with existing fences or walls and other features need to be taken into accout.

Turning posts

These should be about 125-150mm diameter, and the same length as the straining posts. Normally the smaller diameter posts of the batch supplied as strainers are used.

a A turning post is set in a dug hole, normally 1m deep, in the same way as a straining post. A foot and breast plate is fitted at the bisect of the angle.

b No strut is required for a turner if the angle is less than 30 degrees. Above 30 degrees, either one or two struts can be used. If one strut is used, it should bisect the angle as shown. Keep it low, to try and reduce stock damage. An angle greater than 90 degrees normally has a single strut.

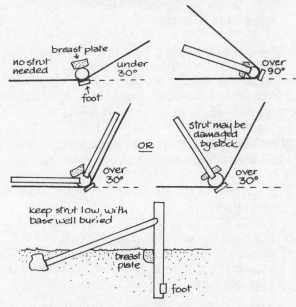

c Fit the strut and thrust plate as described for straining posts (see p74).

d The wire is taken around the back of the post with the wire fastened to a running fit. Two staples can be used, as shown.

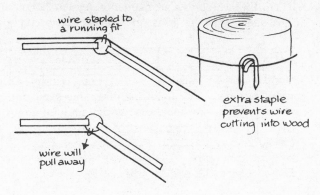

Layout

a Put a strainer, turner or large stake (if the batch supplied is of variable size) at the top of any hump or bottom of a hollow.

b All turning and straining posts at low points should have larger than normal feet, to combat the extra upward force on the post.

c If a stake is driven in at a low point, it may need to be tied down. The need for this depends on the steepness of the dip, the amount of strain, the softness of the ground, and the length and diameter of the post. Tie downs are used more often on high tensile fencing, as fewer posts result in the fence hugging the ground less well than mild steel fencing. They are described on page 80.

d Small dips and hollows can be filled in after the fence has been strained. This requires using either turfs, sods of earth or peat, rocks, extra rails or netting.

e Keep the fence away from any steep banks which could provide a 'launching off' place for animals that jump.

Large hollows, gullies and watercourses

In some situations it will not be possible to make a tie-down in a gully:

a If the gully is too steep to hold the fence down securely.

b If the gully is a watercourse for part of the year. Waterlogged marshy ground at the bottom of a gully will also need to be 'bridged', as it will be too soft to make a secure tie-down.

Where water levels fluctuate greatly during the year, a water gate should be fitted. This is a barrier which swings up and floats when the stream is in spate, and drops to form a barrier as the level drops. See page 127.

Gullies which are permanently dry, or have only a seepage at the most, can have a fixed barrier.

ESTIMATING MATERIALS

Walk the fence line, pacing it as you go, and making a sketch of the position of all straining posts, turning posts and struts. Mark gateways, and note the need for tie-downs, water gates and barriers. Then using the information given in chapter 1 work out the number of intermediates, the length of wire and other fittings required.

mild steel stock netting fence (50m roll length)

100m strain

join rolls of netting

tie down

existing hedge

badger gate

stream

gate

45m strain

short, steep section with water gate – use post & rail

50m strain

gate

43m strain

●━ straining post
○━ turning post

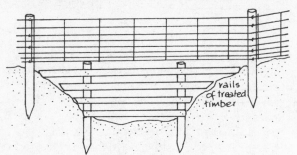

rails of treated timber

5   Strained Fencing – Construction

Order of Work

The basic procedure for any strained wire fence is first to erect the straining posts, and then use a strained wire to give the line for the struts and intermediate stakes. Wires are normally strained from the top downwards, as the top wire has the most leverage on the straining posts. If you strain the top wire last, you may then cause all the other wires to slacken.

The exact procedure will depend on the type of fence, the terrain, and the number of Monkey strainers available. In uneven terrain, don't fasten off the wire before stapling to sufficient intermediate stakes, or you may find the wire is too taut and cannot be pulled up or down. For the same reason, always leave the Monkey strainers in position as long as possible and do the cutting and fastening of the wire as the last stage, so any adjustments in wire tension can be made. Unless the coil of wire is needed elsewhere, do the cutting of the wire as you fasten off. This saves the inevitable wastage of wire caused by having to guess the finished length, and minimises the time that the wire is cut but not fastened, and when it can cause possible injury.

Taking the example of a strained wire fence of stock netting with a line wire top and bottom, a suggested order of work is as follows:

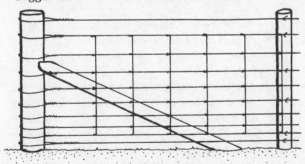

1   Clear the fence line.

2   Dig holes for straining and turning posts, and set the posts in the ground.

3   Strain up the bottom wire to give the line for the struts. Do not fasten off the bottom wire, but leave it held in position by the Monkey strainers.

4   Put the struts in position.

5   Strain up the top wire, leaving it on the Monkey strainers.

6   Knock in the intermediate stakes at the high and low points along the fence line.

7   Staple the top wire to the high and low intermediates, adjusting the tension if necessary at the Monkey strainers.

8   Knock in the remaining intermediates, and staple the top wire to them. Adjust if necessary to final tension, cut and fasten off.

9   Strain the stock netting and staple to high and low intermediates. Staple to remaining intermediates, cut and fasten off. (If you only have two sets of Monkey strainers on site, you will need them both to strain the netting. Take the set off the bottom wire, and if the wire is cut, secure the end by poking it into the ground until it can be re-strained.)

10 Check the tension on the bottom wire, staple to intermediates, cut and fasten off.

Clearing the Fence Line

Often the worst part of preparing to erect a new fence is the clearing away of the old one. Because many fences are 'patched up' for years, rather than being replaced, there is often a tangled succession of fences, with new wire on old posts, new posts knocked in at intervals, wires attached to trees and so on. It is not surprising this is done, when one realised the effort involved in removing an old fence. The job is particularly awkward where there is any barbed wire involved, or where the effects of animals or cultivation have buried the lower part of the fence.

It is not usually worth trying to save the wire, although pieces of hexagonal mesh and stock netting are useful for odd jobs such as tree guards, seed bed covers and so on. Hexagonal mesh can sometimes be re-used, but usually when one has got to the stage of replacing a fence, not much of it is worth re-using. Salvaged stock netting is very difficult to re-strain properly. Barbed wire should not be re-used unless it is in exceptionally good condition. Barbed wire is one of the least expensive fencing materials, and it is dangerous to strain any which is of suspect quality. Avoid the use of any barbed wire where possible (see p44).

Posts are often worth re-using. Any straining posts in the right place, that are solid in the ground and free from rot, can be re-used as they are, or with the addition of struts if necessary. Other sound posts can be lifted or dug out, although this is not an easy job if the post is secure in the ground. One method is to make a small notch at the base of the post, and lever it out using a crowbar. Otherwise, removal requires the awkward job of digging right down to the base of the post.

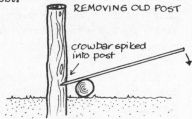

REMOVING OLD POST

crowbar spiked into post

If a whole line of posts have to be removed, it will be worth borrowing a tractor with front loader which will make a quick job of pulling the posts out of the ground. Alternatively, posts can be roped to the bar across the lower links of the tractor, and then rocked or lifted out.

If the site is going to be used for grazing, and not be regularly cultivated, consider leaving one or two posts for stock to use as rubbing posts. This will save wear and tear on the new fence.

Make a tidy job of clearing up the old fence. The quickest way is to cut the wire next to each post, pull the wire free and bundle it up tightly for disposal. If the wire and staples are rusted you may have to cut either side of the staple to free the wire. The posts are then removed with staples still in place, and disposed of. This avoids the danger of leaving staples lying around.

If the posts are to be left in place, or re-used elsewhere, remove all the staples and gather them up carefully for disposal. Fold up all unsalvageable stock netting as tightly as possible, or you'll be left with a huge unmanageable pile of wire to somehow transport away. Avoid at all costs leaving any wire to be cleared up at a later date, because by the time someone remembers it's likely to be half overgrown, and a hazard to man and animal. Hire a skip if necessary, or take the wire to the nearest authorised dump.

CLEARING VEGETATION

Try and choose a line which requires the minimum of vegetation clearance.

In thick woodland or coppice, clear a width of about two metres, to give sufficient room for working whilst erecting the fence, and enough room to walk up and down the fence line. When clearing the line, two or three people can go ahead with billhooks, bowsaws or slashers, keeping a safe distance from one another, whilst another one or two people remove the cut vegetation, and drag it back to a suitable place for burning or removal. In sparse woodland or scrub, cut material can usually be disposed of by scattering, if it will not be a danger to stock. Do not leave cut brambles or thorny branches where sheep are to be grazed, as they will get entangled.

Bonfires can be fun in wintry weather, but are time consuming and inevitably cause damage to the ground on which they are sited. This is acceptable if the area is to be cultivated, but in permanent grass or woodland the site is likely to become invaded with nettles, delaying the return of the original vegetation cover. Depending on the site and the type of vegetation, consider leaving scattered piles of brushwood as 'habitat piles' in woodland or scrub. It is not recommended to pile up the brushwood along one side of the fence, although this may seem a good idea where you want to keep people away from the fence, for example to discourage vandalism. The problem is that the dry brushwood can act like a fuse wire, and rapidly burn along its length, possibly setting fire to woodland or crops. Remember also that brushwood piles may not be a good idea in young woodlands, where they can act as cover for rabbits.

Hole Digging

This is the hard part of fencing! Bear in mind the following:

a   Make absolutely sure you've chosen the best site for the post before you start to dig. See the section on planning the fence (p21).

b   Have available enough of the right tools for the job (see below and p29). Although some people may enjoy hanging upside down and grovelling with their hands in the bottom of a deep muddy hole, it's not sensible to expect everyone to want to do it. It's also a dangerous and very tiring way of digging out a hole.

c   Wear gloves if your're not used to digging. Using a crowbar, which quickly gets dirty and gritty, soon causes blisters.

d   Don't make the hole wider than is necessary. Firstly, you're making more work for yourself, and secondly, the post will be less secure than in a narrow hole. If the hole is wide enough to stand in, it's much too wide! Keep the sides vertical.

e   In most soils you will be able to tamp back in more soil than you dug out, in spite of the hole now containing the post! You may then need to dig a shallow pit nearby to provide enough fill.

f   On urban sites and near buildings, remember there may be underground services.

g   If working on very steep slopes, a temporary 'step' is useful for retaining the spoil.

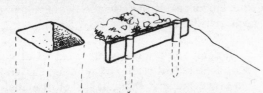

In long grass, old fertiliser sacks or large sheets of plywood make it easier to shovel up the spoil.

h   Separate the top and sub soil, and throw roots and rocks to one side.

Procedure

1   Mark with a spade the size of the hole. This should be the diameter of the post plus enough room to fit the punner you are going to use on at least three sides of the post. Aim to place the post against the side of the hole, so that the greatest pressure is against an undisturbed face. A hole of about 400mm diameter is suitable for a typical straining post. If using a garden spade and shuv-holer in loamy soil or soft clay, a square hole is easier to dig. A combination of crowbar, trenching spade and shuv-holer in difficult ground will normally produce a round hole. In either case, keep the sides as vertical as possible.

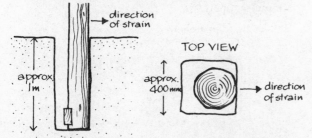

2   Dig down as far as you can with the spade, removing the fill and piling it up far enough from the hole that it's out of your way and won't slide back in, but near enough for ease of action. Some people find it easier to dig by the sequence shown below. Concentrate on half of the hole at a time. Especially as you get deeper, it is easier to prise loose the second half of each layer using a crowbar or spade.

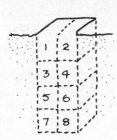
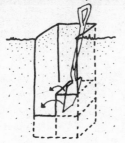

3   Once you have got too deep to remove soil with the spade, start using the shuv-holer to remove the loosened soil. Except in very soft soil, sand or peat, don't use the shuv-holer for actually making the hole, as the blades are not strong enough.

4   Instead of a shuv-holer, you can use a special ladle-shaped tool called a gully-bowl cleaner (as used by road cleaners). This tool is light but strong. Use by placing it in the hole, and then shovel soil onto it using a sideways action with the spade. There is a similar tool called a spoon spade, used by British Telecom, which has a blade bent at a right angle.

The advantage of these tools over the shuv-holer is that they are much lighter and less bulky to transport on site. The gully-bowl cleaner type could be improvised from a light metal container such as a biscuit tin or old metal feed-scoop, securely attached to a long wooden handle.

5   Hole-digging is best done as a two person job, with one person using the spade or crowbar to dig, and the other removing debris with the shuv-holer as the hole gets deeper. This then gives each person a rest while the other works.

As a guide at which to aim, the Forestry Commission allow 56 minutes for two men to dig a hole 850mm deep in soil of clay with a few stones, fit and firm the post and refill the hole (Forestry Commission Standard Times). Conservation volunteers may take a little longer!

Soft soil

In deep loam or soft clay a deep narrow hole can quickly be made using a post hole auger. These are available in various sizes and types (see p30). Depending on the soil type and dampness of the ground, screw the auger down about 200-300mm, and then lift it up, bringing the soil with it. If you can't easily lift it up, unscrew the auger a short way to lessen the load, and then lift it out. In wet clay soils you will need a short stout stick to clean the blade frequently. For hole diameters larger than the auger, make two or more holes immediately next to oneanother, and then clean out with spade and shuv-holer.

Wet soil

If the hole starts to rapidly fill with water while you are digging, stop and consider the alternatives.

If possible, move the site of the straining post or turning post onto ground which looks as if it should be drier. Try a few test holes with a crowbar. If it goes in easily and squelches around in wet subsoil, it is going to be almost impossible to get a straining post firm in the ground, apart from the practical difficulties of digging the hole. If there is no alternative drier site, consider using a box strainer (see p65), which is driven, not dug, into the ground, and which can give a firm structure even in wet soil.

Alternatively, you will have to dig a large pit and use bracing timbers or stones to wedge the post firmly. This is very laborious, and not guaranteed to be successful.

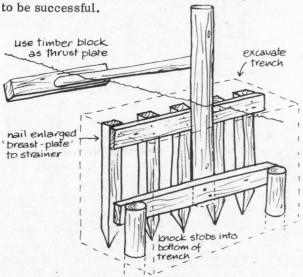

use timber block as thrust plate

excavate trench

nail enlarged 'breast-plate' to strainer

knock stobs into bottom of trench

In many upland areas, fencers select rock outcrops and drill them to fix metal posts (see below) rather than try to secure wooden posts in peat.

The use of high tensile wire is also helpful, as this can be strained over much greater distances than mild steel wire. On some sites it will then be possible to fix straining posts on firm ground, with the fence stretched across the boggy areas.

Rocky ground

This will involve a lot of hard work with a crowbar! A pick can be used for the first 300mm or so, until the hole gets too deep to use one. See page 29 for notes on the use of the crowbar.

If you come across a large rock, you can either try and prise it out, shatter it, or abandon the hole and start elsewhere. Look at the surrounding ground to see if the rock follows the line of any exposed bedrock. If so, either re-align the

fence to avoid it, or if this is not possible, consider using a box strainer. As long as there is 300mm or more of soil over the bedrock, it should be possible to make a firm structure.

Where bedrock at the surface is unavoidable, a rock drill will have to be used.

If you decide to try and shatter or cut through the rock, methodically chip away along any visible sign of weakness. Don't use a lot of muscle unless you think you can split it. Take great care when removing large stones or rocks from holes, as they can easily slip and trap the hand. You may have to split the stone if it is too heavy and bulky to get a grip on.

Rock drills

If bedrock is unavoidable, the only practical way of fixing a straining post is to use a rock drill. These can be hired (eg Pionjar 120), and are available with a special backpack for carrying to inaccessible sites, as the machine weighs 26kg. They are noisy and tiring to use, and should only by used by an experienced operator. Any work using a rock drill should have preferably been done before volunteers start work. The straining post should be of metal (see p40) with a pre-fabricated strut, braced onto a rock outcrop or into another drilled hole. Sites with difficult conditions such as frequent rock outcrops may well not be suitable for volunteer work, and are best done by fencing contractors with specialist tools and experience.

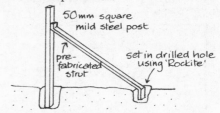

50mm square mild steel post

pre-fabricated strut

set in drilled hole using 'Rockite'

Erecting the Strainer

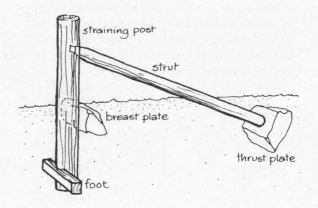

straining post

strut

breast plate

thrust plate

foot

Fixing the foot

The foot or cross-member is very important in resisting the twisting and upward-pulling forces on the straining post. It should be made of a piece of timber about 300mm long by 75mm by 50mm, or an equivalent piece of round timber. Although rot should not normally be a problem deep in the soil, it is advisable to use preserved softwood or durable hardwood, as with other fencing timbers.

A longer foot can be fitted to give extra strength, but the length is limited by the amount you are prepared to dig out in order to fit the foot down the hole. Extra digging is not only time consuming, but means more care is needed to make sure the backfill is really secure.

1 Hold the foot across the butt end of the straining post, about 50mm from the bottom, and mark off lines for cutting.

2 Cut down with a bow saw about 15mm at the mid point of the lines, and then chisel the wood away. Score the wood, and then chisel out the wood in deep strips. Check the foot for a reasonably tight fit in the recess.

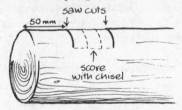

3 Except in heavy impermeable soils, liberally apply creosote or cuprinol to the cut area as a precaution against fungal attack (see p39).

4 Skew nail the foot into the recess.

Firming the post

While one person is fixing the foot, the other can be digging out a slot at the bottom of the hole. This must be at right angles to the line of strain, and on the side away from the strain.

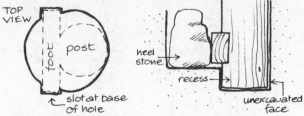

1 If soil conditions allow, try and excavate a recess at the bottom of the hole to receive the strainer, as shown. Otherwise, if the bottom of the hole is level, there will be a gap under the foot which will not be filled and tamped.

2 Estimate the length of the slot using a spade as a measure. It is very awkward to lift a heavy strainer vertically into the hole, and then have to lift it out again when it doesn't fit. You will also tend to dislodge material from the side of the hole as you lift the post in and out.

3 Having got the post in the hole, find a stone of suitable size to use as a heel-stone, for wedging behind the foot. Again, try and measure roughly whether there is enough room, as the stone is likely to be impossible to remove if it wedges in the wrong place. Tamp the heel-stone down as necessary with a mushroom headed crowbar, and drop more stones in to wedge as required.

4 There are many different protagonists of various best ways to backfill a hole! Some people prefer not to use any rocks, but to rely on the soil, as long as it is of the type which can be tamped. This includes loams and clays, provided the clay is not too wet, but excludes very peaty soils or those containing a lot of organic matter, which will rot away. For this reason, turf or vegetation should not be used for backfill.

The backfill in the lowest part of the hole is the most important, so take great care to tamp it thoroughly. The post should stand firm and solid after the first 300mm or so are tamped. Backfill in layers, tamping thoroughly after every three to four spadefuls.

Other people prefer to backfill with rocks where possible. One method is to drop two largish rocks down on both sides of the post, and then ram a wedge-shaped stone between each pair of rocks, so jamming the post in place. This layer is then backfilled with soil or stones, and then the procedure is repeated on the next layer, using the other two sides of the post. If enough rocks are available, this can be done all the way up the hole.

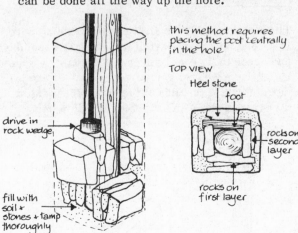

Other people prefer to use smaller rocks with soil, dropped randomly down the hole and thoroughly tamped in layers. The method used really depends on what soil conditions are like, what stone is available, and the wetness of the soil. Wet clay is impossible to tamp successfully. The method using rock wedges requires having a mushroom-headed crowbar or other suitable implement for driving in the wedges.

5 As you near the top. find another suitable rock, if possible, to use as a breastplate. Alternatively, use a piece of wood, such as a third or a half of a fencing stake. This should be placed on the opposite side to the foot, with the top just below ground level.

6 Finish with the soil raised above the surrounding ground level, so that water does not collect around the base of the straining post.

Fixing the line wire

Once at least two straining posts are in position, a line wire can be attached and strained to give the line of the struts, and of the intermediate stakes. As explained below, it is most important to get the strut exactly on line, and it is not sufficient to position it by eye.

1 Attach the wire to one of the straining posts, either by knotting, fence connectors or by stapling (see p57).

2 Unroll the wire (see p53).

3 Strain the wire at the second straining post (see p54). If you have enough sets of wire strainers, it's best to leave this set in position, so alterations to the tension can be made as necessary when the intermediates are in place.

Attaching the struts

The attachment of the strut to the straining post is a very important part of the strainer assembly, and needs to be done with care. Often it is done by cutting a wedge, sometimes called a 'bird's mouth', out of the side of the strainer, wedging the strut in place and attaching it with a nail.

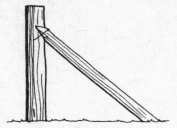

This method is not advised for the following reasons:

1 The cut effectively wastes part of the straining post and weakens the timber, and increases the likelihood of rot starting.

2 Nailing will split and weaken the wood, although this effect can be lessened by drilling a pilot hole.

3 There is not enough resistance to sideways movement. An animal or person can dislodge the strut by leaning or kicking against it.

4 Although it looks simple, it is difficult to make the cut accurately. A small error in the angle of the cut can result in too large or the wrong shaped wedge being removed.

The method recommended below has the following advantages:

1 Only a small amount of the post is removed, and if cut accurately to give a tight fit, the chance of rot starting is slight.

2 As the fence is strained the joint tightens up, and there is no possibility of the strut being removed from the side.

3 No nail is required.

4 Because the joint is made using a chisel, rather than by two drastic cuts with a bowsaw, the novice fencer is less likely to make a mistake. It may take quite a time to get it right, but it is time well spent. Most volunt-eers also find it a welcome break to spend a while chipping away with mallet and chisel, after the hard slog of hole digging!

Fitting a strut is easier with a round straining post, and a strut already chamfered to a point. Fitting a strut to a corner of a square straining post can be rather awkward.

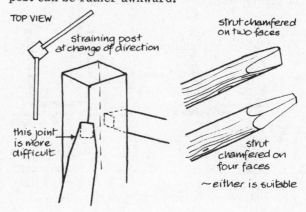

TOP VIEW
straining post at change of direction
this joint is more difficult
strut chamfered on two faces
strut chamfered on four faces
~ either is suitable

If the struts are supplied on site un-pointed, chamfer them with a bowsaw or billhook. It's more efficient if one competent carpenter does the whole lot at the start of the task. Give the cut areas at least two coats of preservative before the struts are used.

It is important that a bottom wire is tensioned to give the exact line of the strut. Part of the strength of the fence relies on the struts being as near as possible in line with the tension of the line wires. If the strut is out of line, the straining post is likely to twist and pull out when the tension is put on the wires. If the ground is undulating, check that the bottom wire is not caught up anywhere.

The exact position of the joint between strut and straining post will vary according to the type of fence wires and the method of attaching the wires to the post. If the wire is stapled to the post, it will run out from the side of the post, and the strut can be put exactly on the centre line. If the wires are attached by fence connectors or knots, the wires will run out from the centre of the post, and a strut placed on the centre line would interfere with the wires.

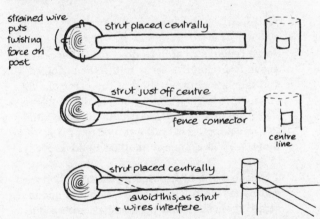

Note that one method of avoiding this problem, as used by Bryce Electric Fencing, is to not use a strut at all, but to rely on an extra heavyweight straining post, raked slightly backwards. The wires are attached through the post, thus giving a perfect line of strain. It is of course more important with electric fencing that the strut does not interfere with uninsulated wires (Chapter 7).

The strut should join the post at a point ½ - ⅔ of the height of the top wire. Note that this is not the same as ½ - ⅔ of the height of the top of the post. If stapling netting to the post, position the strut so the join will not coincide with any of the wires, if possible.

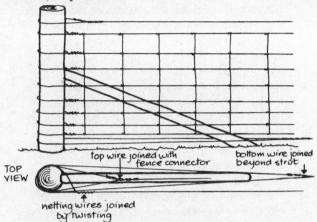

If using fence connectors on line wires, put the strut at the halfway height. This allows the upper wires to be clear of the strut. The lower wires are joined beyond the strut.

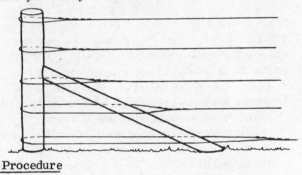

Procedure

1 Holding the strut at the correct height on the straining post, mark with a spade where the base of the strut touches the ground. To allow for the fact that the strut will be rebated by about 25mm, and that the angle will be slightly steeper (see diagram), start digging the slot at least 50mm to the straining post side of the mark. If you start digging the slot too far away from the strainer, more stones or other packing will be needed to get the strut solid. Dig the slot about 300mm deep at its deepest point, sloping up towards the straining post. Cut it just wide enough to take the strut.

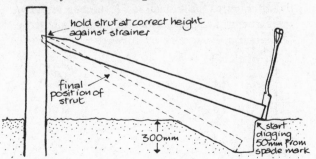

2 Hold the strut in position against the strainer. Then using a suitable straight edge, mark a line vertically down through the point of the strut, parallel to the straining post. Remove the strut and cut along the line, and chisel off the extreme tip, as shown. The length of the cut should be about $\frac{2}{3}$ the width of the strut, to give sufficient surface area at the joint.

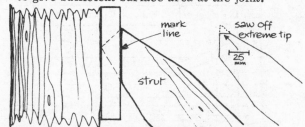

3 Put the strut back in position against the straining post. While one person holds the strut, another marks accurately around the cut end to give the area of the mortise in the straining post.

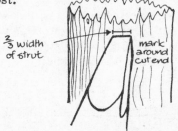

4 Cut the mortise in the straining post. With sharp taps of the mallet on the chisel, mark off the area in squares, the width of the chisel head. Then working from top to bottom, chisel away the slices of wood. Continue until mortise is about 25mm deep. Do not cut along the dotted line shown, as this makes the upper lip of the mortise weak and liable to snap off.

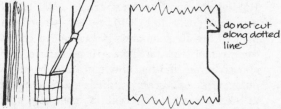

5 The strut should fit exactly into the mortise, with no gaps visible around the edge. Mark round the strut and then remove it, to check the depth to which it is going into the mortise. Usually it is also possible to see the 'imprint' of the strut end on the back of the mortise, which gives an indication of whether the strut is going in to the full depth, or whether it is catching at one side or corner.

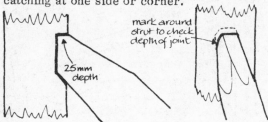

6 Before finally fitting the strut, brush preservative liberally into and around the mortise, and onto the cut end of the strut. Do not nail the strut.

7 Try to find a large and strong stone, that will not shatter or fracture, to use as a thrust plate. It should be long enough to extend well to either side of the base of the strut, and deep enough that the strut cannot slip off the bottom. The top of the stone should not protrude above ground level. Widen the slot already made, to take the stone. Some fencers also put a stone underneath to stop the strut slipping off the bottom of the thrust plate. Then using the spade, lever the strut into position so it is jammed tight behind the stone. If the strut won't fit, dig back a fraction to move the stone back.

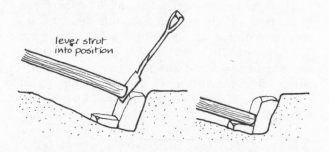

Some fencers prefer to do it the other way around, fitting the strut to the thrust plate, and then knocking the top of the strut sharply down so it 'clicks' into place in the mortise. However this is quite difficult to judge, and it sometimes breaks the top edge of the mortise. The former method is advised.

8 Test the strut by kicking against the bottom, and by trying to lift it out. It should not move at all sideways, and it should require a lot of heaving to lift it upwards. If it comes out it's not good enough. Start again using a bigger rock as a thrust plate, or by wedging the existing one with extra stones.

9 Backfill the hole, tamping the soil down with a punner. Leave the surface slightly higher than the surround, to prevent water gathering around the base of the strut.

If stones are not available, a wooden 'stob' made from a stake cut in half can be used. The usual method of fixing this is to knock the stob in at an angle while the strut is held in place. The problem is that the stob can go out of true if it hits a stone, and there is anyway only a small 'face' where it meets the strut. To do this with round stakes you need to cut a notch in the base of the strut, to stop it slipping off.

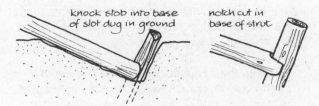

knock stob into base of slot dug in ground

notch cut in base of strut

A better way of using a wooden stob is to dig a trench across the line of the fence, and lay the stob horizontally. This is a stronger structure, as the force is spread along the stob. It can also be placed carefully in position, rather than relying on hitting it just right.

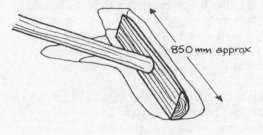

850 mm approx

Intermediate Stakes

The spacing of the intermediate stakes depends on:

a the type of stock being exclosed or enclosed.

b the stocking rate. High stocking rates will put increased pressure on fences as food comes in short supply, and stakes will need to be closely spaced.

c the type of ground. On stretches of boggy ground, it will be more difficult to get the intermediate stakes firm. To compensate, the posts will need to closer spaced, or if available, use longer posts.

On uneven gradients and hummocky ground the spacing will have to be adjusted so that stakes are placed at all high and low points. It is more important to get the stakes firm, and properly spaced according to the gradient, than to have them evenly spaced.

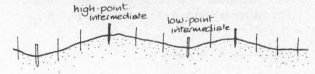

high-point intermediate

low-point intermediate

d the type of wire being used. Intermediate stakes on mild steel stock netting are usually spaced at 2 - 3m intervals, whereas those for high tensile wire can be spaced up to 10m apart. See Chapter 1 for designs of different types of fences.

Procedure

The following describes the procedure for flat land. For undulating land see below.

1 If a top plain wire is being used, attach this and strain. If there are enough sets of strainers, leave this set in position. If not, attach the wire by knotting (except for spring steel wire) so that it can be re-strained if necessary. This wire then gives the exact line for the stakes, and makes it easy to see that they are at the right angle as they are melled in. Do not put in the top wire at this stage if barbed wire is to be used, as it is too dangerous. If barbed wire has to be used, it should be attached last of all.

Where the fence is close up to a wall or to tall vegetation, and you can only use the mell or drivall from one side, it may be easier to line the stakes up by eye, as the top wire may get in the way.

2 Space out the stakes to the required spacing (a measuring stick is useful), laying them with their points towards the wire. If the post sizes are variable, select the fatter ones for any soft ground, and the thin ones for any rocky or stony ground.

3 An experienced fencer will be able to knock the stakes in on his own, but for those less adept, two or three people will be needed. One person holds the stake, another mells it in, and the third checks that the line is correct. The third person is less essential if upper and lower wires are in place.

Start with the post half way along the strain, and then do the posts three-quarters and a quarter way along. This reduces the likelihood of getting out of line. If you start at one end and work along, the whole line can be creeping out of true without it being easy to see, because the end strainer is a long way off. Any small error on the first stake is compounded by the second, etc.

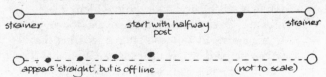

strainer   start with halfway post   strainer

appears 'straight', but is off line   (not to scale)

4 One person places the stake to be used in position against the wires. The other person checks that it is at right angles to the ground. If the post is rather uneven, put the best face towards the wire to give a good surface for stapling. Make sure the same face is towards

77

the wire when you come to knock the stake in. Press the stake down to make a mark on the ground.

5 Lay the stake back down, and then using a crowbar make a pilot hole by dropping the point in and moving the crowbar in a small circular motion. The other person should still be checking that the crowbar is at right angles to the ground. If you find the top wire gets in the way, lean on it just enough to get it out of the way. The pilot hole should be almost to the eventual depth of the stake, to knock any stones out of the way. However, the diameter should be as small as possible, in order for the stake to be firm. As explained on page 62, a post driven in is much stronger then one in a pre-formed hole. In soft ground, a pilot hole should not be necessary.

6 Remove the crowbar and return the stake to the hole, holding it as before. If available, the stake can be held with a 'stob holder' to lessen the chance of being hit by a mis-aimed mell. Most stob holders, however, are designed for use with square posts. Where a drivall is being used, two people can use it together. Take special care that the stake is 'true' in the pilot hole, because once the drivall is in position, it's not easy to check the alignment (see p31).

Keep knocking the stake in until it's the required height. If it won't go in far enough, don't keep on hammering as you will only be smashing the point of the stake against the rock or other obstruction it has met. If the post is firm enough, leave it at that. If not, take it out and try again a short distance to one side.

Continue until all the stakes on that strained section are in place.

On undulating ground the procedure should be as follows:

1 Instead of starting with the half, three-quarter and quarter way stakes, begin by knocking in those at all high and low points along the strain. Then staple the upper and lower wires to a running fit to these stakes, pulling the wires up or down as necessary. You may find that too much strain has been put on the wires, and that the Monkey strainers have to be released by a couple of links. If any of the 'low point' stakes are loosened or pulled up out of the ground by the upward force of the wires, the stakes will have to be tied down (see p80). This is best done at this stage.

Use the measuring stick or tape measure to get the top and bottom wires at the correct heights for the type of fence.

2 Knock in the remaining stakes. The wires should find their own level, and can be stapled as they lie, rather then measuring them against each post. This 'smooths out' the line. Beware however of further high and low points appearing as the wires are attached, especially in very uneven terrain. Keep a check on the bottom line to make sure it's still stock proof. When using a bottom wire with stock netting it's a good idea to leave stapling the bottom wire until after the netting is attached. The wire is then stapled half way between the bottom of the netting and the ground at each stake.

3 Note that intermediate stakes should always be knocked in at right angles to the ground surface, even on slopes (see p63). However, this is rarely seen on fences in Britain, and to most people will look 'wrong'. It is suggested that you check with the client before departing from the traditional method!

Straining the Netting

Procedure

1 Starting at the first straining post, unroll enough netting to go round the post and fasten off by whichever method chosen (see p57). Make sure the netting is the correct way up; ie closer spaced horizontal wires to the base.

You will need to remove the end one or two verticals to give enough wire for fastening off. The vertical wires on welded netting are removed by cutting near to each weld. On hinged netting, cut the vertical half way between each horzontal. You can then untwist the two almost-equal length pieces by pushing against each other. Collect up the pieces of wire for safe disposal. Fasten off at the post, and then unroll the netting to the next straining post.

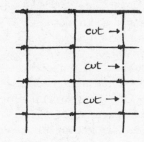

2 If you only have one set of strainers, strain
   the bottom wire first, though this does tend
   to distort the net. Normally you should have
   at least two sets, and can strain the top and
   bottom wires at the same time. Alternatively
   use straining clamps (see p56). Depending on
   the length of the strain, you will need several
   people to help get the net up into position.
   If there aren't any spare hands, go along the
   fence temporarily tacking the netting every
   few stakes, ensuring you place the staples so
   the wire can pull through as it is strained.

3 Strain the netting to the required tension. On
   each stake, staple to a running fit the top,
   bottom, and one or two of the middle horizontal
   wires. Keep to the same pattern on each post.
   Cut and fasten off the netting, and remove
   the wire strainers.

Sloping ground

On an even gradient, the procedure above can be
followed, by starting with the netting held at an
angle, as shown. Get a couple of people to unroll
and hold the first few metres of netting, and you
should then be able to judge the angle by eye.

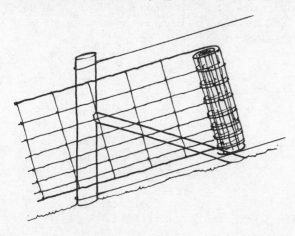

Undulating ground

This is more difficult, as the netting distorts
going over the changes in gradient. The best
method is to attach the start of the roll to the
first straining post with two sets of strainers,
unroll the netting, and then attach it to the next
straining post with another two sets. The netting
can then be temporarily tacked at the high and low
stakes and adjustments made at either end until
the netting is as taut as possible.

Joining the netting

The simplest situation is on flat ground, where
straining posts can be spaced at intervals to
coincide with the lengths of netting. For mild

steel netting, this would normally be 100m
intervals, so that 2 x 50m rolls are joined to make
one strain, and fastened off at each straining post.
However, straining posts cannot normally be so
regularly spaced, and netting has to be cut and
joined. The sequence has to be worked out for
each individual site, but bear in mind the
following:

a The aim should be to finish or cut the roll at
   each straining post, so that the netting can be
   fastened by tying, twisting or by connectors
   However, this may mean cutting the netting
   more frequently than necessary.

b If you don't cut the netting, but continue it on
   to the next straining post, the only way of
   fastening it so the strain is taken is to hammer
   staples in fully, which damages the wire
   galvanising.

Try and balance these two alternatives by making
use of turning posts (see p67). On these the
netting is fastened to a running fit, and continues
on to the next straining post. If the fence has at
least one top wire, this will take much of the load
from leaning animals. It may then be acceptable
to take netting around the back of straining posts
and continue on, where cutting would be wasteful
or inconvenient. However, don't join more than
three rolls of netting before fastening off fully.

Never fasten netting to the 'front' of corner posts,
as it will pull away. Take the netting around the
back, even if this means that the struts will be
on the stock side of the fence. If stock damage is
likely to be a problem fasten a short piece of
netting to protect the struts.

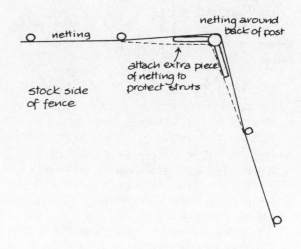

Tie Downs

In undulating ground, straining posts should be sited in the bottom of dips, in order to anchor the fence securely. However, this is not always possible and it may be necessary to anchor intermediate stakes in dips using tie-downs, to prevent them pulling up when the wire is strained. The same techniques can be used in soft ground, where it is impossible to get stakes firm simply by knocking them in.

Tie-downs can also be used on high tensile wires and netting, to pull the fence down at dips that occur between stakes, which may be spaced up to 10m apart. However, these do not always hold firm, and it is better to fill in with earth or rails where possible.

Some different methods of making tie-downs are shown below. The greater the angle the wire is pulled down, the stronger must be the attachment of the tie-down in the ground.

Spanish windlass

This can be used to firm up stakes in mild steel fencing, where they cross soft ground.

a Knock two fencing stakes as shown, as far as possible into the ground, but leaving at least 150mm protruding.

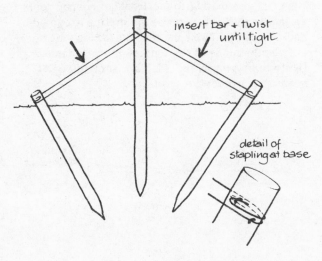

b Run a length of 4.00mm mild steel wire as shown, and staple. Repeat for other side.

c Then with one person each side, insert a stout piece of wood or wrecking bar between the wires and twist until tight. The wood or bar can then be removed.

d Cut off the stake tops if protruding more than about 150mm.

Stake

This is used in both mild steel and high tensile fencing, to anchor stakes and droppers. Tie downs for droppers are available from electric fencing suppliers such as Gallagher Fencing. The tie down is pre-drilled for easy fastening.

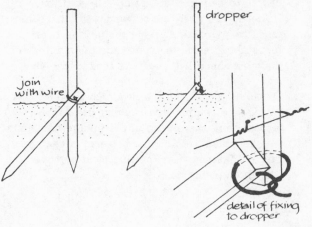

Buried object

Sometimes it is possible to use a large log, rock or even a piece of scrap machinery to anchor a high tensile fence in a dip. Attach a wire to a dropper and fasten it around the object. Fill in to hide the object as necessary, and to make the fence stockproof.

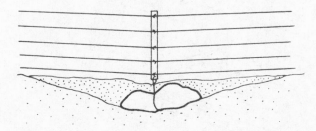

Anchor disc

This is a special metal disc with a wire threaded through, which is screwed down into the ground with an anchor disc driving tool. These are very strong, but there is the disadvantage that if the disc hits a rock before it goes deep enough, it cannot easily be retrieved.

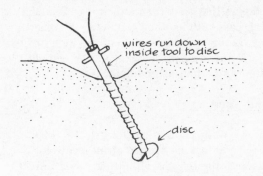

Other Procedures

Dropper fencing

Strain up a bottom and top wire as described above, and knock in the intermediate stakes. Fasten off the top wire, and then run out, strain and fasten the remaining wires in turn, from the top downwards. Take care to put the same tension on each wire, in order that you don't loosen wires already fastened off.

Wooden battens should be of 50 x 38mm pressure treated timber. A quick method of spacing the battens evenly between the intermediate stakes is to use a piece of elastic with the number of battens marked on it, and stretch this between the stakes. If obtainable, use barbed staples, and staple alternately as shown, to help prevent the batten from sliding on the wire. The staples should be driven until they are just gripping the wire.

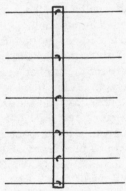

High tensile steel droppers are available from Hunter Wilson and Partners Ltd. These are cheaper than wooden battens, and do not need clips or ties to fit. They are also lighter and less bulky to transport on site, and make the final fence weight lighter than if wooden battens are used. The dropper grips the line wires tightly so that it cannot slip.

The dropper is fitted as follows:

1   Locate the centre twist of the dropper on the centre wire. Holding the bottom half of the dropper, rotate the top half around the wire. Tug sharply to lock it into the vertical position.

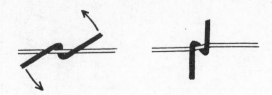

2   Repeat process on next wire up, twisting the dropper to the left. Continue to top. Repeat from centre to bottom strand.

3   Secure top and bottom by using a wire twister (see p33). Ensure top tail is turned down.

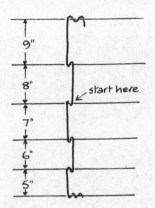

Mending strained wire fences

a   Never cut or undo wires while they are under tension, as they will spring back. Always use wire strainers at a straining post to take the tension, and then undo or cut the wire as necessary.

b   Wire strainers can be used as shown to pull together the ends of a broken wire. Join with a fence connector or figure of eight knot. Take care not to put excessive tension on the wire in order to join the two ends, but put in an extra piece as necessary.

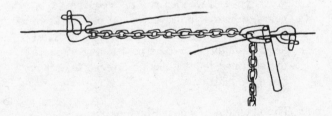

6 Wooden Fencing

Wooden fencing is generally used where attractive appearance and long life are important. Close-board fencing is used for privacy and security.

Wooden fencing compares to strained wire fencing in the following ways:

a The strength of a wooden fence is in its rigidity, formed by the strength of the posts and rails, the method of jointing, and the firmness of each post in the ground. In contrast, strained fencing is flexible, and its strength comes from the elasticity of the wire, and the strength of the straining posts.

Any extra load on a strained fence is spread along its length. Extra load on a wooden fence is borne by that section with its adjacent posts.

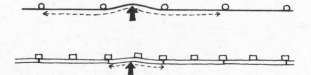

In general, there is a greater margin of safety with wooden fencing. If one component, such as a rail, breaks, the rest of the fence is not affected, although of course it may no longer be stock proof. If one component, such as a wire or straining post, fails on a strained fence, the whole section may be affected.

b Most types of wooden fencing require posts to be set in dug holes, at pre-determined distances. This can be awkward in difficult ground conditions. The positioning of posts for strained fencing can be altered to suit the ground conditions.

c The erection of wooden fencing requires no specialist tools, and most types can be built by semi-skilled labour. In comparison, the safe handling of wire, especially high tensile spring steel, requires wire strainers, dispensers and cutters, and is potentially hazardous because of the danger of wires breaking if overtensioned.

d Strained fencing is at its most effective over long, and preferably straight, fence lines, where the straining posts can be placed at the maximum distance apart. It is more difficult to keep strained fencing taut over short distances, and more straining and turning posts are required that for the equivalent total length in one long strain.

Wooden fencing can be built in short lengths, round corners, and for most types, up and down slopes, with little extra effort or cost compared to a straight run.

Materials

TIMBER

Post and rail and other types of timber fencing are costly in materials and time-consuming to erect, and only good quality timber, either naturally durable or treated with preservative, should be used.

Information on choice of timber and suitable preservative treatments is given in chapter 4.

Traditionally timber fencing has been built of oak or chestnut which are the most durable native timbers. The old method of splitting the timber to produce posts, rails and pales (thin, narrow panels) gives the most durable product, because the cells of the timber are not cut through, as they are if the wood is sawn. Split wood therefore absorbs less water than sawn timber, and is more resistant to weathering. Split rails are about a third more expensive than equivalent sawn and preserved softwood, but are stronger, and to most people, more attractive because of their traditional appearance.

Oak and chestnut, although not requiring drying for preservative treatment, should be seasoned before use. Otherwise, rails may warp, and become loose in the mortises as the wood shrinks.

Another traditional style in fencing is the 'arris' rail. This is diamond-shaped in section, the sharp top edge being designed to shed water and so lessen rot. Arris rails are fitted into mortises. Half-arris rails are sawn to give a vertical face for attachment of panels or pales.

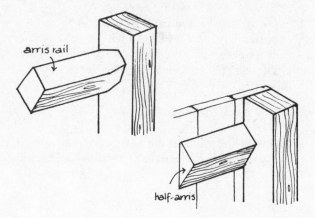

In addition to the preservatives described on page 38, there is a very wide range of products designed to protect and colour timber, for use on wood that is naturally durable or treated with preservative. These products come under the general name of 'exterior stain finishes', and provide a porous coat that is absorbed to some degree, depending on the type of timber, and whether it is split, sawn or planed. Absorption and colour is best on rough timber, in contrast to paints and varnishes which require a smooth surface. The porous nature of the skin allows any moisture that does penetrate to escape by evaporation.

The main use of stain finishes in fencing is on timber out of ground contact, where an attractive appearance is required, for example panel fencing for screening purposes. The stain is easy to apply by brush, and maintenance is minimal. If the colour fades after two or three years, another coat can be applied with no preparation other than brushing the wood to remove any dirt. The Countryside Commission for Scotland have done detailed trials on exterior stain finishes, and their leaflet, 'The Treatment of Exterior Timber against Decay', lists 27 manufacturers of stains, which they have found satisfactory. Timber merchants and large DIY stores should stock a reasonable range. Most stains are harmless to plants and animals when dry, but check this when you buy it. It is stressed that exterior stain finishes are not a substitute for preservatives.

Paints and varnishes are not recommended for fencing. These products function by making a waterproof skin, and any failure of this skin allows moisture to enter, so encouraging the onset of rot. Frequent maintenance is needed to give good results.

FITTINGS

Always use galvanised nails and screws in fencing. Non-galvanised fittings will wear loose as they rust. Nail length should be 2½-3 times the thickness of the timber held.

The main problem with using nails is that the wood is liable to split. This occurs particularly when nailing close to the end of a rail.

Splitting can be lessened by:

a blunting the point of the nail by tapping it with a hammer. This causes the nail to cut through the fibre of the wood, rather than splitting it.

b pre-drilling a hole through the rail.

c using longer nails, driven at an angle as shown.

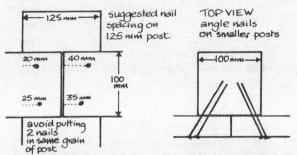

The traditional method of mortising rails without additional nailing (see below) avoids this problem.

The usual size of nails for post and rail fencing is 4mm x 100mm (to BS 1722 Part 7). The plans in chapter 1 give the sizes of nails required for different designs of wooden fencing. Numbers per kg of common sizes are given below. Always bulk-buy nails, screws, staples and other fastenings where possible, as they will be very much cheaper than buying small amounts.

Plain round head nails, galvanised

Length (mm)	Gauge (mm)	Number per kg
150	6.0	31
125	5.6	42
"	5.0	51
100	5.0	66
"	4.5	79
"	4.0	101
75	4.0	128
"	3.75	145
"	3.35	187
50	3.35	284
"	3.0	342

Some designs of fence require bolts, for example to secure rails for attaching vertical boards on screening or security fencing. Bolts give a much stronger join than using nails or screws. Coach bolts are the most secure, because they have a square collar which locks in the wood as the nut is tightened.

The length of the bolt should be equivalent to the thickness of the timbers, two washers and a nut, plus 5mm. For a neat finish, a shorter bolt can be used, with the nut countersunk into the wood. Bolts with a diameter of 6 or 8mm should be sufficient. Preferably obtain galvanised bolts, but these may need to be specially ordered. If not obtainable, use those with a black japanned finish.

Brackets for attaching fencing panels to posts are available from the manufacturers of fencing panels. These are described on page 92.

'Metposts' are metal spikes which are driven into the ground to hold wooden posts, mainly for panel fencing. They are quick to use and durable, but more expensive than the length of post and concrete which they replace. They are useful for fence repair. Bolt-down metposts are available for use on concrete or wood foundation.

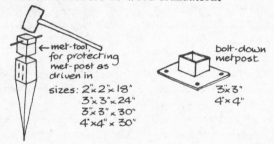

Post and Rail Fencing

In choosing the design of post and rail fencing, consider the following alternatives:

Mortised or nailed rails?

The rails can either be set into mortises cut into the post, or nailed onto the post. Mortised rails are stronger, because they cannot be dislodged by leaning animals and they are more difficult to vandalise than nailed rails.

Traditionally, no nails were used on mortised rails, and good craftmanship and properly season-ed timber allowed tight joints to be made. Now-adays, manufacturers of mortised fencing recommend using nails although this should not be necessary if the timber is dried before the mortises are cut. If nails are used, 75 or 50mm size are adequate, compared to the 100mm normally used for non-mortised rails. Details of nail and timber sizes are given with the designs in chapter 1. The length of the taper allows the nails to be knocked in at a good distance from the rail end, thus lessening the chance of splitting the wood.

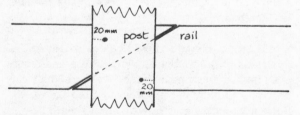

Timber for mortised fencing is more expensive than the equivalent for nailed fencing, because of the cost of cutting the mortises and tapering the rails. It is not usually worth trying to do this yourself:

a Cutting mortises without power tools is a slow job. This is done using a mallet and chisel, or

alternatively by drilling through with a brace and bit and then cleaning the mortise with a chisel.

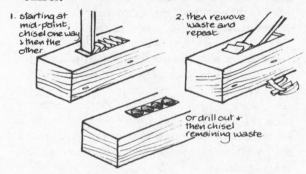

Mortises can be cut by power drill, using a mortising bit and a drill stand.

b If mortises or tapered rail ends are made in treated softwood, the preservative-impregnated layer will be cut, allowing moisture to enter. Any cut areas therefore have to be re-treated by hand. Manufactured mortised fencing is usually treated after cutting, so this problem does not occur.

Mortised fencing can only be constructed using posts that are set in dug holes, which is slower than driving the posts into the ground. Mortised rails are also more difficult to mend than nailed rails.

Driven or dug posts?

As explained on page 62, posts that are driven into the ground are firmer and quicker to erect than those set into dug holes and then firmed with backfill.

Both half round and square posts for nailed fencing can be driven into the ground, but care must be taken that the post does not twist as it goes in. If this happens, the face to which the rail is attached will be out of true.

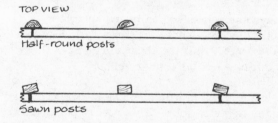

In deep loamy soils it should be possible to knock the posts in accurately, preferably aided by hold-ing the post with a stob holder, to keep it true. If the post hits any stones in the soil, it may be difficult to keep it in line. Making a deep pilot hole with a crowbar will help in stony soils, by forcing any stones out of the way. Otherwise, post holes will have to be dug.

A traditional post and rail design has the main posts set in dug holes, with smaller alternate posts, called 'studs' or 'prick posts' driven into the ground. These strengthen and stiffen the rails.

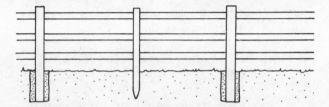

There may also be a problem with posts that have weathered tops. Some fencing manufacturers make a special metal tool called a 'dolly', which fits over the top of the post and protects it as it is driven in. Different sizes and designs are made to exactly fit the weathered top. A temporary one can be made out of a piece of fence post, but this will crack after only limited use.

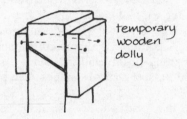

temporary wooden dolly

Posts with only a shallow weather can be driven in directly using a rubber mell.

DESIGNS

Various designs of post and rail fencing are given in chapter 1. These can be adapted to suit the intended use. the material available and so on. Most designs are based on the traditional 6ft interval between posts. with 12ft rails. The rails are either overlapped between equal-size posts, or mortised with alternate posts and studs.

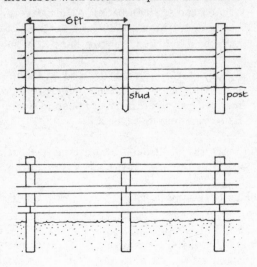

The British Standard size for rails in nailed post and rail fencing (BS 1722:Part 7) is 38 x 87mm. This, or a near equivalent is suitable for most uses. Lighter rails, of 30 x 75mm, may be adequate for light stock control, to support rabbit netting, and pedestrian control where the fence is unlikely to be climbed. Heavier rails, of 50 x 100mm, may be worth fitting on fences which are likely to be frequently climbed, whether this is an intended use or not.

Posts range from 100mm diameter half round for light nailed fences, to 125 x 75mm for heavy nailed and mortised fencing.

In addition to the designs in chapter 1, which are based on British Standards and commercial timber sizes, some traditional designs of wooden fencing are given below. These are given not only for historical interest, but to show well-tested designs that are still in use, and which could provide inspiration for some present day fencing.

The following design is of the timber fence which surrounds Charlecote Park, Warwickshire, now owned by the National Trust. The fence is at least 400 years old, and as in Shakespeare's time, encloses a deer park. The fence is made of split chestnut. with the lower rail mortised into the 'godfathers', and the upper rails nailed. Barbed wire has been added to stop people climbing through.

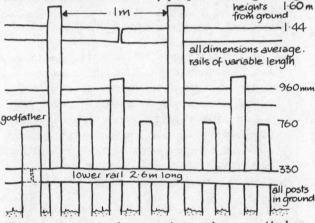

This is a more modern version, using sawn timber, around a deer park near Alton in Hampshire.

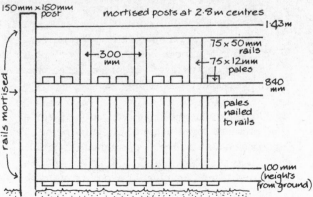

This post and rail fence near Ullswater, in Cumbria, has tall posts, drilled through to take wires. These discourage animals from jumping, and make the fence more difficult for people to climb.

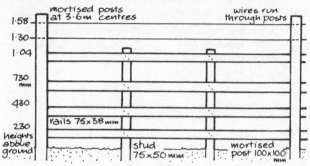

ERECTING THE FENCE

There are two basic methods of erecting a post and rail fence:

a Erect the posts all along a section of fence, and then attach the rails. This requires very careful measurement of the post spacing, as they have to be set at the exact distances predetermined by the rail length.

b Erect the posts and attach the rails in one operation, in effect building the fence as you go. This method has be used for mortised fencing.

With nailed fencing the choice will depend on:

a The type of ground: On level ground with easy soil conditions it should be safe to proceed with putting in posts some distance ahead of the rails. The method described below of laying out the rails on the ground is the usual method of measuring the post spacing. On undulating land where measurement is more difficult, and rails may need to be adjusted to fit, it will be easier to attach the rails as you proceed.

b Available labour: In order to effectively employ a group of volunteers on a single run of fencing, it may be necessary to erect the posts ahead of the railing to keep all hands busy. In stony soils where hole digging is slow, post erection takes must longer than nailing the rails. Where a group can be split into twos and threes working on separate sections of fence, each can erect and nail as they go.

c The importance of appearance: It is easier to achieve the illusion of the rails being 'continuous' if they are attached last of all. This gives a very attractive appearance to nailed fences, particularly on curves and undulating land.

d The present use: If replacing an existing fence which is in use, you will have to build as you go, leaving the fence stock-proof each evening.

Procedure

The following procedure is for building a nailed fence with overlapped rails.

1 Mark the line of the fence in one of the following ways:

a Use a bricklayer's line, or a line made of a strong length of twine attached between two pegs. Preferably have a length long enough to stretch between all adjacent corner posts or changes of direction. Place temporary canes or stakes at the changes of direction.

b An alternative method is to use wire as the line, on fences which are going to have one or more wires in addition to the rails. The partly strained wire gives a good true line. A bottom wire is useful to make the fence lamb-proof, and wires are also useful as anti-vandal devices (see p112).

Erect the first post permanently, to give a reasonable anchorage for the wire, then mark the remaining corner posts with temporary stakes. Tie the wire off at the first post (tying method given on page 58), and run it out to the end of the fence line and fasten with wire strainers, loosely strained. Prop the end post with a temporary strut as necessary, to provide sufficient anchorage for the wire.

This method is best used for posts which are to be driven into the ground, as the wire can get in the way of post hole digging, and be a danger if people trip or the wire is broken and springs back. Alternatively, lay the wire to one side once the post positions have been marked, making sure it is secure.

c A surveyor's tape can be used as a line over short distances, but is not generally recommended as it is difficult to keep it sufficiently taut over long distances.

2 To mark the positions of the posts, lay out a double row of rails on the stock side of the line.

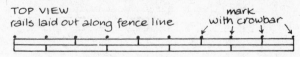

Start one of the rows with a half length rail, and butt all the ends up close, to give a double overlapping row as shown. At each join mark the position carefully with a crowbar, held up against the line. When all are marked, remove the line.

This is easy to do over level ground and short-cropped grass, but more difficult on uneven ground where the rails tend to slip out of position. In this case it is safer to measure out the distance between each post. The sequence is also displaced if rails are of varying lengths. If you suspect that the batch supplied is uneven, check through them before you begin, and put to one side any that are either too long or too short.

3 See page 70 for information on post hole digging. Put all the spoil to one side of the fence line, or else it gets in the way. Ensure that the correct face of the post is towards the line of the fence, with the rails on the stock side. Rectangular section posts on nailed fences should have their long face to the rails, to give the maximum area for nailing. Mortised posts are prepared the other way, with the long face across the line of the fence.

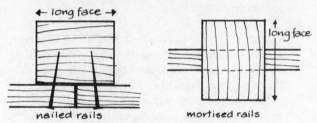

Check the following for each post:

a Post spacing. Use a tape measure, measuring stick, or the rail you are going to use. The rail can be attached ahead of the post, as shown below. This avoids any error, and reduces the chance of wastage from having to cut rails to fit.

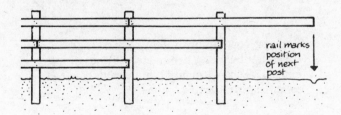

b Line. Check that the post is up against the line or wire, and that the line isn't caught up anywhere.

c Trueness. The post face must be correct for nailing. Check this using the line.

d Verticality. Check this with a spirit level, on two adjacent faces.

e Depth/height. This can be done with a tape measure or measuring stick. Take care that the base of the measurement is taken at the average ground level. If necessary, lay a small piece of wood across the hole and measure from there.

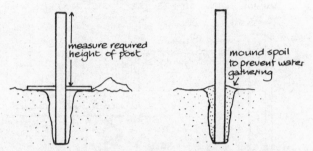

If you hit bedrock or a large stone near the base of the hole, it may prove impossible to set the post down the required depth. If it is only a few centimetres short, this should still be deep enough to get the post firm, as long as this is not taken as the general rule for all posts. Cut the necessary amount off the bottom of the post, rather than the top. This is because the cut will remove the treated layer (on preserved posts), but this will not matter deep in the soil, where the absence of oxygen excludes rot. If the hole is more than about a quarter short of its required depth, the post may need to be concreted in (see p121).

4 On a wire fence, the strained wire can be pulled up or down to the high and low points, and then allowed to find its own line on the remaining posts, so evening out any small undulations. On a post and rail fence with overlapping rails, a similar 'general line' needs to be followed. If you try and measure each post from the base upwards on uneven ground, you will be unable to fit the rails. This is shown, exaggerated, below.

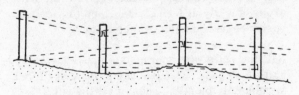

One method of lining up the rails is to use a length of twine, stretched between several posts, and held or tied at the measured height, starting with the bottom rail. The measurement should be of the top of each rail. Then place the rail up to the line, and nail in place. Re-position the line for the second rail and repeat.

Another method is to use a measuring stick, cut to the height of the post and marked with heights of the rail tops. Several of these are useful if a large group is working on the fence. The stick can be used at each post, or in conjunction with a line. Always mark the positions of the tops of the rails. It is then easy to see that the rail is being held to the mark, and if the rails are supplied in slightly uneven sizes, at least the tops of the rails will be level.

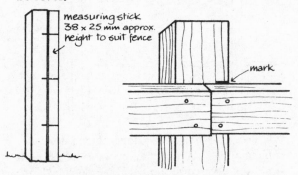

measuring stick
38 x 25 mm approx.
height to suit fence

mark

A third method is to use measured blocks, made from an old rail or other suitable piece of timber, cut to lengths equivalent to the gaps between the rails. Mark each block clearly with either its size, or its position in the sequence. For a large group have several sets of blocks.

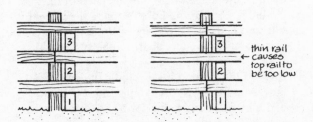

thin rail
← causes
top rail to
be too low

These are easiest used from the bottom upwards, so that they wedge on the rails and leave the hands free for attaching the rails. They are best used on even ground, which they will copy to give even railing. As described above, on uneven ground they will result in uneven railing. Blocks will also be inaccurate if the rails are of slightly differing sizes, and they cannot easily be used on slopes (see below).

5 Nail the rails with appropriate sized galvanised nails (see p83). Using a waste piece of timber as an anvil, blunt the ends of all the nails required, to lessen the chance of them splitting the rails. If this is done as you go along the fence, inevitably the post tops get used as convenient anvils, leaving indentations on the surface.

Attaching the rails is easiest done as a two-man job. Hold the rail to the mark on the post,

and nail first one end and then the other, using two nails driven in skewed at each end. The skewed nails make it more difficult to pull the rail off. Finally nail the centre of the rail, also using two nails. If you have to do this job on your own, use a small block temporarily nailed to support the rail end.

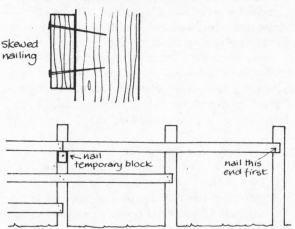

skewed nailing

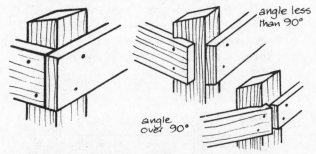

← nail
temporary block

nail this
end first

Avoid using rails with knots or other faults on curves in the fenceline, as they may break when forced into position. If possible, reject and return such rails, or use them for half pieces at either end.

Corners and changes of direction can be made as shown below. It is best to keep any cutting of rebates to a minimum, because they weaken the post, and are time consuming to make. Where necessary, cut rebates with a tenon saw or small bowsaw, and clean out with a chisel and mallet. A surform is useful for finishing off. Paint all cut surfaces with preservative.

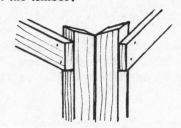

angle less
than 90°

angle
over 90°

Fencing contractors often make changes of direction by using two posts. Although more expensive in materials this avoids having to cut the timber.

Slopes

Follow the general procedure given above, laying out the line along the route of the fence, placing temporary stakes at corners, angles and breaks of slope. The aim should be to try and get each section between these stakes making as smooth a profile as possible, as otherwise you will have problems fitting the overlapping rails. There is a certain amount of 'give' in a 12 ft rail, allowing it to be curved either 'round' or up and down, but obviously this must not be over done as either the nails will give or the rails will break at a knot or any other weak point.

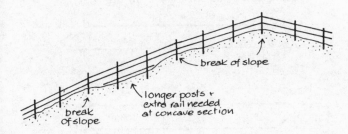

Note the following:

a   Longer posts may be needed to compensate for less stable ground conditions.

b   Longer posts, and extra rails or a strained bottom wire may be necessary to keep the fence stockproof across concave sections of slope.

c   It is not possible to keep the same overall height and rail spacing as on level ground. In the diagram below, gap 'a' is smaller than gap 'b'.

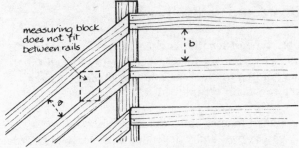

d   On very uneven sections of slope it will not be possible to overlap the rails, which will need cutting at each post. Rail ends will also need cutting to fit at breaks of slope. Treat all cut ends with preservative.

e   At awkward changes of direction, especially where combined with changes in gradient, two posts can be used as shown on page 88.

Curves

A loosely strained wire is useful for laying out nailed fences along curves. Use the following procedure:

1   Erect the two end posts firmly, and then knock temporary posts in at intervals along the proposed curve, spacing them at approximately 3-4 times the final spacing of the fence posts.

2   Run a wire out round the temporary posts and strain loosely, leaving the monkey strainers in position.

3   Using the procedures described above, erect the fence along the line of the wire, removing the temporary posts as you proceed.

Mortised fencing

The rails of mortised fencing must be fitted at the same time as posts are erected. The general procedure is as follows:

1   Run a line out along the route of the fence, using temporary stakes as necessary at changes of direction.

2   Dig the first post hole to the measured depth and erect the post. checking that it is vertical, and tamping the backfill thoroughly.

3   Saw off the tapered end on the first set of rails, so they fit neatly into the mortises. Treat the cut ends.

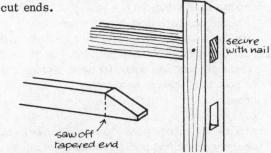

4   Using one of these rails as a measure, position the next post hole. Allow for the tapered section of rail, which fits into the mortise.

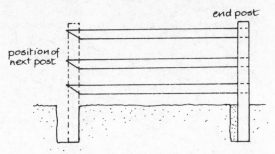

5   Dig the second hole. Make sure that the hole is at least 3" (in the example above) wider than

the post, to give sufficient room to fit the rails. Dig the hole as shown, with the undisturbed face towards the start of the fence.

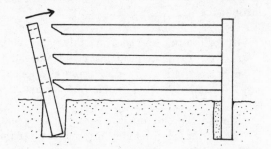

6 Put the post in the hole, leaning it away from the start of the fence. Push the rails through the mortises in the first post. Then with one or two people to help, hold the rails in the horizontal position, while the second post is straightened into place with the rails pushed into the mortises. Check that the post is vertical, and all rails securely in position, and then firm the post. Repeat all along the fence line. Nail the rails if required as each section is completed.

7 On slopes, the mortises may need enlarging in order to fit the rails.

Repair of nailed fences

a Re-attach or replace nailed rails as necessary.

b Posts which have rotted or broken must be replaced or repaired. To replace the post requires digging out the stump of the old one. For fences with driven posts it may be possible to lever out the old post (see p70), and then drive a slightly larger post into the old hole. Normally the old post will need digging out, as a hole will anyway need to be dug for the new post.

c To repair a post which is sound above ground, but rotten or broken at ground level, set a short post immediately next to the broken one, either by digging a hole or by knocking the post in. Then nail or bolt the posts together as shown.

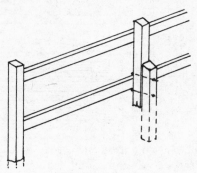

Repair of mortised fences

a Depending on the amount of 'give' in the post, it may be possible to force the two posts apart just sufficient to fit a replacement top rail. Do this by putting one end of the rail in position, pushing it as far as it will go into the mortise, and then forcing the other post away, until the rail end can be slipped into place.

b ·If the above is not possible, or lower rails need to be mended, use the following method. Force the rail as far as it will go into the mortise. Then holding it against the other post, cut off the tip flush with the post.

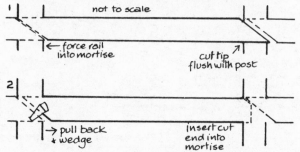

c Then pull the rail back slightly, so that it slides into the second mortise, with just enough to hold it at either end. If loose, wedge with small wooden wedges knocked into the mortise.

d Mortised arris rails can be repaired with special brackets. These are available from Jacksons Fencing.

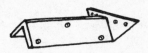

Board and Screen Fencing

This type of fencing is used for privacy and security, for windbreaks and shelters, and for the holding of stock in confined places. There are two main types:

a Board fencing is basically a mortised or nailed post and rail fence, with vertical boards, sometimes called pales, added. This makes an extremely strong and durable fence, but has to be built on site and is thus expensive to erect. A fence with gaps between the pales is usually called a paling fence, and is mainly used for garden and ornamental fencing.

b Screen or panel fencing is made of prefabricated panels, fastened on site to posts set at pre-determined distances. Many different types of panels are available. These are quick to erect, but are not as strong as board fencing, as the panel is normally only held in place by small brackets.

All timber should be pressure treated softwood, except for pales which may be made of cleft oak. Gravel boards are often included in the design. These are wooden or concrete boards fitted along the base of the fence, where there is the greatest wetting and drying action, which encourages rot. The gravel boards can be replaced as necessary. Post tops should be weathered, or have wooden post caps to protect the end-grain. Careful erection, particularly firming the posts properly, adds greatly to the life of the fence, as any 'wind rock' action will soon loosen the fence.

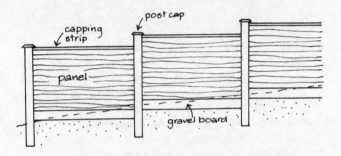

Board fencing can be erected on slopes, but panel fencing is not so suitable, as shown. Longer posts are needed, and part of the fence is buried in the slope. On shallow slopes a concrete gravel board 300mm high can be used. On steep slopes, board fencing should be used instead of panels.

BOARD FENCING

The following design is of a typical board fence. Posts are 125 x 100mm (5" x 4"), and 600mm (2ft) longer than the fence height, with weathered tops and mortises for the rails. Two rails are used for a 1.2m (4ft) high fence, and three rails for taller fences. The pales are 100mm(4") wide, sawn to a taper, above a 150mm (6") gravel board. All wood is pressure treated softwood.

75mm galvanised nails are used for attaching rails and gravel boards (1kg for 75ft of fence), and 50mm galvanised nails for attaching the pales (1kg for 30ft of fence).

The procedure for erection is basically the same as for a mortised fence (see p89), except that posts are concreted in position (see p121). Great care must be taken that posts are vertical. Once the post and rails have been erected, the gravel board is attached. Finally the pales are nailed

on in the sequence shown. A gauge can be made up for easy fitting of the pales.

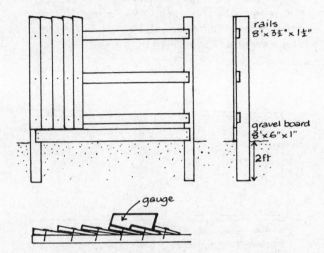

The following design is for a cheaper fence, with nailed rails and spaced boards. Height, board size and spacing can be altered to suit the requirements of the fence.

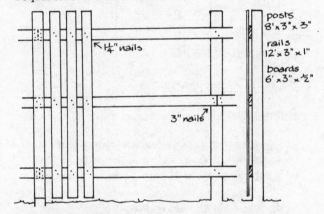

Alternate-board fencing can be constructed, with either vertical or horizontal boards. These have the advantage of looking the same from either side, ie there is no 'right' side. When set vertically, the boards give a varying sense of enclosure, according to the angle at which they are viewed. Total screening can be made by overlapping the boards.

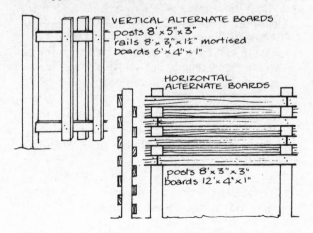

PANEL FENCING

The following designs of panels are available. All are produced in 1.8m (6ft) lengths. Most are available in heights of 2, 3, 4, 5 and 6ft. Some suppliers are listed on pages 133-135.

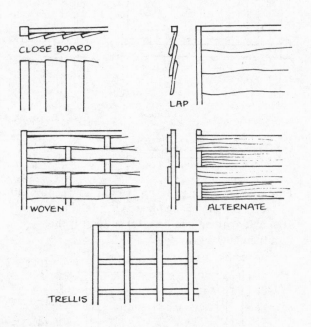

CLOSE BOARD

LAP

WOVEN

ALTERNATE

TRELLIS

Procedure

The general procedure for erecting a panel fence is as follows. The exact method of fixing the panel to the posts will vary with the manufacturer.

1 Clear the fence line of obstructions.

2 Dig the hole for the end post. This will normally be 600mm (2ft) deep, and the width of the spade. This allows a sufficient volume of concrete to hold the post firmly. Use a spirit level to check the post is exactly vertical. Backfill with concrete (see p121).

3 Run a line from the post to the end of the run of fence, stretching it taut. Measure along the length of the panel, and dig the next hole. Panels are normally attached between the posts, so the panel length must be measured from the edges of the posts, not the centres.

4 Set the second post in the hole, but don't back-fill. Either get someone to hold it, or use battens temporarily nailed to prop the post in position.

5 Set the panel in position, checking it is the right way up and correct side facing.

Chock the panel up with blocks to give sufficient room for the gravel board. Attach to the posts as recommended by the manufacturer. Some brackets have to be attached first to the post, with the panel then being slid into place in the manner of a mortised rail.

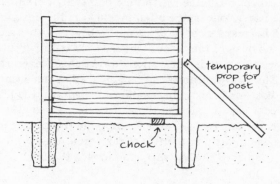

temporary prop for post

chock

6 Concrete the second post in position, and then repeat the procedure for the remaining length of fence. Do not go on ahead putting up posts because there is no way of compensating for any slight error in measuring either the distance or the verticality of the post.

7 Attach gravel board, post caps and capping strips as necessary.

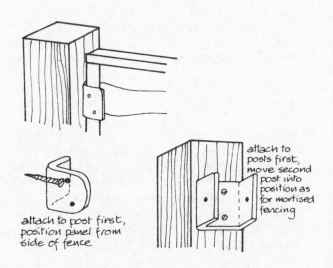

attach to post first, position panel from side of fence

attach to posts first, move second post into position as for mortised fencing

7 Electric Fencing

Temporary electric fencing has been in use for many years in this country. This has traditionally been a single wire. powered by a battery. and moved daily to give dairy cattle fresh grazing of grass or fodder crops. This principle has now been extended for use with other stock. particularly sheep. and a new development has taken place of erecting permanent electric fencing for boundary and field fences. This has been made possible by the development. in New Zealand, of high powered energisers which are capable of electrifying many miles of fences.

Electric fencing is a fast-developing and competitive business at present, and advice is readily available from the various manufacturers, importers and installers of equipment. Addresses are given on pages 133-135.

Electric fencing is a psychological, not a physical barrier. It follows therefore that:

a Stock must be trained to respect the fence. Young or untrained stock may rush and break through a lightweight electric fence because they have no fear of it.

b For most animals the fence must be kept working all the time that stock are in the field. Otherwise they soon realise that they won't get a shock. and will lean through or break down the fence.

c Electric fencing needs regular checking by someone who understands the system. Unlike conventional fencing there is little margin for error, as if a fault occurs, the entire 'barrier' may be lost. Most types of conventional fencing will keep functioning as some sort of physical barrier, even when not perfectly maintained.

d Because it is not a physical barrier, components are lightweight compared to conventional fencing. This keeps down costs and erection time.

Electric fencing works by making a circuit between energiser, fence, animal and ground. The output along this circuit is weakened if current is lost through long vegetation or stray wires touching the live wire. It follows that:

a Electric fencing will not function efficiently through lush vegetation,   where animals are grazed only on one side of the fence. This may include fences which on one side have woodlands. arable land, roadside verges or hedges. High powered energisers will burn off grass growth. but scrub or

woody growth may encroach, particularly where fences are not 'live' all the time. Although herbicides can be sprayed to keep fence lines clear, this method is expensive in chemicals and time, ecologically unsound, and only proves that the wrong fence has been chosen for that situation. Fence lines may look suitable for electrifying in winter, but the lush spring and summer growth can make the situation look very different. Part-electrifying, using scare wires or top electric wires may be suitable, as these can more easily be kept free of vegetation.

b Electric fencing will not function against animals which jump the fence, as they will not receive a shock. A scare wire set to one side of the fence may be effective however (p98).

c Some animals are more sensitive than others to electric fencing, because they present little electrical resistance. Most animals will first touch the fence with their noses, which being moist, conduct the current effectively to the ground to complete the circuit. Pigs have very wet noses and good memories, and may refuse even to cross lines where electric fences used to be. Dogs are also usually very sensitive, which can be useful against strays, but requires careful handling of working dogs. Sheep, on the other hand, may feel little effect through thick fleeces.

Permanent electric fencing of boundaries and fields is possibly best suited to large areas of stock land, particularly in the uplands. Here the advantages of lightweight components, easier transport of materials and saving on erection time can be gained, without the problems of lush vegetation growth.

Combined electric and conventional fencing

This is a form of permanent electric fencing, but is simply an electric wire added to a conventional 'physical' barrier. This has several advantages:

a It increases fence life by keeping animals off the fence, and stops damage from them leaning and rubbing on the fence. It is much more effective in this than barbed wire, and is less damaging to both animals and people.

b On new fences. an electric wire can be combined with high tensile netting or wires to give a relatively lightweight but stockproof fence.

c An electric wire can be used to make stockproof an existing dilapidated fence, wall or hedge.

d If the electric system fails, there is still the physical barrier of the fence to keep stock in until the power is restored.

Conservation uses

Electric fencing is of course primarily of interest to large scale stock farming, but it can also have uses in conservation:

a Temporary or permanent fencing of grassland, heathland and other open areas of land, to allow grazing to keep down the growth and spread of scrub and trees. Grazing is essential for the maintenance of some grassland and heathland reserves, and fencing can be a major expense. Electric fencing is suitable on heathland, as neither heather or bracken have much effect in shorting out fences.

Temporary electric fencing, powered by battery, can be used to rotationally graze areas of open land, where otherwise stock control would be impossible. This does need regular attention, but is only what the stock should anyway receive. The grazing or sale of stock may provide some income for the management of the reserve or country park.

b Scare wires can be used to keep stock away from fences being used to enclose young wood-lands. Temporary electric fencing can be used to protect young or recently laid hedges, or as a 'stop-gap' measure to keep walls stockproof until repair can be done.

c Low electric fences have been developed for use against rabbits. This could be a cheap and effective way of keeping a young woodland free of rabbit damage (see p108).

Electric Fencing Principles

How it works

Electricity flows only when it can complete a circuit, for example from the source of power along a conductor, such as a wire, and back to the source again. The electricity flows as a result of and electrical pressure which is measured in volts. Fence controllers are designed to work on a certain range of voltage (220 - 240 volts). The quantity of flow is measured in amperes (amps or A).

In electric fencing, a series of current pulses are passed through the wires of the fence. The current is in pulses to allow the person or animal touching the wire to release their hold in the interval between pulses. The current comes from the mains supply via a mains operated fence unit, also called a controller or energiser, or from a battery via a battery-operated fence unit. Most battery-operated units run off 12v wet cell car batteries. These are normally recharged every 1-2 weeks from the mains or a generator. Altern- atively, solar or wind powered units are available which under suitable conditions keep the battery charged.

Many different modles of energisers are available, which vary according to their maximum discharged energy per pulse, and their ability to maintain current flow under lush vegetation conditions. They are normally sold by the estimated length of fence they will power, but this will vary consider- ably according to the climate, vegetation growth, fence construction, number and gauge of wires.

The diagram below shows the pathway of the current. The value of the current passing through the animal depends on the voltage along the line, determined by the output of the energiser, and the type of ground which forms the 'earth return pathway'. Wet ground is a good conductor. and current flow is increased. Dry, stony or rocky ground has a higher value of resistance to current flow. The contact made between the animal or person and the ground also affects the current flow. A soft-footed animal such as a dog has less resistance than an animal with hooves. A person in wellington boots will have more resistance, and so feel less 'shock' than a person in canvas shoes.

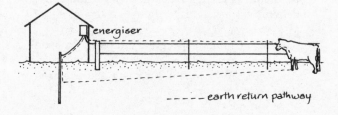
------ earth return pathway

Installation of mains energiser

The manufacturer will include detailed instruct- ions on the installation of a mains energiser. If a second-hand energiser is obtained, send for instructions from the relevant manufacturer. Note the following:

a The output earth terminal of the energiser must be connected to a separate earth point, and not to the earth of the mains supply. The energiser earth must be at least 10m from the

94

energiser or from any other metal, such as a shed roof, water pipe, or mains earth.

b The mains energiser should be mounted near the mains supply, with output pulses led out to the fence by a lead-out wire. If the energiser is installed at a distance from the mains, there are potential hazards with the wire connecting the two. In order of effectiveness, types of lead-outs are as follows:

   i A single 3.15mm aluminium wire (aluminium is the best suitable conductor)

   ii Four or five wire electric fence (several wires offer less resistance than one wire)

   iii Two parallel 2.5mm high tensile wires

   iv A single 4mm mild steel wire

   v A single 2.5mm high tensile wire

c The mains energiser must be safely installed under cover, out of reach of children, and in a place where no mechanical damage can occur.

Earth for mains energiser

This should be installed in the wettest possible place, such as a stream bed or permanently waterlogged ground. Use either:

a A series of galvanised stakes or pipes knocked into the ground to a minimum of 2m, and at least 3m apart from one another. The depth is important, and one stake 3m deep is more effective than three stakes at 2m deep. Join the stakes to the earth terminal of the energiser with one length of galvanised wire, attaching it securely to the stakes with heavily galvanised bolts or clamps.

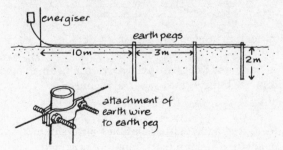

b Bury as deep as possible, and at least 2m deep, a large galvanised object such as a water tank or galvanised sheets. Connect with galvanised wire to the energiser earth terminal, and use a heavily galvanised bolt or clamp, sealed against corrosion, to attach the wire to the buried object.

Once the fence is erected, the effectiveness of the earth can be tested as follows:

a Drive a metal stake into the ground adjacent to the fence line and at least 100m from the energiser or energiser earth. Connect the stake to the fence with a piece of wire.

b Place one hand on the ground, and with the other hand touch the earth lead as near to the energiser earth as possible. No shock should be felt. If a shock is felt, increase the amount of buried metal.

The information given above on installation of mains energiser is intended as a guide only. For full details see the manufacturers' instructions. Installation should only be done by a competent electrician.

Other safety requirements

a More than one energiser should never be used on the same fence line.

b Fence lines on separate energisers should at no point be nearer than 2m to one another.

c Warning signs should be fitted on all fences to which the public have access. Plastic warning signs, which meet requirements of size, colour and wording are available from electric fencing suppliers.

d Stiles and gateways on public paths must be insulated or non-electrified (see p100).

e Electric fence lines should not be attached to electricity supply poles.

f Electric fences in the vicinity of power lines should not be more than 2m above ground.

g If electric fences have to pass beneath power lines, they should do so at right angles. Fence lines should never run parallel to power lines.

h High-powered battery energisers in a faulty condition can be as dangerous as a mains energiser. If 'multi-pulsing' occurs, ie the interval between pulses becomes shorter than normal fatal conditions can result.

i Crossing of a public road must be made with either an underground cable, or an overhead wire at least 5m above the road surface. The relevant road authority must be consulted.

j An electrified fence line should not run parallel and close to a telephone line.

Electric Fencing Materials

Posts

The following types can be used:

a   Pressure treated softwood, used with insulators. These are the most commonly used, as posts and insulators are readily available, insulators and staples are easy to attach, and the posts can be used for conventional fencing as required.

b   Self-insulating hardwood. This has been recently introduced for electric fencing, as the wire can be held directly against the post, without the additional expense and problems of using insulators. The wood is extremely hard and staples cannot be driven into it, so wires are fastened with tying wires (stirrup wires) in machined grooves. The wood is an Australian hardwood called ironbark. The posts supplied by Gallagher Fencing are from Pilliga State Forest in New South Wales, which is a managed forest resource.

Insulators

The following types are available:

a   Porcelain. These are the best, but also the most expensive. They are usually used only on straining and turning posts, as they are stronger than other types of insulators, and can take the strain of the wire without breaking.

b   Thermoplastic. These are the most commonly used type, being cheap and easy to fit. They are best used on posts where they support the wire only, with little lateral strain. The black ones are best, as the coloured type tend to deteriorate more quickly in sunlight. Choose the design with the maximum distance between fence wire and staple or nail.

screw-in insulator

plastic nail-on insulator

c   Insultube. This is a specially developed material, supplied in 2m lengths, which can be cut into pieces of about 140mm length and threaded onto the wire, and then stapled to the post. It has the advantage of being simple with little to break or fail, but care must be taken to thread on the correct number when the fence is being erected, as they cannot be fitted afterwards. Like other insulators, it has the advantage of protecting the wire from wind damage against the post. The same material in longer lengths can be used for insulating wires at stiles, above water troughs and so on.

d   Home-made. Alkathene water pipe is often used, in the method described above, but is not as durable.

Off set insulators

These hold the wire at a distance from the fence, and are designed for either:

a   carrying the lead-out wire from the energiser to the fence

b   carrying a scare wire to keep animals off the fence.

Two sizes are available, as shown on page 98.

Stakes with insulators

These are used for temporary fencing, and are available in either metal or plastic, usually with integral insulators. Many designs are manufactured. Separate insulators are also available which can be attached to metal stakes as required to give variable wire heights. The newest types of stakes are plastic multi-wire stakes, which have up to eight wire positions, giving great flexibility of use.

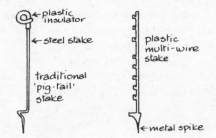

Combined insulator and straining device

These are used on straining posts for permanent electric fencing. Two types are currently available.

a   Insulator pad. This combines an insulated pad with a device that grips the strained wire. A hole must be drilled through the straining post. Produced by Bryce Electric Fencing.

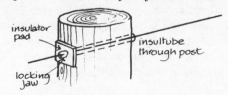

b Strain insulators. This is an insulated tube with an internal metal strip reinforcement.

Porcelain insulators can be used at straining and turning posts, tied as shown below. Note that the wire pulls from the centre of the post and the centre of the insulator.

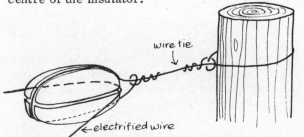

Wire

Barbed wire must never be electrified, or used in any fence that has part of it electrified. If an animal or person gets entangled in the barbed wire, there is a danger of injury or fatality from prolonged exposure to a series of electric pulses.

The gauge of the wire has to be balanced between the following:

a The finer the wire, the greater its resistance to current flow. This can be significant on long lengths of fencing.

b The thicker the wire, the greater its weight and cost. There are also more problems with change in tension due to temperature differences.

Because there should be no direct pressure on electric wires from stock, lighter wire at lower tension can be used than for equivalent conventional fencing. Likewise there is less strain on straining and turning posts. The wire normally used for permanent multi-wire fences is high tensile 2.5mm gauge wire, strained to 100kg. This is also used for electrified top wires, used with high tensile netting.

Provided straining posts are adequate, scare wires can be made of the same high tensile 2.5mm wire, or alternatively, of 2.5mm mild steel wire.

Temporary fences for strip grazing used to be made of 2.00mm (14 gauge) or 1.60mm (16 gauge) wire, but most systems now use a plastic braid containing several strands of this conductive stainless steel wire. This has the disadvantage of higher resistance, therefore is used only for lengths of up to about 600m. Its advantage is that it is lightweight, can be coiled neatly on a reel, and is available in bright colours for greater visibility.

Types of Fence

Permanent

One system of permanent electric fencing is described on page 15. Some other recommended wire spacings are shown below. In the case of sheep fencing, the bottom wires can be connected with flexible connectors, so they can be disconnected when vegetation is lush to prevent current leakage. Alternatively, a simpler system is to leave the bottom wire on sheep fencing non-electrified. All wires on cattle and pig fencing are electrified. Anyone considering installing a large system of permanent electric fencing should study the available manufacturers literature (some are listed on page 139), to find the system that suits their situation.

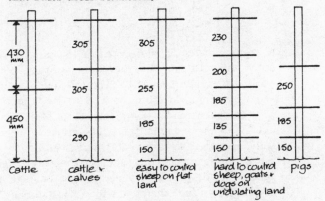

The layout should be planned with a 'trunk line', with other circuits running off it. By installing cut-out switches, these can be isolated as necessary when not in use. Cut-out switches should be installed anyway every half mile or so, to facilitate fault-finding. Straining and turning posts are erected in the same way as for conventional fencing (see Chapter 5).

Combined electric and conventional fencing

a Line wire fences. These can be designed with any number of wires, one or two of which are electrified, at heights chosen to discourage particular types of stock from pushing their heads through the fence. This is an alternative to using droppers or battens for this purpose, and can be effective against the 'targeted' animal but the fence may be damaged if other types of stock are enclosed. It is cheaper than (b) below.

b Netting with electrified top wire. This is possibly one of the best types of stock fencing, as it is proof against most types of farm stock, and is undamaged by cattle or horses. It is fairly expensive, becuase of the cost of the netting. The top wire can be attached by any of the insulators currently available.

c Scare wire. This can be attached to new or dilapidated fences, to keep stock off the fence. Off set insulators or brackets are available from most electric fencing stockists.

The wire should be fixed at about two-thirds the height of the animal being controlled, with brackets spaced about 10-12m apart on flat ground, with extra ones at rises and hollows on undulating land. The 225mm size is suitable for farm stock, and the 450mm size for control of feral animals and farm deer. Note that any existing barbed wire should be removed before the scare wire is fitted.

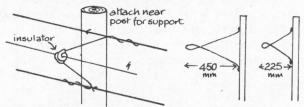

A scare wire can also be used to discourage stock and wild animals from jumping stone walls. It should be about 600mm high and about 500mm away from the wall. Attach the wire to short wooden posts at 10-15m intervals, using any cheap and suitable insulator. Drifting snow can be a problem near stone walls, and can pull staples and nails away from posts. If this may be a problem, use barbed staples, or attach the wire with a short piece of plastic twine.

Temporary systems

a Reel systems. Several different models are available. The basic type consists of an insulated reel containing a length of plastic braided or galvanised wire, any length of which can be unreeled to form the fence. The reel hooks onto a stake or over an existing wire to terminate. Up to four reels can be used to make a sheep fence. The fence can be run off a battery, or connected to a mains powered system. Insulated stakes are needed every 5m or so to support the fence.

One gadget designed to make it easier to reel up and move the fence is the 'Ridley Rappa'. This comprises a 'wheelbarrow', which holds two, three or four reels, and winds or unwinds up to 400m of wire as it is pushed along the fence line. The barrow also holds the stakes.

b Netting. Flexible plastic netting is available in 50m lengths in three heights, to stop sheep, rabbits, or horses and goats (see p105). The horizontals are of braided polywire, and the verticals of plastic. In ideal conditions, up to 20 lengths of netting can be powered by a high powered energiser. This system is useful for 'instant' fencing, but has some disadvantages.

i The vegetation needs to be very short along the fence line, or the net distorts. It may be necessary to cut the vegetation along the fence line first.

ii The netting is not very strong, and can easily be torn by careless handling or storage. It should never be used without power, as stock, especially those with horns, can get badly entangled and damage both themselves and the fence.

iii Goats have been known to chew through the non-electrified verticals.

iv The portability of the fence can attract thieves (see p112).

When not in use, roll the netting carefully as shown. Do not roll straight from one end to the other, or the netting will become entangled.

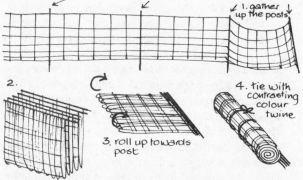

c Tumblewheel. This is designed for temporary cattle fencing, and is especially easy to move to allow a fresh strip to be grazed each day. The wire is passed along one spoke of the wheel, and the legs not touching the ground are also ive, to keep stock away. The fence is moved by rolling the wheel along, and can also be lifted up to allow stock or vehicles underneath. This system is available from Gallagher Fencing.

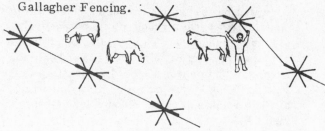

Gateways

The live wire of permanent systems must be taken either over or under gateways. Under is more satisfactory, as overhead wires can be brought down. Dig a trench at least 400mm deep, and use a length of double insulated galvanised wire, encased in plastic pipe, and about 2m longer than the width of the gateway. Connect it as shown, with the ends turned under to prevent water getting in. Do not use ordinary fence wire, as it will corrode. Copper wire is also unsuitable, as this creates corrosion at the join with the fence wire.

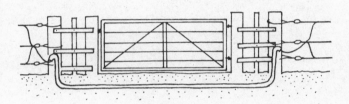

Some people advise leaving a section of about 3m either side of any gateway unelectrified, to make it easier to move large numbers of stock through it. If electrified to the edge of the gateway, stock may be wary and difficult to drive through. This is not essential but may be useful in some circumstances. It may also be advisable where walkers and horse riders frequently use the gateway, to prevent accidental shocks.

In some situations the gate itself may need electrifying, to stop stock rubbing and damaging the gate. (Note that all-electric paddocks should always include separate rubbing posts to allow animals to scratch themselves.) A single scare wire can be run right around the gate, flexing at the hinged end.

Alternatively, electrified gates can be used. These are widely used in New Zealand, and are currently being devloped in the UK. The example shown below is produced by Bryce Electric Fencing.

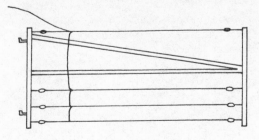

Other gateways include the following:

a   Spring gate. This is a very simple and economical gate, formed by a high tensile steel spring that stretches to at least 6m, with an insulated handle. These cost about £4 each which is a considerable saving on conventional gates.

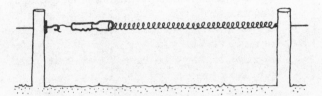

b   Swing gate. This gate is pushed open by a vehicle driving through, and then swings back to close. It is a cheap alternative to a cattle grid at frequently use access points. There is no chance of getting a shock when driving through, because the tyres provide insulation, but these gates do tend to discourage visitors who are not used to them! The gates must be driven through slowly or they tend to get damaged. Insulated handles are provided for pedestrian use.

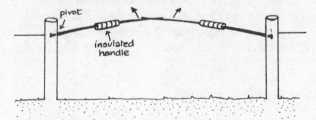

c   Offset lift gate. This can be constructed at infrequently used access points.

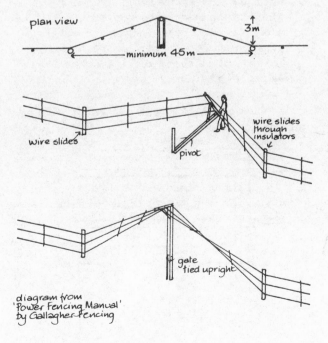

diagram from 'Power Fencing Manual' by Gallagher Fencing

d Grateway. This resembles an electric cattle
grid, held about 100mm off the ground and can
be used at busy access points up to 6m wide.
The grid is made of heavy duty plastic rope
with twelve strands of stainless steel wire,
attached with springs. As a vehicle drives
over, the rope is pressed to the ground and
shorts out; the vehicle also being insulated
by its rubber tyres. Available from Gallagher
Fencing.

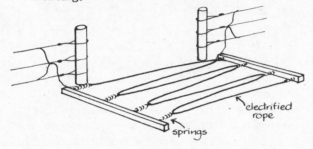

Water gate

This consists of lengths of vertical electrified
wires, suspended over the stream bed or gully
so keeping it stockproof. When the stream or
river is in spate, a resistor isolates the power
from the water gate. Very long gates of 50m
or more can be installed to span wide, shallow
river beds. Available from Bryce Electric
Fencing.

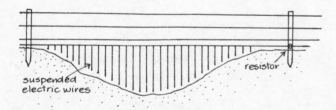

Stiles

Stiles must be insulated with a length of polythene
pipe or 'Insultube'.

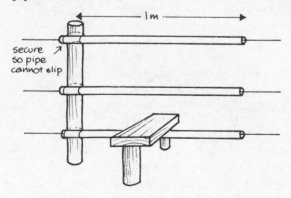

8 Fencing – Special Uses

Fences with Walls

Fences are sometimes needed to heighten or reinforce a wall. Situations may include:

a A change in the type of stock, resulting in the wall no longer being effective.

b The need to discourage feral animals, such as deer and goats, from jumping in to fields.

c A lack of stone may have forced the original builder to include a wall top fence.

d Lack of time or labour to repair a dilapidated wall may require a temporary wall side fence to be erected.

e The need to discourage people from climbing over the wall.

Where walls were designed to be topped with a fence, the posts were usually set into the wall, or less frequently attached to the side of the wall. The wall and fence below, near Ambleside in Cumbria, has wooden posts set in special long 'through stones' which have holes cut in them.

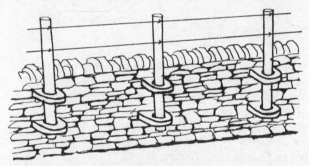

Because of the difficulty of adding wall-top fences, often walls are heightened by using tall posts either leant on or immediately next to the wall. The problem with this method is that often the ground is too stony to knock posts in, and that the use of materials is not very efficient as only the top part of the posts are being used to actually support the wires.

MATERIALS

Posts

Metal posts are usually used for wall-top or 'jump' fences. This is because they are durable, and have a small cross section for their strength, making them easier to fit in the wall top than a bulky wooden post. A suitable type is a flat mild steel bar. drilled to take the required number of strands. Suitable sizes of bar are 5mm thick, and either 25 or 40mm wide, depending on the

use and the length of wire to be supported. This can be bought from steel stockholders in about 6m lengths, and then cut to the required lengths and drilled. For maximum durability, the bars should then be taken to a galvaniser for treatment. Galvanisers are listed in the Yellow Pages Telephone Directory. Prices will vary, but a minimum charge of about £20 is to be expected. Other materials can be used as available, particularly of salvaged material. Angle iron is strong, though rather unsightly. Rather than use drilled holes, wires can be attached with short pieces of wire called 'stirrup wires'. These are best cut from lengths of 2.50mm high tensile or mild steel wire. Thicker wire is difficult to twist neatly.

Depending on the length of fence and the type of wire used, adequate straining posts must be included. These are simply a small version of a normal straining post, and can be made out of flat steel bar, with the top of the strut bent and bolted to the strainer. The larger size given above (40 x 20mm) should be used, or angle iron, preferably of the size 50 x 50 x 6mm. The wire can be terminated at the straining post with eye bolts, which are neat and allow for re-tensioning.

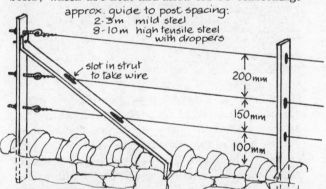

An alternative arrangement for a straining post is to use a full height post set in the ground at a wall end or gateway. Provided a good sized post is used, and it is set sufficiently into the ground, no strut should be necessary as the wall end will provide support.

Wire

The best type of wire for jump fencing is high tensile spring steel, as this allows maximum spacing of intermediates, so reducing material and erection costs. Alternatively, use a heavy mild steel wire, such as 4.00mm, and use eye-bolts or radisseurs to permit retensioning.

Spacing of the wires will depend on the situation, the wall height and the use. Traditionally the top wire is about 450mm from the top of the wall coping, and spacings as shown should be suitable for most uses.

Barbed wire should only be used on wall top fencing to discourage people from climbing over, as it will be no discouragement to stock. Similarly, electrified wires are no advantage, as the animals will be on or over the wall before they discover the wire is electrified. If using electric fencing, erect a scare wire instead (see p98).

An alternative method is to use stock netting for wall tops. This has the great advantage that animals cannot easily push their way through if they do manage to get onto the wall top, and deer and goats are deterred from jumping. A recent introduction is high tensile netting in the size suitable for wall tops. Details of sizes are given on page 47.

Stock netting can be attached to metal straining posts by knotting or fence connectors (see p59). and to metal intermediates with stirrup wires.

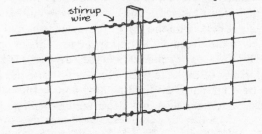

FENCE TYPES

Jump fence

If the fence is constructed as part of a new wall, or one being rebuilt, the posts can be set in as the wall is built. The traditional method is to set the base of the post in a hole cut in a through stone. This can be done using a cold chisel and lump hammer, making a quarter turn with each blow. Alternatively, a power drill, powered by a generator, can be used.

Another method is to rest the base of the post on a through stone and mortar it in position, propping it in place as necessary until the mortar is set. A quicker variation of this, which saves having to wait for the mortar to set, is to prepare hollow concrete blocks with posts set in mortar. These are then built into the wall so that the blocks are hidden.

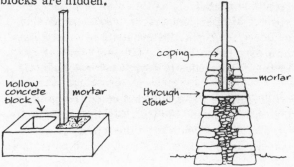

If the wall needs to be stock proof from one side only, set the posts to that side to prevent stock jumping onto the wall.

Adding a jump fence to an existing wall can be done by removing the coping stones and sufficient fillings to reach a through stone. The post is then mortared in place and the wall rebuilt. Alternatively, if the coping stones are large enough, they can be drilled to take the post. This saves any dismantling of the wall. Use a cold chisel or power drill to make a hole about 50mm deep. Set the post in with 'Rockite' cement.

Cornish hedges or stone faced banks, which are earth filled, can be heightened by knocking in wooden stakes and building a normal strained wire fence. Further details of walling are given in Dry Stone Walling (BTCV 1977).

Wall side fence

Before deciding on the design, consider the following:

a Can posts easily be knocked into the ground beside the wall? Try a few trial posts.

b Does the fence need to be stock proof from both sides?

If the posts can be knocked in and only one side needs to be stock proof, the fence can be built as a normal stock fence, with the netting 'suspended' at the required height. Overlap the fence below the wall top as shown, so there is no risk of a gap being forced if the wire loses tension. Turning posts at inside corners will need to either be tied back through or over the wall with spanish windlasses, or alternatively a strut fitted on the stock side. Keep the strut low to discourage animals rubbing on it.

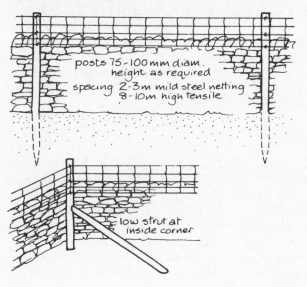

Where posts cannot be knocked into the ground, you may have to tie them through the wall with wire. Thread the wire through the wall, round the post and back again, then tie with a reef knot and tighten with a batten. Do this twice for each post.

To make a wide wall stock proof from both sides, the posts can be set alternately on either side, and either knocked in or tied to the wall. Because of the zig-zag line made by the posts, if netting is used it can only be attached to alternate posts ie on the same side of the wall. On the other side, one or two line wires are attached to discourage animals from jumping up. This solution is expensive in materials, as long posts are needed, and you are effectively making two fences for the same boundary.

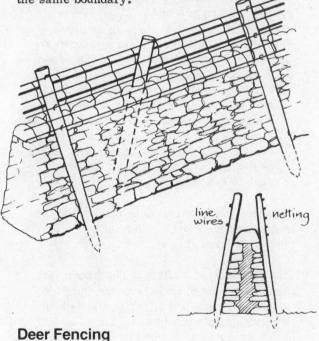

Deer Fencing

Deer fencing is erected for one of two purposes:

a To exclude deer from commercial woodlands, or where woodlands are being re-established for ecological or landscape reasons in upland areas. Exclosure fences may also be needed to protect high-value horticultural and agricultural crops.

b To enclose deer in a park or deer farm.

EXCLOSURE FENCES

Because of its height, deer fencing is expensive in materials, bulky to transport to the site and difficult to erect. It is important therefore to:

a ensure the need is essential. If a commercial crop is being protected, it may be the case that the fence costs more than the eventual economic return from the crop. This is more likely with small or awkwardly shaped areas, as a fence becomes cheaper per unit area enclosed as the area increases. Other forms of protection such as individual tree guards or chemical repellants may be an alternative. The Forestry Commission reckon that these other forms of protection are unlikely to be competitive with fencing in effectiveness or cost on areas larger than four hectares. In other words, a deer fence may be an expensive way to protect a woodland smaller than four hectares.

b ensure that as much as possible is found out about the species, numbers and movements of the deer, as well as other animals such as hares and rabbits. This is important in choosing the type of netting, and possibly in the placing of the fence. If rutting areas are enclosed within the fence, deer will try to break through.

Designs

Three designs of strained wire deer fence are shown on pages 10 and 11. Two of these are well-proven Forestry Commission designs. For further details see 'Forest Fencing' (Forestry Commission, revised 1985).

Deer fences of line wires only are not recommended as they are very time consuming to erect and require closely spaced droppers to prevent deer squeezing through.

Barbed wire should never be used in deer fencing as deer can become entangled and die if they try to jump it.

Electric scare wires (see p98) have been found to be successful in keeping deer out of woodlands. A single wire should be fixed at a height of about 1.2m, and 450mm out from the rabbit or stock fence enclosing the wood. Hang coloured tape or similar at intervals along the rabbit fence to encourage the deer to investigate, and they will get a shock as they do so.

ENCLOSURE FENCING

Deer parks were traditionally enclosed by high stone or brick walls, or by wooden fencing, an example of which is shown on page 85. Modern deer farms and deer in wildlife parks are enclosed by strained wire fences, basically similar to those detailed on pages 10 and 11.

However, provision must be made for:

a the increased pressure on fences from enclosed but non-domesticated animals. If frightened, they may attempt to jump or break through any fence, however high and secure.

b the need to minimise the chance of animals escaping. Unlike domestic animals, once through the fence, the deer are unlikely to be recaptured.

c the need for special provision at gateways to prevent animals escaping while, for example, feed is being brought in. This may require a system of double gates, as shown below.

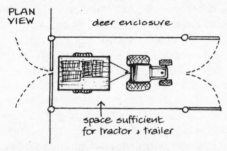

PLAN VIEW

deer enclosure

space sufficient for tractor & trailer

d handling systems, for deer to be restrained for examination, treatment and so on. These should be of close vertical board fence, at least 2m high, with no gaps where the animals can see out. Deer can jump or clamber over extreme heights when cornered.

Fences to enclose deer therefore have to be built to the highest specification so there is no risk of fence failure. Fences for deer farming are a specialist subject beyond the scope of this handbook. For further information contact the Deer Farming Association, or fencing contractors with experience of deer farming systems.

ERECTION OF DEER FENCING

The basic procedure is the same as a normal height strained wire fence. Note the following:

a Posts and full-height deer netting are extremely heavy and bulky to carry. Hire or borrow suitable transport (see p34) to ensure that carrying by hand is kept to an absolute minimum.

b Take care when putting straining posts into post holes. Place the post on the ground so the base is its diameter distance from the edge of the hole. With the aid of another person as necessary, lift the further end and gradually raise the post to the vertical. Then lift it just high enough to move it sideways and gently down into the hole. Don't try and hoist the post directly into the hole or you will dislodge soil back down into the hole.

c There are various ways to reach to the height required to knock in intermediate stakes:

i The easiest method, if you have a suitable vehicle, is to drive close enough to stand safely on it and knock the post in with a mell.

ii Use a drivall in the following way. Lay the stake down with the point to the pilot hole in the ground. Slip the drivall over the stake top and then raise the stake to the vertical. You can then reach up and use the drivall as normal. Take care when removing it from the stake top as you will be lifting its base up to head height, and it can easily topple over. A strong person is needed! Safety helmets are advisable.

iii Another method is to make a temporary platform of some sort, which can be moved from stake to stake. However, the platform has to be fairly heavily constructed to be safe and useable on uneven ground. This makes it cumbersome to move around, and requires it to be made up and dismantled on site. If you can get the platform there by vehicle, you can probably use the vehicle to stand on.

It is only the erection of the stakes that requires extra height; all other work can be done from ground level.

d The stakes must be firm in the ground, as their height gives extra leverage compared to normal height posts, and pressure from wind or animals can loosen them. Keep knocking the posts in until they are solid, even if this takes them below fence height. Add an extra piece, nailed on as shown, to give the required height.

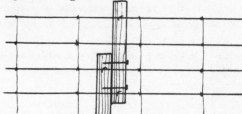

e If using the Forestry Commission system of two widths of netting lashed to three spring steel line wires, follow this procedure:

1 Erect the straining and turning posts and run out the bottom and centre wire.

2 Knock in the intermediate stakes, and run out the top wire. Staple all wires to stakes, and then strain to final tension and fasten off at straining posts.

3 Unroll the top netting and tension as required. Attach it to the top wire with lashing rods.

4 Roll out the bottom netting and attach it, together with the bottom wire of the top netting, to the centre wire.

5 Attach netting to the bottom wire.

6 If using rabbit netting as the bottom netting, this is easier to attach with netting rings. In this case attach the top net to the top and middle wires first with lashing rods, and then attach the rabbit netting. Turn under and cover with sods or secure with wires (see p108).

Remember to gather tools etc to your side of the fence before you start attaching the netting, or you may have a long walk round!

Goat Fencing

Goats are notoriously difficult to enclose by fencing, and it is partly for this reason that they were traditionally tethered. Note the following:

a Goats are adept at climbing, and struts for straining posts will provide a suitable foothold. Either place all struts on the non-field side, or if both sides are to be grazed, attach an extra piece of stock netting on the far side between the straining post and the first stake, to make the strut inaccessible.

b Likewise, the rails of post and rail fencing can provide a foothold. If this type of fence is already in place, it will need covering with netting, and heightening (see below). Gates must be treated similarly.

c Never use barbed wire, as goats may injure or kill themselves if they try to jump it.

d Goats can be restrained with electric fencing, provided they are taught to respect it.

<u>Stock netting</u>

The most suitable height netting presently available is 1200mm high, in the lightweight 'Universal' range from Sentinel Fencing (although any size can be made to order by Balfour Westlar). This needs to be heightened by the addition of line wires to make a fence about 1500mm high. Posts will need to be specially ordered, as they are not stock sizes.

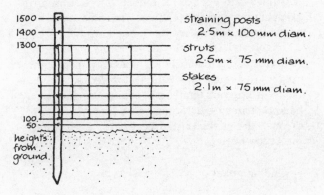

<u>Converting existing fences</u>

This can be done by heightening, or by adding an electric wire.

A standard post and rail fence will need heightening by about 500mm, and the rails covering with netting to deter climbers. One method is to use a combination of two sizes of stock netting, for example the 900mm and 650mm high 'Universal' netting. Heighten the posts by nailing on additional pieces. Use the 650mm net at the bottom, straining it lightly before stapling. If you simply unroll the netting and staple it as you go the netting will be very loose.

The end post can be strengthened to use as a strainer by attaching a small strut, or by fitting and extra rail and loop of wire to make a box strut, as shown.

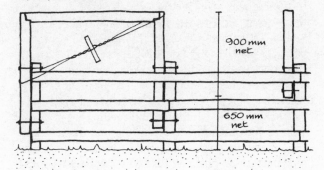

Alternatively, fix a scare wire at about 800mm, held out from the fence on offset brackets (see p98). Additional electric wires above the original fence will serve no purpose, as the goats may not touch them before they jump.

Electric fencing

Goats will usually respect electric fencing, but are intelligent enough to exploit any weaknesses. If single wires are used, three are needed at about 200 500 and 800mm high. To train the animal, let its natural curiosity lead it to touch the wire, so that the shock is mentally connected with the fence, and not for example with a person leading it to the wire. It is also advised to 'not put ideas into receptive minds', for example by stepping over electric wires yourself, as the goat may follow suit.

Flexinet electric netting is available in 1100mm height, designed particularly for goats. Never leave this in use unelectrified, as the goats may become entangled. Some goats learn to chew through the unelectrified verticals, even when the fence is live.

Excluding goats

In some upland parts of the country feral goats may be a nuisance. Action taken depends on the economic loss they cause, but if necessary fences will have to heightened by adding another roll of stock netting. It is likely that deer may also be a problem, in which case increasing the height to exclude them may make the job worth doing. Check around the boundary fences and remove or make inaccessible any branches or rocks which allow goats to climb over. A scare wire may be effective, particularly if there are just a few animals which persistently 'break in'.

In contrast, there is a New Zealand technique for capturing feral goats to use them to graze and 'improve' rough land. This involves placing wooden planks or similar up against boundary fences, to positively encourage intruders!

Badgers, Foxes and Rabbits

BADGERS

Badgers move around at night between setts, watering places, latrines and feeding sites, often on tracks which have been in use for many years. Badgers are very strong, and can push their way underneath or between tightly strained wires and stock netting. Tracks should be easy to recognise. Look for tunnels, 150-300mm high, through hedges and scrub, bare scuffed ground beneath fences, and clearly defined paths across permanent pasture that look like narrow footpaths, but lead to badger-height gaps in boundaries.

In many situations there may be no need to make any special provision, as even if new fences are put up across the tracks, badgers will find their way through, although possibly damaging the fence to some degree. Problems arise when:

a gaps forced by badgers make the fence no longer stock proof, for example allowing young lambs to get through. This may not be a serious problem if that gives the lambs access only to another field, and if they are fairly closely shepherded and can be returned to their mothers if they can't find the way back. It will usually be possible to keep young lambs in more secure fields for the week or so that they are small enough to escape through badger gaps.

b badger gaps make the fence no longer proof against pest species, in particular allowing rabbits into tree plantations. This requires either totally excluding badgers (see below), protecting the trees by other means such as tree guards, or fitting badger gates (see below).

c badgers themselves do damage. This can be a problem with high value agricultural crops, horticultural crops, nurseries and gardens. Badgers do damage by digging holes to get at worms and slugs, disturbing seed beds and young plants.

Badger-proof fencing

As badgers can get under fences by digging in most soil types, possibly the only totally badger-proof fence is a close-board wooden or rigid metal fence, set over a concrete foundation. For gardens, some form of close-board fencing set over a concrete gravel board, set partly into the ground, may be suitable. The fence need only be close-board for the first 600mm height.

For a larger area, chainlink (heavy grade, mesh size 50mm), heavy Twilweld (mesh size 50 x 50mm) or Weldmesh (mesh size 50 x 50mm) can be used. To discourage badgers digging underneath, lay a separate section of mesh on the ground in the direction of attack, fastened to the bottom of the fence with gordian rings or sacking ties. Peg it down with wire loops as for rabbit fencing. Hexagonal mesh is not strong enough as badgers can tear through it. Try using either light Twilweld, which is available in 300mm width, or cut sections of heavy Twilweld or Weldmesh into 300mm wide strips. The reason for using a separate strip is that it can be replaced separately if it gets damaged or rusts badly, whilst leaving the main fence intact.

Another easier and probably cheaper solution is to

use electric fencing. Electric netting will provide short term protection, possibly for young crops. Alternatively, use permanent electric fencing, with electrified wires lower than usual at 100mm and 200mm. These can be connected with flexible connectors, so they can be disconnected at times of year when the badgers are no threat, although this may result in establishment of paths, whose use is later difficult to discourage. Fence lines may need to be kept clear with herbicide to prevent loss of voltage. Keep a check that badgers are not digging underneath the fence, and if necessary block with rocks or similar, to force the badgers back onto the wire to reinforce the shock deterrent.

Badger gates

These can be put in to prevent badgers damaging fencing, and to allow access for them but not for rabbits. Their construction and use is described in 'Badger Gates' (Forestry Commission leaflet 68, 1976).

On new fences, the badger gate must be assembled in stages, to allows the badger to get used to using the gap, before the gate is fitted. On existing fences where the gap is already in use, it may be possible to proceed a little quicker, but it should still be done over a few days.

Work is best done in early summer when badger activity is high; and in the season before young trees are planted.

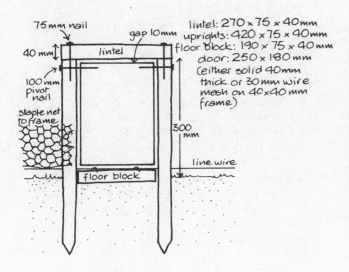

1 Erect the new fence, cutting away a piece about 200mm across and 270mm high in the rabbit netting. Disguise the bottom line wire by putting sods of earth beneath it, and loose earth over it. Leave this for a week or so, until you are sure it is being used. Check by looking for footprints in the loose earth, but placing a

small stick across the hole (though this may be dislodged by other animals), or by watching. In early to mid summer badgers emerge regularly at dusk, and if the run is near a sett you are fairly certain of seeing them.

2 Fit the floor block in position, stapling the line wire to it. Cover this with loose earth and leave for a week or so, and check it is being used.

3 Fit the uprights and lintel, and staple the netting in place. Leave for a week or so.

4 Fit a temporary wooden half door, about 1200mm high, and allowed to swing freely. Leave and check for use.

5 Fit the full door, and check for use.

If necessary, creosote can be used as a short term deterrent to discourage badgers pushing under the fence elsewhere, as they do not like the smell. Paint it liberally along the bottom of the netting, either side of the gate.

Foxes are recorded as using badger gates, but rabbits apparently either do not learn the trick, or are not heavy enough to push the gate open.

FOXES

There is no entirely satisfactory method of fencing fields against foxes, which is why controlling the fox population is the normal method of trying to reduce losses of lambs, geese and poultry. However, it is claimed that foxes are deterred to some extent by electric fencing, and enclosure of electric netting, used in addition to the existing fencing, may provide some protection. Permanent electric fencing of line wires is probably less effective, because the fox can jump between the wires, and gateways usually remain unprotected. However, a fox can easily jump clear over an electric fence of 1m height or so, therefore the fence cannot be relied upon. Extra high fences, of about 2m height, or roofed-in enclosures are needed for poultry and game.

RABBITS

Rabbit fencing must include netting with a mesh of 31mm size or smaller. The usual method is to use hexagonal mesh 1050mm high, with the bottom 150mm turned over in the direction of attack, so giving a fence 900mm high.

For a new fence for rabbits only, or for rabbits and sheep, use the design shown on pages 9 or 10. To convert a stock netting or post and rail fence, simply add the hexagonal mesh. The mesh should not be strained, as this pulls it out of shape. Unroll it, attaching it as you go. Fasten it by its top selvedge and again just above ground level, using 15mm staples on posts and rails, and netting rings (see p61) on horizontal wires, spaced about every 500mm.

The recommended practice used to be to bury the bottom 150mm, but this is not now thought to be necessary. Instead it can be covered with turves or sods of earth, or pegged down with wire loops about 100mm long, cut from old wire, and spaced about 300mm apart. On a new fence, a tractor and plough can be used along the line of the fence, and then the furrow folded back afterwards to bury the netting.

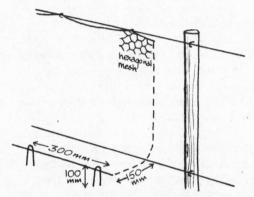

Electric netting has been successfully used as a temporary fence to keep rabbits off young crops. Another system produced by H Ridley and Sons is a three-wire electric fence on short stakes designed specifically against rabbits. The fence comprises three reels of wire with a reel post and sufficient stakes and insulators for a 400m length fence. The fence can be reeled out using the Ridley Rappa (see p98).

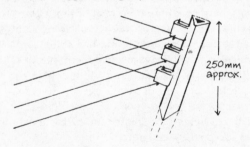

Tree Protection

Much of the fencing work done by conservation volunteers is to protect newly planted trees, or to enclose woodlands where increased natural regeneration is required to ensure their long-term survival. Tree protection needs planning carefully if resources are not to be wasted, as often the fencing or other protection costs more than the young trees themselves.

The aim of tree protection may be to:

a prevent damage from animals browsing on the leaves and young shoots, gnawing at the bark and rubbing themselves on the trunks.

b prevent damage from vandals

c prevent damage from machinery and tools. This can occur in amenity areas and roadsides cut by machine, and where plantations are weeded with brush cutters or hand tools.

d encourage growth. Fences can include wind-break material to give protection to young trees, and individual 'tree shelters' are also available.

Protection is divided below into three different types; fences for small woods, exclosures for individual trees, and tree guards. Tree guards are usually used in association with one of the other types of protection.

FENCES FOR SMALL WOODS

Planting small woods and copses has several advantages over planting individual 'specimen' trees:

a Instead of the typical standard tree with stake and tie, small feathered trees called whips can be used. These are much cheaper, establish quickly and do not normally need stakes and ties. Whips are not usually planted in individual exclosures (although they will often do better than a standard tree), presumably because they look rather 'lost', and the cost of the whip hardly justifies the cost of the exclosure.

b An interesting series of habitats evolves as the copse grows, and the mutual shelter improves the microclimate for tree growth. This is especially important on exposed sites.

c If an understorey of shrubs is planted, these can be cleared later to give a single or group of 'specimen' trees, as desired. The extra land used and lost to grazing is only that which will eventually be shaded out by the mature trees.

d The cost per tree of fencing a small copse is much less than building individual tree exclosures.

e This type of planting is a less obvious target for vandalism.

In choosing the design and materials of the fence, it is important also to consider for how long the fence is going to be required. The length of time will depend on the type of planting, and what the site is to be used for. On non-grazed amenity sites, fencing may be used to keep people, rabbits and deer away from the young trees, until they are well enough established to withstand vandalism and browsing. This may take 5 to 50 years, depending on the site and the size of the trees at planting. Short term fencing of non-durable timber should be suitable for a 5 to 10 year life. Fencing of trees in mown grass also protects the trees against machine damage. The situation is similar for trees in arable land, although individual tree protectors against rabbits may be sufficient where vandalism and deer are not problems.

On grazed land, the situation is different, as planting may need protecting for a much longer period if not indefinitely. Single trees, or groups of 'specimen' trees will need almost indefinite protection against sheep and horses, which may tear at the bark of mature trees, especially in winter when grazing is in short supply. Cattle are less likely to cause damage once the trees are large enough, and merely give a neat 'parkland' appearance by browsing the leaves and young branches to an even height.

More natural groups of mixed trees and shrubs, may be able to fend for themselves once they have become established. Where species such as hawthorn and blackthorn are included, and allowed to grow to dense shrubs within the protection of the fence, the main stem will be safe from browsing when the fence is removed. If planted around the perimeter, thorny shrubs can give protection to standard trees with more vulnerable bark. However, sheep are still likely to find their way in, and graze the ground flora and any tree and shrub seedlings, so the wood will not regenerate naturally. Sheep can also get badly entangled in thorn, bramble and wild rose, so it may be necessary to fence to protect the sheep. In the past, small woods were often protected by a proper laid hedge of thorny shrubs.

Type of fence

a   High tensile fencing is not usually used on lengths of fencing less than about 100m, as its benefits result from using it over long distances. However, it may be worth using to enclose a new copse where no existing fencing is being incorporated, and the fence can be made in one strain, with only one straining post (two if a gateway is included), plus three or so turning posts. Where the ground is undulating and

frequent tie-downs would be needed, mild steel fencing or post and rail may be more suitable.

CATTLE EXCLOSURE

b   If deer are a problem, they will have to be excluded by a high fence, an electric scare wire, or by the use of chemical repellents (supplier listed on p135). If the rabbit population is high, it is probably worth building a deer fence, with rabbit netting as the lower section.

c   Rabbit netting is fairly expensive to erect and is not essential for excluding any other animals; ie cheaper stock netting can be used against deer and sheep. For planting young trees, it may therefore be satisfactory to omit rabbit netting and use plastic tree guards or tree shelters instead. If however the aim is natural regeneration of the woodland, rabbit netting may be essential.

d   Where sheep are to be grazed, stock netting is essential. Bear in mind that young lambs may be able to squeeze through, and can do damage by nibbling and pulling at the shoots.

e   Provided trees are planted at a suitable distance (see Table 8.1) from the fence, horses and cattle should present no particular problems. Increase the fence height if for any reason you want to plant especially near the fence.

Shape of wood

The plan of the fenced area is important in determining the cost of the fence per unit for the total area enclosed. Ground plans of fences, in order of cost effectiveness, are firstly squares, then rectangles, triangles and finally complex shapes.

Circular clumps of trees look very attractive, and are a classic shape for hill tops and hangers (woods on steep slopes), but circular or curving fences are more difficult to build than straight ones, and are not very convenient for the operation of machinery in the adjacent land.

Strained mild steel fencing can be constructed in a circle, but is expensive, because of the frequent turning posts and struts required.

Another fairly easy design for a curving fence is to use a post and rail fence with non-overlapping rails. This is best built with round posts and half round rails, so there is no problem with the angles. Use fairly large diameter posts (at least 100mm) to give sufficient timber for nailing.

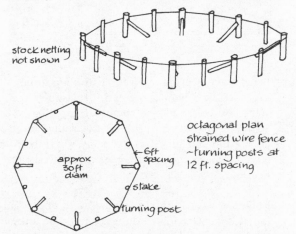

stock netting not shown

octagonal plan strained wire fence —turning posts at 12 ft. spacing

approx 30 ft diam

6ft spacing

stake

turning post

Planting is often done at field corners, in which case two sides of the copse are already enclosed, although fences may need upgrading. In other places the line of the fence will be determined by the shape of the 'waste ground' which is being planted up.

FENCING INDIVIDUAL TREES

This is an expensive way of protecting trees, and should only be used for formal planting of avenues or 'specimen' trees in parkland.

When designing them, consider the following:

a Are deer and/or rabbits a problem? See point (b) above.

b What is the reach of any animals to be grazed around the tree? Unless it is certain that only sheep will be grazed on the land in the following years, it is usually worth providing fencing for horses or cattle, as a single animal can destroy several years' growth, or kill a tree by debarking it in just a few hours. See the Tables below.

c How will a person get into the exclosure to tend the tree? If vandalism is not a problem, a section of climbable fence is an advantage.

d Consider using a herbicide or mulch to kill all ground flora within the exclosure. This not only greatly aids the growth of the tree by reducing competition for water and nutrients, but also reduces the pressure on the fence from grazing animals, as they will have less inducement to lean through.

Table 8.1

HEIGHT OF GUARD REQUIRED (metres)

Horses	2.50	2.25	2.00	1.75	1.50	1.15	1.15	1.15	1.15	
Cattle	1.85	1.70	.150	1.15	1.15	1.15	1.15	1.15	1.15	
Man	2.25	1.90	1.70	1.50	1.35	1.15	1.15	1.15	1.15	
Red Deer	2.10	1.75	1.45	1.20	1.20	1.20	1.20	1.50	1.80	zone A
Fallow Deer	1.80	1.60	1.25	1.10	1.10	1.10	1.35	1.80	1.80	
Goats	1.85	1.70	1.35	1.20	1.15	1.15	1.15	1.15	1.15	
Roe Deer	1.60	1.35	1.10	1.00	1.00	1.00	1.60	1.80	1.80	
Sheep	1.10	0.90	0.90	0.90	0.90	0.90	0.90	0.90	0.90	zone B
Hares	0.85	0.85	0.85	0.85	0.85	0.85	0.85	0.85	0.85	
Rabbits	0.75	0.85	0.85	0.85	0.85	0.85	0.85	0.85	0.85	

0   0.25   0.5   0.75   1   1.25   1.5   1.75   2   2.25

DISTANCE FROM TREE (metres)

Table 8.1 shows the height of the guard required against various animals, and the distance it should be from the tree. In zone A, the barrier must be of netting or timbers which are close enough to prevent the animal putting its head through and reaching the tree. In zone B, the barrier need only be sufficient to prevent the passage of the animal. The spacing of the horizontal and vertical members of netting or timber are shown in Table 8.2. Note that in Table 8.1 the height of the barrier against deer increases as the distance from the tree increases. This is to prevent deer jumping into the exclosure.

Table 8.2

SPACING OF VERTICALS AND HORIZONTALS

	zone A	zone B
Horses	100	500
Cattle	100	500
Deer	75	225
Goats	75	225
Sheep	50	150
Hares	30	30
Rabbits	30	30
	vertical and horizontal spacing (mm)	horizontal spacing (mm)

e It is not possible to build an exclosure simply out of three or four posts with strained wire or netting, as sufficient strain to keep the wire taut will cause the posts to move. Horizontal rails must be included.

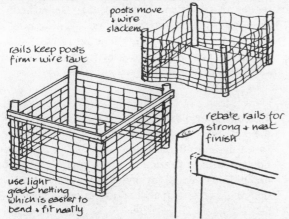

f All sorts of stock may use the exclosure for rubbing against, so build it strong enough to withstand this, with horizontal rails as shown. Sheep and cattle may also tend to use the exclosure as a place where they lie to chew the cud and to sleep. This will result in loss of grass cover and possible soil erosion at the base of the fence, which may then need extra wires to keep it stock proof.

g It is not usually a good idea to try and increase the distance of the top rail from the tree by slanting the posts outwards, as this makes it difficult to fit netting neatly and securely. The top rail also then has to be long, and being unsupported in the middle, needs to be a fairly large timber. In this case, resources are probably better used on extra posts.

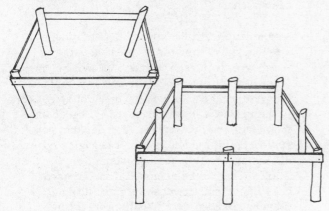

h Don't automatically top the exclosure with barbed wire, except against vandals, as this does not stop animals leaning over and makes it difficult to climb in to tend the tree.

Designs

Some designs for tree exclosures are shown below. These should be adapted, using the above tables, to fit the space and materials available.

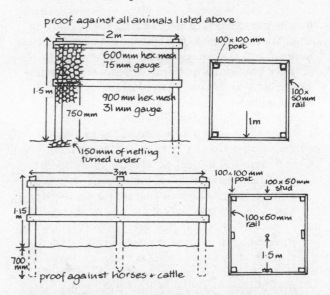

Triangular shaped exclosures for single trees are not generally recommended, because although they use one less post, they use about 50% greater length of rail than a square, spaced an equivalent distance from the tree. They may be worth building around the trunks of tall standard trees, similar to a tree guard. These need to be maximum height for the animal concerned, and with closely spaced netting or rails. The designs shown below should be quite cheap to make, as short lengths of waste timber can be used for the rails (treat with preservative as necessary).

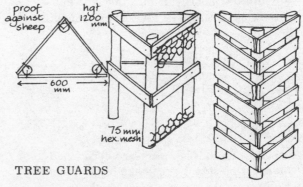

TREE GUARDS

There are three main types shown below. The use of tree guards is discussed in Woodlands . (BTCV 1980).

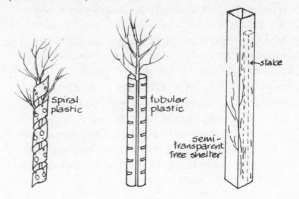

Anti-vandal Devices

In some areas fences may attract vandalism, or even theft of parts of the fence. This may be due to dislike of the fence in principle, because it changes traditional patterns of access, or simple vandalism, or organised theft of fence materials and components.

a If new fences are to be erected in sensitive areas where public access will be altered, make sure that local people are consulted or informed before work commences. Provide suitable gates and stiles on public rights of way, and consider putting them at any other traditional access points, if this seems likely to avert problems. It may be necessary to display notices at these extra access points, explaining that they are permissive paths, in order that they are not 'presumed dedicated' in the future as public rights of way (Footpaths, BTCV 1983).

b Build fences well so that they are strong and difficult to vandalise. In particular make sure that the struts on strained fences are tightly rebated. Nailed struts can be pulled or battered out of position. Do not use box struts as they are easy to undo.

c Run a single wire along rails, up posts and so on, to discourage chain saws being used on the wood. Staple closely to make the wire difficult to remove, or sink the wire in a groove so it cannot be levered off and cut.

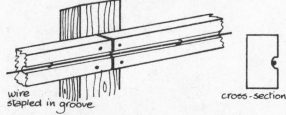

wire stapled in groove   cross-section

d High tensile 3.15mm wire has been found to be the most resistant to damage from children clambering on fences. Other wires quickly sag and lose tension.

e Use posts of metal or other synthetic material (see p41) to discourage firewood gatherers.

f Hang gates so that they cannot be lifted off (see p120).

g Beware of temporary electric fencing attracting thieves, as batteries, fencing units and lengths of netting may disappear. If possible use mains power, or place battery and unit under a secure lockable cover. A vandal-proof box which protects the battery and unit is available from the Rutland Electric Fencing Co.

112

Sand Fencing

The principles of sand fencing are described below, together with some recommended designs. For further details, and information on the positioning of fences in sand dune systems, see Coastlands (BTCV, 1979) and Sand Fencing (CCS Information Sheet: Plants 5.2.5). Sand fencing is built primarily to trap sand and encourage dune stabilisation, but may also be part of schemes for access control.

a The optimum porosity of a fence for trapping sand is 40%. This means that 40% of the fence is open, and 60% is impermeable. Individual components of the fence should not be more than about 75mm wide in order to avoid local eddying and scour around the component.

b Given suitable sources of dry sand and correct wind conditions a mound will accumulate to leeward of the fence, and extending horizontally 12-16 times the fence height.

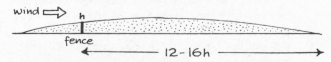

wind ⇨   h
          fence   ◄──── 12-16h ────►

It is therefore important to choose the height to suit the intended extent of the trapped sand. The strength of the fence must increase with increasing height in order to withstand the force of the wind in the period while sand is accumulating. However, in spite of using heavier posts and other components it is more cost effective to build one very high barrier where necessary, rather than build successive lines of low fences.

c As the fence will be buried hopefully within a few months, there is no point in using preserved or durable timber. However, the fence needs to be robust enough to withstand the wind and not to look too much of an eyesore in the period it is still exposed. Degradable materials are preferable, in order that no evidence of the fence is left if changing conditions eventually cause erosion of the dune. Plain wires can be removed if re-exposed, but wire or plastic mesh is more difficult to tidy up. Barbed wire should never be used in sand fencing.

Brushwood fencing

At its simplest, this type of fence is made only of brushwood. This has the advantage of being degradable, and well suited to volunteer labour because it is usually a 'free' material, needing only the labour to gather and transport it. The cut lower branches (brashings) from commercial woodlands are suitable, spruce and fir being the best species. Pine and birch can also be used, but larch is not sufficiently bushy. Erect the brashings as shown below, locking them against one another to make the fence strong enough to withstand the wind.

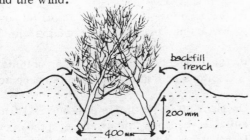

A more robust type of brushwood fence uses posts and strained wire. Straining posts should be set with about 900mm in the sand, with foot and breastplate. Wide-topped holes can usually be dug fairly quickly in dry sand, using a shuv-holer. Sand does not compact with tamping, so the hole is merely refilled. Struts are not usually necessary as only low tension is needed on the wires, and fence lines are normally fairly short. Other posts can be driven in using a drivall or mell.

Many methods of wire and brushwood fencing have been used, two of which are shown below. It requires specialist knowledge and experience of local conditions to place sand fences effectively, and normally a few trial fences should be built before embarking on any large programme of sand fencing.

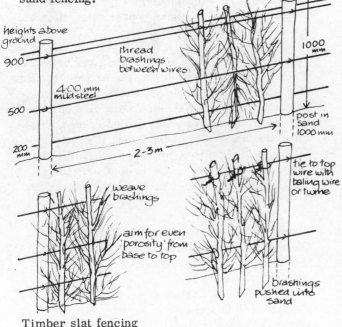

Timber slat fencing

In areas where brushwood is not available, or where a less labour intensive method of fencing is needed, timber slat fencing can be erected. The advantage of this is that the panels can be made in a workshop, and quickly erected on site.

Attach the panels to the posts with wire, to avoid weakening the wood by nailing it. The design below is recommended in 'Sand Fencing' (CCS leaflet 5.2.5), which also gives details of different sizes of posts required to support several tiers of panels, one on top of the other. These high barriers are used across dune gaps. Wires and ground anchors are needed to hold them firm against the wind.

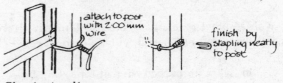

bearers: 2500 × 40 × 30 mm
posts: 1650 × 75 × 50
slats: 1000 × 75 × 8, with 75mm spacing (use 15-18mm thick slats where area is in recreational use)

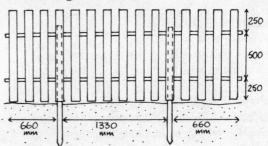

Chestnut paling

This is expensive, but is effective also as a barrier against people, and is quick to erect. For maximum efficiency in sand-trapping, use the size with 50mm gaps between the pales. Chestnut paling can be simply strained by hand, and stapled direct to posts, but this is liable to sag and lose tension. A more wind-resistant fence is made by attaching it to separate strained wires, 4.00mm diameter, using gordian rings or short lengths of wire.

Another method is to only attach the paling at the top of the posts, so that when it is half-buried it can be pulled up and re-attached to continue the dune building process. Extra supporting posts will be needed.

Synthetic fabrics

These have the advantage of being lightweight and easy to transport to remote sites, but they are expensive compared to other methods. Both Tensar Cladding and Paraweb (see p50-52) have been used, with varying degrees of success. Severe coastal conditions can cause tearing of the fabric before sand trapping is complete. Other fabrics being tried, with promising results so far, include Wyretex, Enkamat and N33 (see p134 for suppliers).

113

Access Control

Fences for access control may be necessary to:

a discourage intruders, and reduce disturbance to farm stock or wildlife.

b reduce erosion. This happens mainly on 'open land', such as heaths, dunes, grasslands, moors and mountains, when the recreational pressure becomes greater than the land can bear without damage.

SECURITY FENCES

In order of security, types of fences are approximately as follows:

a Steel paling fences. Mainly used for industrial premises, and need to be built by contractors. Steelway-Fensecure manufacture a large range.

b Concertina barbed wires. Impossible to climb, and difficult to cut and disentangle (see p44).

c Welded steel fencing, eg BRC Weldmesh. Hard to climb, but can be cut with boltcroppers.

d Chain link with barbed wire at top. Can be quickly cut with wire cutters.

e Close vertical boarding with barbed wire top. A recessed wire (see p112) can be added to discourage people trying to remove the boards.

f Chestnut paling (see p52). Difficult to climb, but pales can be broken and wires cut.

g Brushwood fencing. Difficult to climb, but can be pulled apart and set alight.

h Barbed wire. If spaced at 150mm intervals from the ground up to 1200mm, and not too tightly strained this is difficult to climb, but can be quickly cut.

i Stock netting, topped with two lines of barbed wire.

j Permanent electric fencing. Discouraging, but can be vandalised.

EROSION CONTROL

The success of erosion control fences depends on them being perceived not as barriers to be climbed, but as guide rails to be followed. Where they are being used to block eroded routes care must be taken that:

a the new path looks attractive and interesting

b the new surface looks more comfortable to walk on than the old one

c the old route is disguised as far as possible by turfing, planting or screening with brushwood

d there is good information and publicity for visitors so that the scheme is respected.

On many sites, a simple post and rail fence is suitable, because this can be erected over short lengths, has a 'hand rail' appearance, and can often be taken down and re-used as necessary. Where control is more difficult, chestnut paling or brushwood fencing will have to be used. For further details see 'Footpaths'(BTCV 1983) and 'Bridleway Management' (Countryside Commission 1985).

Fedges

This rather rustic word has been coined elsewhere to describe a cross between a fence and a hedge. This is made by planting climbing plants to scramble over a fence, making it appear like a hedge. This is obviously useful in gardens and parks for disguising ugly fences, but is no use where stock are concerned as they will eat the plants. This technique may be applicable for conservation use in school conservation sites and country parks.

Some suggested plant species are given below. Preferably grow these from seed or from cuttings in a nursery bed or pots, and transplant when growing strongly. Wild plants can also be transplanted from an area which has an excess, provided the landowner's permission is granted. It is illegal to dig up any protected species. The following species are robust, common and useful to birds and insects.

Ivy (Hedera helix)
Honeysuckle (Lonicera periclymenum)
Old man's beard (Clematis vitalba)
White bryony (Bryonia cretica)
Hop (Humulus lupulus)
Bramble (Rubus fruticosa)
Vetches (Vicia spp)
Dog rose (Rosa canina)

Avoid garden cultivars such as variegated ivies, introduced species of honeysuckle, and the very vigorous Russian vine (Polygonum baldschuanicum).

9 Gates and Stiles

Most fences require access points of some kind through them, whether for vehicles, stock or people. Provision must also be made for public rights of way.

Gateways and Gates

TYPE OF USE

Vehicles and machinery

In choosing the width of the gate and the layout of the gateway, consider what vehicles and machinery are likely to need to use it. Normal field gates are 3.66m (12ft) wide, to allow for access by tractor. Wider gates may be needed for special farm or forest machinery. The splay and layout of the gateway, and the way that the gates open, are also important to permit easy manoeuvring of vehicles. Badly designed ones will soon be damaged.

Stock

Gates must be as proof against stock or wild animals as the fence itself. Consider:

a the height of the gate. All agricultural gates are 1.2m (4ft) high when hung, which is suitable for most stock. Deer gates need to be specially made, usually out of timber. Two designs are shown on page 122. Otherwise, height can be increased by improvising vertical extensions to support an extra rail or netting. This is not very satisfactory as it upsets the balance of the gate, and is difficult to do neatly.

b the spacing of the gate members, and the clearance above the ground. Hexagonal mesh will need to be attached to most types of gates to make them proof against lambs, piglets, dogs and so on. Manufacturers of metal gates should be able to supply them with welded mesh or steel panels welded to the bottom section, as required.

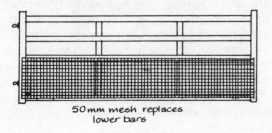

50mm mesh replaces lower bars

Usually 50mm clearance is allowed between the bottom rail and the ground. Additional netting or rails may be necessary where gates have to be hung on sloping ground. Rabbits present a particular problem, as they are only stopped by 31mm mesh, turned under in the direction of attack. For frequently used gateways with a hard surface, such as a vehicle entrance to a tree nursery, burrowing should not be a problem. To cover the ground clearance gap, fix a strip of hexagonal mesh which brushes the ground, to be replaced as necessary. On infrequently used vehicle entrances, where there is no surfacing, a buried strip will have to be fitted to discourage burrowing. This can be left partly buried and driven over while the gate is in use, and then re-attached when work is finished.

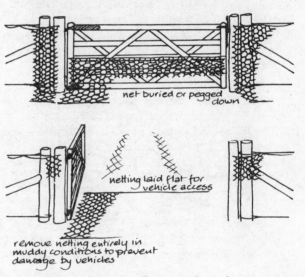

net buried or pegged down

netting laid flat for vehicle access

remove netting entirely in muddy conditions to prevent damage by vehicles

c the gate catch. Horses, cattle and goats may learn to operate gate catches.

Frequency of use

Gates, posts and fittings are expensive to buy and time consuming to erect. If gateways are to be used only infrequently, for example for access to a woodland for management work, slip gates or rails will be adequate (see p123).

Emergency use

This may include flood or fire, when stock have to be moved quickly, and access is needed for firefighting. It is especially worth being prepared for such emergencies on long stretches of strained wire fencing, as if this has to be broken through, repair can be a tedious job. By comparison, a post and rail fence can be breached by removing a few rails, which are easily replaced.

In areas liable to flood, provide a gateway which leads to higher ground so that stock can be quickly moved to safety. For firefighting, especially likely in woods and heaths, make sure gateways are at least 3m wide, and that they cannot be blocked by parked cars.

Personnel or stretcher gates, for removing casualties from mountain areas, can be built into strained wire deer fences (see p123).

Provision may also need to be made for removing animals from exclosures, such as young woodlands. Animals may either jump in and be less keen on jumping out, or may walk in when snow covers the fence. Provide one-way ramps (see p127) or gateways with slip gates.

Selective use

You may wish to provide access for one type of use, but exclude another. For example, the gateway shown below can be negotiated by horse-riders, but discourages motor cyclists as it is difficult to lift a bike over the barriers.

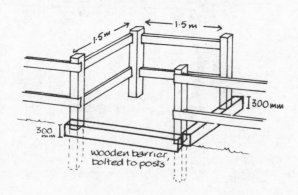

Cattle grids can be used for busy vehicle entrances, where stock need to be excluded. They should be manufactured to BS 4008, and are available in various weights and widths from 9' to 16' wide, from agricultural merchants and suppliers of fencing. They are very expensive however (£200-£400) and an electric 'grid' or gate may be a suitable alternative.

SITING AND DESIGN

Where possible, avoid low lying ground and badly drained soil, as gateways get muddy and poached (heavily trampled) in wet weather. Choose the higher points along the fence line. Also avoid sloping ground as this causes problems with the hanging and opening of the gate.

Gateways are usually sited so that stock and machinery can be moved around farms, nature reserves and so on, without having to use public roads. Gateways onto public roads also tend to

encourage trespass, as the gateway provides a pull-in for cars, and access for people to picnic or dump rubbish. On the other hand, the need for all-weather access to fields, and for emergency access, requires some gates onto public roads. Planning permission may be needed for gates opening onto public roads (see p25).

Gates are normally hung so that they open into fields, and away from tracks and roads. However there are many exceptions to this, due to sloping ground, corner sites or other special requirements.

Gateways can be designed so that gates can be used in more than one position. In the example below, the gate gives access to a field shelter from one of two paddocks. This is useful for stock which like access to shelter at all times, such as horses and goats, and allows paddocks to be rested alternately.

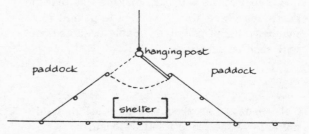

The following arrangement is useful for moving stock, as the gates are designed to close off the adjacent tracks.

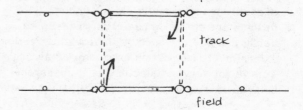

Wood

Traditionally gates were made out of wood, preferably oak because of its durability. Most wooden gates now available are made out of imported hardwood such as keruing, or of pressure treated softwood.

Wooden gates look attractive, and if well made and properly hung can be extremely durable. If one or two bars get broken, repair is possible, and some manufacturers stock replacement parts for their gates. Wooden gates should always have a brace, which runs from the base of the heel to the top rail. As shown, this transfers the strain down to the base of the hanging post. All wooden gates, however narrow should be built to this basic design.

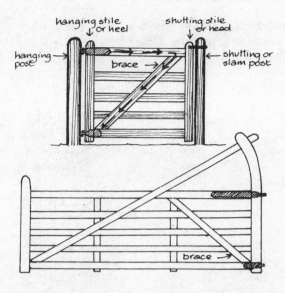

hanging stile or heel
shutting stile or head
hanging post
brace
shutting or slam post
brace

For good appearance, and to function properly as a barrier the gate should match the fence it adjoins, for example a palisade fence should have a matching palisade gate. Wooden gates are fairly easy to make, although they will not be as durable as manufactured mortised gates.

The disadvantage of wooden gates is that they are heavier than equivalent metal gates. This restricts them to a maximum length of 3.6m for hardwood gates and 4.2m for softwood gates. For gateways wider than this two gates are required.

Gate widths are unfortunately confusing. Because imported timber arrives in metric lengths many wooden gates are now being made in metric sizes, although imperial sizes are still manufactured. Most metal field gates are made in imperial sizes. Make sure you measure exactly any existing gateway you wish to close, and check with the supplier that the stated size is exact, and not an approximate metric or imperial conversion.

The following are some examples of field gate sizes available from national suppliers. Dimension refers to external width (see diagram).

Wooden gates Metric	Wooden gates Imperial	Metal gates Imperial
2.4m (7'10½")	8'	8'
2.7m (9')	9'	9'
3.0m (9'10")	10'	10'
3.3m (10'9½")	11'	11'
3.6m (11'9½")	12'	12'
	13'	13'
	14'	14'
		15'
		16'

Metal gates

Metal gates are used for their lightness and strength allowing single gates up to 16' wide to be made. Gates should be made of round or square section tube, which is stronger than metal angle and supplied galvanised or painted with non toxic Red Oxide primer. Single braces usually run the opposite way to those on wooden gates, and act in tension to keep the gate a true rectangle.

Most metal gates have adjustable eyes, so they can be adjusted as necessary to fit the hooks on existing gate posts. Metal gates are also supplied with the latch ready fitted. In contrast, wooden gates are usually supplied without fittings or latch, which adds further to their cost, which is already on average higher than for metal gates.

A disadvantage of lightweight metal gates is that they are easily buckled by the impact of a vehicle, making them difficult to operate and liable to rust because of damage to the galvanising.

GATE HANGING

Normally gates are hung behind the posts. This allows the gate to be opened fully through 180 degrees, and keeps the gate and fittings out of the way of vehicles and animals passing through. Gates should be hung between posts only when it is necessary for the gate to swing in both directions. However this method is easier for hanging wooden gates with non-adjustable eyes, as the upper hook can then be used to its full adjustment. The effective width is about the same for either method, as shown below.

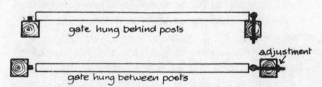

gate hung behind posts

gate hung between posts

adjustment

The thrust of a wooden gate is taken as shown. The top hook is on a through bolt, to resist the pulling force and the bottom hook is driven part way, to take the pushing force of the gate.

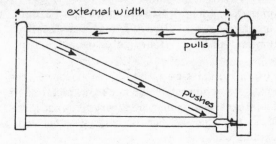

external width
pulls
pushes

Posts

Gates should be hung on posts which are separate from the fence, and should never be hung on straining posts, as either the gate or fence or both will be adversely affected. A method recommended to span the gap between the gate post and straining post is shown below. Note that the short rails are not attached to the hanging post, so that if the gate post gets knocked by a vehicle, the fence is not affected.

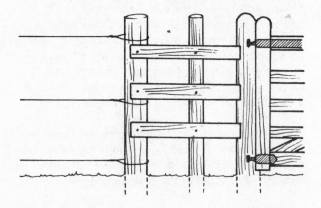

Wooden posts should be made of hardwood, or pressure treated softwood. Suitable sizes are:

Hanging posts:

150 x 150mm x 2.4m	Gates up to 3m wide
175 x 175mm x 2.4m	Gates over 3m wide
200mm diameter x 2.4m	Gates over 3m wide

Shutting post:
Normally 150 x 150mm x 2.4m

Both hanging and shutting posts should be supplied with weathered tops, to shed rain water. Fit a piece of aluminium or tin to protect the tops of railway sleepers or other flat-topped posts.

Metal posts are set in concrete and can therefore be shorter than wooden posts. The post usually has an integral 'foot' to help hold the post firm. New metal gates should be supplied with matching posts. The following sizes are a guide to those available:

Diameter x length:

90mm x 1.8m	Lightweight gates up to 3.6m
115mm x 1.8m	Medium gates up to 3.6m
115mm x 2m	Heavy gates up to 3.6m
140mm x 2m	Heavy gates over 3.6m

If fitting an existing gate to a new post, or vice versa, remember that the hooks on metal posts are integral and cannot be altered. Most metal gates are fitted with one or both eyes that can be adjusted.

Fittings for wooden gates

Standard fittings are shown below. These can be used for gates hung either between posts, or hung behind posts.

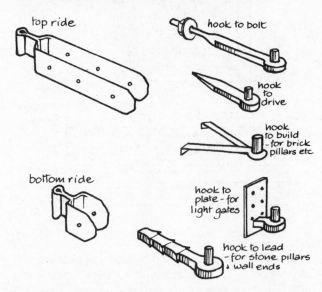

Gates are normally hung as shown below. The gate should rest in any position in which it is placed.

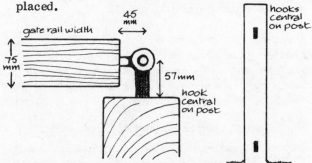

However, there are several variables which can be altered to affect the way the gate hangs and opens, and the position at which it comes to rest. These are used for gates on slopes, or where the gate needs to be self closing.

a Hooks can be directly above oneanother, or offset. This is done by altering the position of the holes which are drilled through the posts.

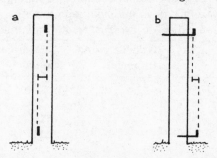

b The hooks can project equally, or by different amounts. This is altered by the amount the top hook is tightened, and the bottom hook is driven into the post.

c   The positioning of the eyes of the gate rides which may be directly above oneanother or offset.   Adjustable bottom rides are available.

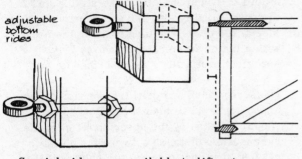

adjustable bottom rides

Special rides are available to lift gates as they are opened.

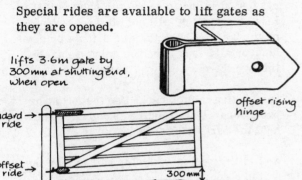

lifts 3·6m gate by 300mm at shutting end, when open

offset rising hinge

standard ride →
offset ride →
300mm

The following method can be used to make a one way gate swing shut.

a   Offset the top hook 30mm in the direction of in which the gate closes.

b   Project the bottom hook 5mm further than the top hook.

c   Project the bottom (adjustable) ride 30mm beyond the top ride.

HANGING POST

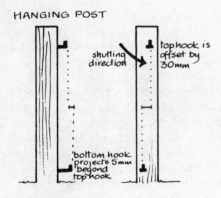

shutting direction

top hook is offset by 30mm

bottom hook projects 5mm beyond top hook

Latches for wooden gates

A good latch should be:

a   self latching when the gate swings closed

b   designed to function for a long time, even if the gate 'drops' with time and use.

c   stock proof.

The following latches are commonly used.

Spring latch:
Advantages.   Easy to operate from either side, and still works if gate drops.
Disadvantages.   Awkward to fit so that the tension is enough to keep the gate closed without being difficult to operate.   Action of using lever puts strain on the hinges.   Not usually self-latching.

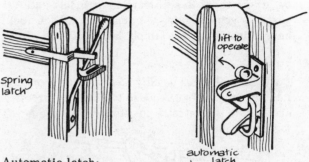

spring latch

lift to operate

automatic latch

Automatic latch:
Advantages.   Easy to fit and durable as long as the gate does not drop.   Self-latching.
Disadvantages.   May be awkward to operate from far side.   Only used on gates hung behind posts.

Loop latch:
Advantages.   Easy to fit and operate.   Durable if made of rigid metal or chain.   Works even if gate drops.   Useful on double gates.
Disadvantages.   Can be worked by animals.   Often improvised with wire or baler twine, which are not durable.

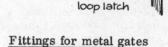

loop latch

Fittings for metal gates

Metal gates are supplied with ready-fitted eyes for hanging, one of which at least is usually adjustable.   Hooks on metal posts cannot be altered so no special adjustments can be made for particular sites.   On the other hand, they are simple and quick to erect, with less to go wrong.

Latches are also ready fitted, and are usually either sliding latches, automatic or heavy loop latches, the latter being mainly on double gates.

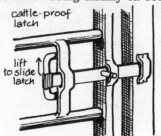

cattle-proof latch

lift to slide latch

Double gates

Double gates are needed for entrances over 3.6m for hardwood gates, 4.2m for softwood gates, and 4.8m for metal gates. Wooden gates, usually used for driveway entrances, have a drop bolt to locate the head of the gate in the closed position, and a loop latch to hold the two gates together. Equal size gates normally both have a drop latch, but where there is a pedestrian or bridle gate next to a vehicle gate, the smaller gate does not have a drop bolt, but simply latches to the larger gate.

Double metal gates usually have a large loop-over latch. This is heavy enough to be cattle-proof, and to hold the gates in position without the need for drop bolts.

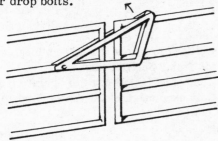

Procedure for gate hanging

A well hung gate should open easily and stand open clear of the road or track, swing slowly shut without crashing against the shutting post, and latch easily.

The following is the basic procedure for hanging a wooden gate:

1 Fit the top and bottom ride to the gate level with the top and bottom rails. Do not fit the top ride if inverting the top hook to prevent the gate being lifted off.

2 Dig the hole for the hanging post, which should be not less than 1030mm deep. For good appearance, the top of the post should be about 50mm above the top of the hanging stile. See page 70 for information on tools and methods for digging a deep and neat-sided hole. The straining face of the post should be against an undisturbed face, as shown below.

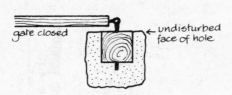
gate closed   ← undisturbed face of hole

Check that the post is exactly perpendicular, and then backfill the hole, tamping each layer.

3 The lower hook is fitted first. Measure the distance from the base of the heel to the eye, and add 50mm for ground clearance. Using a drill or brace and bit, make a pilot hole in the post, slightly smaller and shorter than the size of the hook, and then drive in the hook with a lump hammer. Drive in to leave sufficient protruding, as described on page

4 Measure, mark and drill the position of the upper hook. The main weight of the gate should be taken by the upper hook, so make sure that the distance between the hooks is not less than that between the rides. If it is less, the top ride will not sit down properly on the hook. Check that the drill is being held horizontally, and that it is going squarely through the post.

If inverting the top hook, use the following procedure. This requires several people to hold the parts in position.

a Drill the holes in the top rail to take the top ride.

b Fit the top hook to the post, with the hook pointing down, and hold the top ride in place on it.

c Then lift the gate into position, sliding it onto the top ride, and bolt the top ride through the pre-drilled holes.

5 Mark the position for the shutting post, dig the hole and set the post in position, checking that it is vertical.

6 Fit the latch.

The basic procedure for hanging a metal gate is as follows:

1 As the metal post already has the hooks fitted, it is important to set the post at the exact height required. Measure the height of the lower eye on the gate, set at the mid-way point if adjustable, and add 50mm for ground clearance. Then measure off this same amount down from the lower hook of the gate post, to give the ground level position. Mark this temporarily on the post.

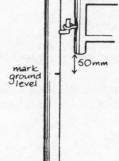
mark ground level   50mm

2 The post is set in concrete, and to make a foundation for the post, the hole must be about 100mm deeper than the base of the post.

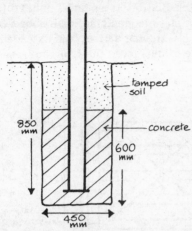

Dig the hole about 450mm square to give sufficient volume of concrete. A narrow 'collar' around the post will not be effective. Take special care that the hole does not narrow towards the bottom, as this is the most important part for holding the post firmly. Finish the bottom neatly and compact it thoroughly by tamping.

3 Use a mix of either:
1 Portland cement : 2 sand : 4 aggregate (20mm)
or
1 Portland cement : 6 all-in aggregate

All-in aggregate is also known as ballast, and contains both fine and coarse materials. The mix can be used either wet or dry, and either way the post must be left for several days before the gate is hung. The dry mix method is easier, and is suitable in all but very dry soils or conditions.

As a guide, you will need approximately two barrows-full of mix per post, which will be about 4 shovels of cement to 24 shovels of aggregate. Mix thoroughly. Shovel some into the hole, tamping it lightly, until you reach the height of the post base. Set the post is place and adjust the height as necessary with more mix. Fill the remainder of the hole. If using a wet mix, vibrate the concrete thoroughly with a piece of wood to force all the air from the mix. Prop the post in position using two pieces of timber.

4 Measure the position of the shutting post, and set in as described above. If the soil is suitable, the shutting post can be set simply in tamped soil as it takes no strain.

5 Leave for three to four days, and then remove the props and hang the gate.

Special Gates

Kissing gate

This is a 'captive' gate, which is proof against large stock, whatever position the gate is in. Kissing gates are usually used on popular footpaths, especially those likely to be used by elderly people. Kissing gates have the advantage of stopping motor bikes, but can also be awkward for walkers with large rucksacks.

Kissing gates are not normally sheep proof, but can be made so if hung to be self-closing with a spring and latch.

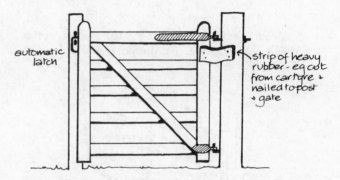

The significant dimension of a kissing gate is the area of the space made by the guard rails, when the gate is in mid-position. Various designs are shown below.

a This is sheep proof, but rather a squeeze for people with rucksacks.

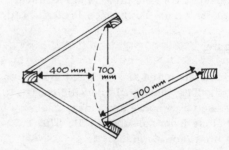

b This design is easy for walkers, but needs a spring and latch to be sheep proof.

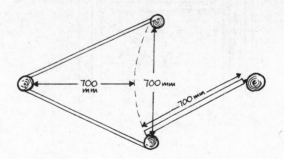

121

c The following design is by the Countryside Commission for Scotland (see CCS Information Sheet 4.8.4). It is easy to construct as it is based on a square, so the joints between rail and post are easy to make. However, the 400mm gap is rather small for most people.

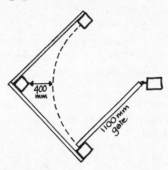

d Traditional metal kissing gates are attractive and very durable, but not normally sheep proof.

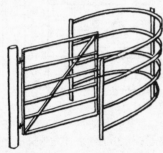

For more details on kissing gates, see Footpaths (BTCV, 1983). Kit-form kissing gates, comprising wooden gate posts and rails with gate fittings, are available from British Gates and Timber Ltd. Metal kissing gates are available from Goodman Croggan, through agricultural merchants, and from Townscape Products Ltd.

Hunting gate

Hunting or bridle gates are designed for use on bridleways. The gate should be wide enough to be safely used by a horse and rider, and easy to open and close from horseback. BS 5709:1979 specifies the following sizes.

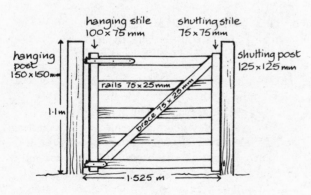

Hinges can be fitted so that the gate swings both ways, with a self-closing action. These work best on fairly heavy gates. Such hinges are available from British Gates and Timber Ltd, as is the complete 'equestrian' gate shown below. This has a self-closing action, and extended shutting stile to be accessible from horseback.

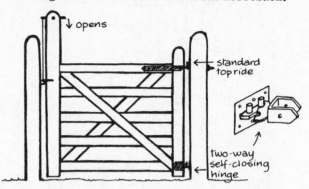

If possible, gates should be positioned so that there is room for the horse to stand to the side while the rider leans over and opens the gate.

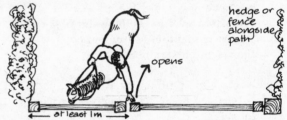

Deer gates

Vehicle gates through deer fences should be 1.8m (6ft) high, and normally 1.8m (6ft) wide, hung in pairs. They must be reasonably strong, but of lightweight construction because of their height. Pressure treated softwood fencing rails, available in 3.6m (12ft) lengths, are suitable material. Two possible designs are shown below.

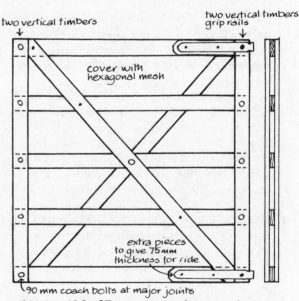

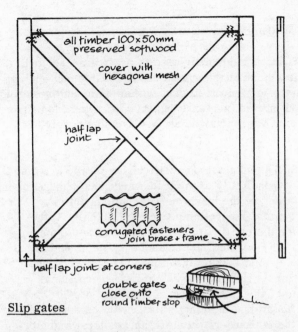

all timber 100 x 50mm preserved softwood

cover with hexagonal mesh

half lap joint

half lap joint at corners

corrugated fasteners join brace + frame

double gates close onto round timber stop

Slip gates

As their name implies, these are slipped open and closed, rather than being swung on hooks. They are suitable for infrequently used gateways for vehicles and stock, and having no fittings, are easy and cheap to make.

The simplest are slip rails, often used in horse paddocks.

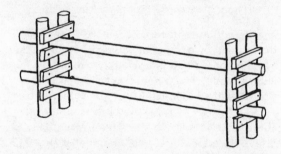

A slip gate can be made out of fencing rails as shown below. Dimension (a) must be sufficient to safely span the gateway, while (b) allows the gate to be slipped to one side. It can then be lifted clear of the other post, and removed as necessary.

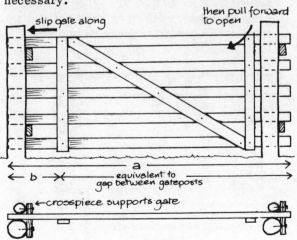

slip gate along

then pull forward to open

a equivalent to gap between gateposts

b

crosspiece supports gate

Personnel gates

These work in the manner of a badger gate or cat flap, to allow a person access through a high strained wire fence. On Forestry Commission design fences, with netting hung on three strained wires, the gate can be fitted between the strained wires. On fencing of high tensile netting, some of the horizontal wires will have to be cut off and tied around the stakes.

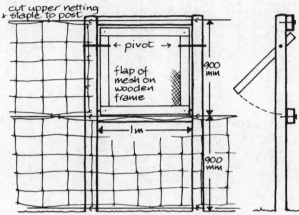

cut upper netting & staple to post

pivot

flap of mesh on wooden frame

900 mm

1 m

900 mm

A useful material for slip or personnel gates is the Weldmesh roll-top panel. This is light-weight but rigid, and can be used without further strengthening. The simplest method of making a slip gate is to fit four metal hooks, onto which the gate is lifted. For a more secure 'flap' gate, hang the roll-top panel on wire loops, or on a piece of metal or timber threaded through the 'roll'. Rolltop panels are manufactured to order by BRC.

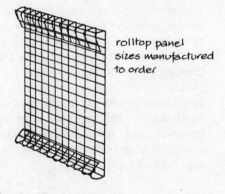

rolltop panel sizes manufactured to order

Flexible gates

Flexible gates, also known as 'Hampshire', 'Irish' or 'New Zealand' gates, are not ideal, but are a useful way of spanning a little used but wide gateway, that is too wide for a slip gate. These types of gates are not permissible on bridleways. They are best made of stock netting, so that they are reasonably stock proof even if not taut. Do not use barbed wire. The normal method is to simply tension the 'shutting stile' with a loop of wire at the top, but this is often either too slack, or impossible to close. One method of closing and tensioning the gate is

123

shown below (from Gates for Farms, MAFF leaflet 712). This uses a metal crank, either home made or from a welder or blacksmith, which is bolted to the post top. Adjust the wire loop on the shutting stile until the gate closes neatly.

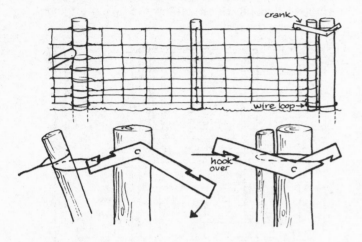

Flexible gates should always be left closed when the entrance is not in use, or they can become a hazard to vehicles or stock, especially when tangled in long grass. If the gateway needs to be left open for stock, roll the gate up neatly and tie it out of the way against the fence.

The 'Rambler'

This is a new design from British Gates and Timber Ltd, which is an alternative to both the kissing gate and the stile. The metal pivot posts are fastened by a loop. When released, the posts can be pushed apart to allow the walker to step through. When let go, the pivots fall back into place. This design has the advantage of being accessible to walkers of all ages and sizes, but some people find it rather unattractive and untidy in appearance. The 'Rambler' retails at about £88, and is available only from British Gates and Timber Ltd.

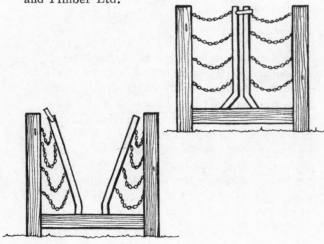

Stiles

Stiles are normally used to provide access over fences on public rights of way. They may also be used for private access within farms and reserves, but should be clearly marked as private in order to avoid confusion, as they are so strongly associated with public access.

Stiles and gates on public rights of way are the responsibility of the landowner, and must be maintained by the landowner in a safe condition. Grants are available from the Highway Authority for the repair of gates and stiles, and from MAFF for new and replacement gates and stiles on public paths. In National Parks, Heritage Coasts and other areas of high recreational use, the authority concerned may provide, install and maintain stiles, with the agreement of the landowner. In other areas, local amenity groups may do likewise.

There is no statutory width or height for a stile, although guidelines are laid down by BS 5709:1979 amended 1982.

The type of stile chosen will depend very much on the expected level and type of use. Points to note are:

a   A stile which is used frequently, especially those used by groups of walkers, field study groups and so on, is obviously worth building with a more robust construction than one which is used infrequently.

b   If the stile is near to a village centre, or on a favourite local walk, it is more likely to be used by elderly people, who may appreciate extra steps and handholds. Alternatively, fit a kissing gate or a 'rambler'.

c   If the stile needs to be stock-proof against sheep and lambs, consider how people will get their dogs through the stile. Fitting a dog-latch on popular walks may avert problems from people damaging the fence in order to let their dogs through.

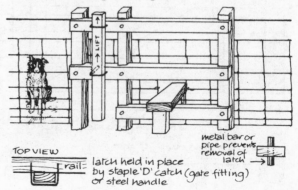

Stile design

The basic dimensions, as recommended by BS 5709:1979 amended 1982 are as follows. These apply only to 'step-over' stiles. 'Step-through' and ladder stiles are different in principle (see Footpaths, BTCV 1983).

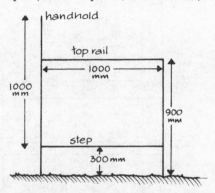

Width between uprights	1000mm min
Height of top rail above ground	900mm min
Height of bottom step above ground	300mm max
Rise between steps	300mm max

The maximum rise between the step and the top rail is 600mm.

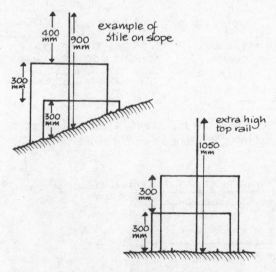

Two steps will be needed if either the stile is on sloping ground, or the top rail needs to be higher than 900mm in order to be stock proof. The rise between the upper step and the top rail should not be more than 450mm.

The basic structural dimensions for step-over stiles are as follows. Timber sizes are given for each design.

Maximum space between rails	300mm
Depth of stile post in ground	750mm
Depth of step support in ground	500mm

Materials and construction

Pressure treated softwood is recommended. Durable hardwoods are also suitable, but are more difficult to cut, drill and nail, and heavier to transport to the site.

BS 5709 recommends mortised joints for rails. These are strong, but are tedious to make except in a workshop. This may be suitable for easy sites on flat land, but prefabrication is more difficult for stiles on sloping or rocky ground, where variable conditions may require unexpected alterations.

A more practical alternative is to use a rebated joint, which can be cut and assembled on site, and thus be altered or replaced as necessary. The joints can be fixed with a coach bolt or a length of studding fastened at each end with a washer and nut. A neat and secure finish is made if this is counterbored and tightened with a socket.

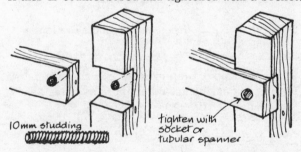

The step should not rest on a rail, or a see-saw action can develop as the step supports settle into the ground with use. The step should over-hang its support by about 40mm, to help protect the top of the support from wear and weather. The easiest method of fixing is to drill and skew nail using two 125mm galvanised nails at each end. A more secure fixing is made by using a coach screw.

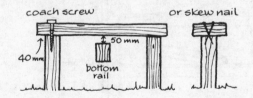

PROCEDURE

This describes the procedure for erecting a stile, taken to the site in kit form, and bolted together through rebated joints.

Concreting of posts is not normally necessary, but if the ground is very wet or otherwise unstable it may be advisable (see p121).

1 Dig holes for stile posts to the required depth.

125

2 Lay posts and rails on the ground, assemble with coach bolts or studding, but do not fully tighten nuts.

3 Set posts into position, check uprights and rails with spirit level, and tighten nuts.

4 Ram soil around posts using punner or other suitable tool compacting it in layers.

5 Dig holes for step supports, positioning them so the step projects about 40mm beyond the support.

6 Set step supports in position. Level, using step and spirit level. Ram securely.

7 Attach step to supports using nails or coach screw.

8 Chamfer step and top rail to give neat finish. Weather and chamfer handhold.

9 Attach wire as necessary to make the fence stock proof.

Three designs of step-over stile are shown below. For more designs and other types of stiles see 'Footpaths' (BTCV, 1983).

British Standard

This is based on BS 5709. The rails are stub-mortised full size into the posts for a depth of 50mm. The step should be set at an angle of between 45 and 90 degrees to the top rail.

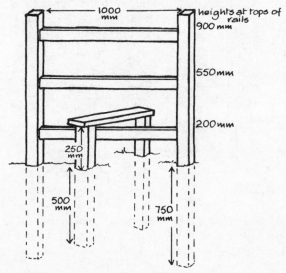

stile posts :	2 of 100 × 100 × 1750 mm
rails :	3 of 75 × 50 × 1100 mm
step :	1 of 175 × 50 × 900 mm
step supports :	2 of 150 × 75 × 750 mm

Rebated stile

This example is shown with two steps, for use on a slope, and a handhold to aid the less agile. The heights of the steps and rails are given as an example only, and will have to be adapted to fit the slope.

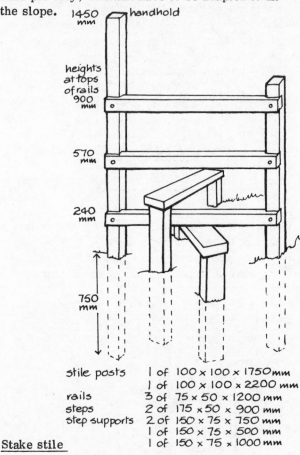

stile posts	1 of 100 × 100 × 1750mm
	1 of 100 × 100 × 2200 mm
rails	3 of 75 × 50 × 1200 mm
steps	2 of 175 × 50 × 900 mm
step supports	2 of 150 × 75 × 750 mm
	1 of 150 × 75 × 500 mm
	1 of 150 × 75 × 1000 mm

Stake stile

This stile is quick and easy to erect, but is not as durable as the designs shown above.

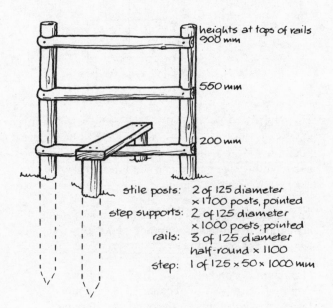

stile posts:	2 of 125 diameter × 1700 posts, pointed
step supports:	2 of 125 diameter × 1000 posts, pointed
rails:	3 of 125 diameter half-round × 1100
step:	1 of 125 × 50 × 1000 mm

Water Gates

These are used to keep watercourses stockproof, whatever the level of the water. The gate is designed to swing up and float as the water rises, allowing water and debris to flow underneath.

A water gate must be carefully made to fit the profile of the gully it crosses. The gate should be of a simple but strong construction, and attached very securely to withstand the force of flooding water. The best method of attachment is to use lengths of chain, joined with shackles. Wire and staples are not strong enough.

On post and rail fences, the gate is attached to the bottom rail. On strained wire fences, a bottom rail must be attached, with extra posts as necessary. A typical design is shown below.

An alternative is to use post and rail fencing, especially in combination with high tensile fencing, where severe tie-downs are difficult to make.

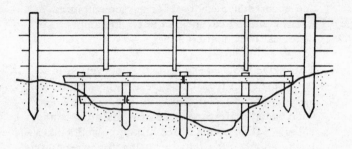

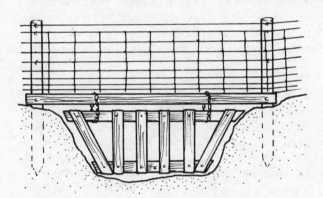

Electric water gates are shown on page 100.

Extra barriers may be needed to span steep sided gullies, where it is awkward to build a fence to follow the gully profile. The ground is often soft and waterlogged, making it difficult to make a secure tie-down for a strained wire fence. The structure shown below was built in an area where stone was plentiful.

Sheep Ramps

These should be included in any exclosure such as a fenced woodland, where animals may get in when snow covers the fence, and then be unable to get out. These are useful in remote woodlands which are not frequently visited, as they allow animals to make their own way out, although of course they may not choose to do so.

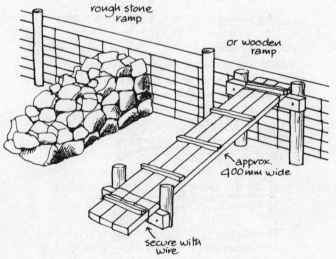

rough stone ramp

or wooden ramp

approx. 400mm wide

secure with wire

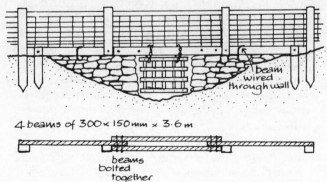

beam wired through wall

4 beams of 300 x 150mm x 3.6m

beams bolted together

Conservation and the Volunteer Worker

The British Trust for Conservation Volunteers aims to promote the use of volunteers on conservation tasks. In addition to organising work projects it is able through its affiliation and group schemes to offer advice and help with insurance cover tool purchase and practical technical training.

To ensure the success of any conservation task it is important that the requesting person or agency the volunteer and the leader all understand their particular responsibilities and roles. All voluntary work should be undertaken in the spirit of the Universal Charter of Volunteer Service drawn up by the UNESCO Co-ordinating Committee for International Voluntary Service. Three of its most important points are:

1 'The work to be done should be a real need in its proper context and be directly related to a broad framework of development'. In terms of conservation, this means that tasks should be undertaken as integral parts of site management plans, not as isolated exercises. Work should never be undertaken solely for the benefit of the volunteer. Necessary follow-up work after tasks should be planned beforehand to ensure that volunteer effort is not wasted.

2 'The task should be a suitable assignment for a volunteer'. Volunteers cannot successfully tackle all types of work and they should not be used where there is a risk of serious accident or injury where a financial profit will be made from their labours, where the job is so large that their efforts will have little overall effect, where the skills required are beyond their capabilities so that a bad job results and they become dispirited, or where machines can do the same job more efficiently and for a lower cost.

3 'Voluntary service should not replace paid local labour'. It should complement such work, not supplement it. Employers should make sure in advance that the position of volunteers and paid workers is clear with respect to any relevant labour unions. Further advice may be found in 'Guidelines for the relationships between volunteers and paid non-professional workers' published by the Volunteer Centre, 29 Lower King's Road, Berkhamstead Hertfordshire HP4 2AB.

Volunteers are rarely 'free labour'. Someone has to pay for transport, materials tools, insurance refreshments and any accommodation charges. Before each party makes a commitment to a project it should be clear who is to pay for what. While volunteers may willingly fund their own work, 'user bodies' should be prepared to contribute and should not assume that all volunteers who are already giving their time and effort will be able to meet other expenses out of their own pockets. Several grant-aiding bodies may help pay the cost of environmental and conservation projects, notably the Nature Conservancy Council the World Wildlife Fund and the Countryside Commission. Details may be found in 'A guide to grants by the Department of the Environment and associated bodies for which voluntary organisations may be eligible' available from the Department of the Environment, Room C15/11, 2 Marsham Street London SW1P 3EB.

It is important that volunteer workers be covered by some sort of public liability insurance for any damage or injury they may cause to property or to the public. Additional insurance to compensate the volunteer for injury to him- or herself or to other volunteers on task should also be considered.

The volunteer group organiser should visit the work site well before the task, to check that the project is suitable and that volunteers will not be exploited and to plan the best size of working party and the proper tools and equipment. Volunteers should be advised in advance on suitable clothing for the expected conditions. They should be physically fit and come prepared to work and they should genuinely want to volunteer – those 'press-ganged' into service are likely to work poorly may do more harm than good and may be put off a good cause for life. Young volunteers need more supervision and are best suited to less strenuous jobs, and it is recommended that where they are involved the task should emphasize education. Note that the Agriculture (Avoidance of Accidents to Children) Regulations, 1958 legally restrict the riding on and driving of agricultural machines vehicles or implements by children under 13 years.

Volunteer group organisers and 'user bodies' both should keep records of the work undertaken: the date of the project jobs done techniques used, number of volunteers and details of any notable events including accidents, unusual 'finds' publicity etc. Such information makes it easier to handle problems or queries which may arise after the task. It also provides a background on the task site for future visits supplies practical data by which the site management plan can be evaluated and allows an assessment to be made of the volunteer effort.

Training

The British Trust for Conservation Volunteers run weekend and week-long training courses on all aspects of practical conservation work, including fencing, throughout England, Wales and Northern Ireland. The Scottish Conservation Projects Trust run similar courses in Scotland. Details of courses are available from the BTCV and SCPT headquarters.

Courses on fencing are run by the Agricultural Training Board which is organised on a county basis, divided into local training groups. These are only open to people employed in agriculture or horticulture. However, the local ATB office (address in local telephone directory) may be able to find instructors for groups wishing to organise their own training course.

Some agricultural colleges run short courses of one to five days in estate skills, including fencing. Recent examples include courses at the following colleges:

Capel Manor Institute of Horticulture and Field Studies, Bullsmoor Lane, Waltham Cross. Herts EN7 5HR

Northumberland College of Agriculture Kirkley Hall Ponteland, Newcastle upon Tyne, NE20 0AQ

Other colleges may be able to set up short courses in response to requests from organisations or voluntary groups.

The Forestry Training Council organise short courses in various aspects of forestry, including fencing, for the private sector of the forestry industry, and local authorities.

Competitions

In recent years the National Federation of Young Farmers Clubs, in collaboration with fencing manufacturers, have organised a national fencing competition. The final is held at the Royal Show. The competition involves a team of people erecting a specified length of strained stock netting fence.

The Farmers Weekly National Field Boundaries Event, of which the National Hedgelaying Championships is a part, includes trade stands and displays of different types of fencing. The event is held each autumn. Further details from the Farmers Publishing Group, Room 1117, Surrey House, 1 Throwley Way, Sutton, Surrey SM1 4QQ.

Addresses of other organisations given above are listed on pages 136-138.

Grants

The Ministry of Agriculture, Fisheries and Food can give grants directly for fencing to established agricultural and horticultural businesses. Other grants may be available, indirectly for fencing, from the Countryside Commission and the Nature Conservancy Council where the fencing is part of a planting or management scheme for landscape or nature conservation purposes. Local authorities, public bodies. voluntary organisations and private individuals may be eligible.

COUNTRYSIDE COMMISSION

The Countryside Commission may grant-aid fencing where it forms part of a scheme for the planting or management of small woods under $\frac{1}{4}$ hectare. These woods must normally be of native broadleaved species and be on sites visible from public roads, rights of way or viewpoints. There is no size restriction on publicly owned sites, where the planting is for amenity purposes. The rate of grant is 50% (discretionary).

Grants for the planting or management of private woods over $\frac{1}{4}$ hectare. and planting for timber production on public land may be obtainable from the Forestry Commission.

Fencing to protect and restore other features, such as ponds, hedgerows and hedgebanks may be eligible for grant if the restoration of such features is part of an overall farm conservation plan.

Further details are given in the booklets CCP171 'Conservation grants for farms and landowners' and CCP172 'Conservation grants for local authorities, public bodies and voluntary organisations' (Countryside Commission 1984). The above information applies to England and Wales. Details about schemes in Scotland should be obtained from the Countryside Commission for Scotland.

NATURE CONSERVANCY COUNCIL

A discretionary grant of 50% of acceptable costs of fencing work may be available, where the primary objective of the work is to enhance wildlife habitats or species on sites of high conservation importance. Geological sites are included. This applies to England. Scotland and Wales. Contact your NCC Regional Office for further details.

MINISTRY OF AGRICULTURE, FISHERIES AND FOOD

Grants are currently administered under the Agriculture Improvement Scheme. This replaces the Agriculture and Horticulture Development Scheme and the Farm and Horticulture Development Scheme, for which applications closed in December 1985. Only established agricultural and horticultural businesses are eligible. Details of eligibility are given in the Agriculture Improvement Scheme Handbook AIS 1.

The following information applies to England. Similar schemes are operated by the Welsh Office Agriculture Department, the Department of Agriculture and Fisheries for Scotland, and the Department of Agriculture - Northern Ireland, from whom advice should be obtained.

In a National Park, the Broads Authority Area, a Site of Special Scientific Interest or a National Nature Reserve you must notify the relevant authority and get its written agreement before you start any work. Otherwise grant may not be paid.

Grants are only given on items which are new and reasonably permanent. Renewals and replacements are eligible, but maintenance and repair are not. Work must be done to a good standard. It must:

a have a design life of at least 10 years (except for temporary protective fencing)

b be properly designed for the agricultural purpose for which it is to be used

c satisfy all relevant statutory requirements

d comply with all relevant British Standard specifications and Codes of Practice, or other suitable standards acceptable to the Ministry.

Grants for fencing are available under two sections of the Agriculture Improvement Scheme:

Improvement Plan

As part of an Improvement Plan (explained in Agriculture Improvement Scheme handbook AIS 1). grants are available towards providing, replacing or improving:

a fences, including safety fencing, protective fencing security fencing, stock and pest-proof fencing including to protect woodland or allow moorland to regenerate. Also for additional fences along farm boundaries, ie alongside a neighbour's fence, to prevent spread of infection

b top-wiring of existing walls

c gates, either for a new gateway, or a higher or wider gate for an existing gateway. Rate of grant is that applicable to the boundary of which it is a part.

An improvement to a fence must make its design or specification better. Adding another wire, or substituting stock netting for line wires would be eligible improvements.

Permanent electric fencing, either from batteries or mains controllers (to BS 2632:1980) are eligible.

Grant is not available for amenity fencing for agricultural dwellings, nor for temporary or movable fencing. (However, temporary fences to protect newly planted hedgerows or shelter belts qualify for the Farm Environment grants described below.)

There are two rates of grant:- the Basic rate, and the rate for Less Favoured Areas (LFAs), which are mostly in the uplands. Any of the fencing work described above, as well as the installation of cattle grids, qualifies for 15% Basic rate, and 30% in LFAs. You must not start work before your application for an Improvement Plan is acknowledged. Further details are given in the AIS Handbook, and in the leaflet 'Roads, paths and fences' AIS 11 (MAFF).

Farm Environment grants

Work which qualifies for these grants does not have to be part of an Improvement Plan, but can be a single project. If not part of an Improvement Plan, you do not need prior approval from the Ministry.

Eligible work includes:

a   protective fencing for hedge planting, replanting in a 'gappy' hedge, and hedgelaying

b   planting shelter belts or hedges to protect crops or livestock

c   protective fencing for single trees planted to shade stock

d   gates and stiles of traditional materials or associated with hedges, walls, banks and dykes of traditional materials. Rate of grant is that applicable to the boundary of which it is a part.

Work	Rate of grant	
	Basic	LFA
Fencing in association with hedges	30%	60%
Shelter belts with at least 50% broadleaved	30%	60%
Shelter belts (other)	15%	60%

The above rates apply whether or not the Farm Environment grant is part of an Improvement Plan.

Under either of the two sections described above, you can choose for grant to be paid either on the actual cost of the work done, or on Standard Costs, which are costs set by MAFF, based on the estimated cost of labour and materials to do the work to a certain specification.

Some of the current Standard Costs (1986) for fencing work are given below. These apply in England, Scotland, Wales and Northern Ireland.

	per metre
STRAINED LINE WIRE FENCE	
With intermediate posts	
- posts up to 2.7m apart	£ 1.10
- posts over 2.7m to 3.5m apart	.91
With intermediate posts and droppers	
- posts up to 14m apart	.83
- posts over 14m to 50m apart	.78
Heavy pattern	1.50
Each additional line wire	.07
WOVEN WIRE FENCE	
Intermediate posts up to 2.7m apart	
- C8/115/30*	1.55
- C6/90/30	1.40
- C8/80/15	1.35
- C8/80/30	1.45
Intermediate posts over 2.7m to 3.5m apart	
- C8/115/30	1.35
- C6/90/30	1.20
- C8/80/15	1.15
- C8/80/30	1.25
Heavy pattern	2.20
Each line wire above or below the roll	.07
(*for explanation of codes see page 46)	
WOODEN POST AND RAIL FENCE	
Three rails	7.30
Each additional rail	.89
PROOFING FENCE AGAINST RABBITS AND HARES	1.10
SAFETY OR CHILD RESTRAINT FENCING	7.05

GATE	Per 300mm of width
Timber field	6.00
Steel field (light duty)	4.35
Steel field (heavy duty)	5.25
Steel cattle yard	6.35

GATE POST	Per post 17.60

TIMBER STILES	Per stile
Single-step stile	12.90
Double-step stile	19.30

CATTLE GRID	Per grid 349.00

British Standards

British Standards cover many aspects of fencing including the manufacture and galvanising of wire, the preservation of timber and the methods of fence erection. These standards are mainly of interest to manufacturers of fencing materials and components, and to specifiers of fencing for building contracts, road schemes and so on. Work which qualifies for MAFF grant may need to comply with certain British Standards (see page 130).

For the purposes of this handbook, the main point to note is that materials purchased should comply with the relevant British Standard. In particular, pressure-treated timber should comply either with BS 913 (creosote) or BS 4072 (CCA), and wire should be manufactured to BS 4102 where appropriate, and be galvanised to BS 443. The British Standards relevant to fencing are listed below. County reference libraries should hold copies of all British Standards.

BS 443:1982	Galvanising of agricultural products
BS 913:1973	Wood preservation by creosote
BS 1485:1983	Specification for zinc coated hexagonal steel wire netting
BS 1722	Specification for fences Each part contains information on materials, construction, workmanship, size and spacing of components, use etc
Part 1:1972	Chain link fences
Part 2:1973	Woven wire fences
Part 3:1973	Strained wire fences
Part 4:1972	Cleft chestnut pale fences
Part 5:1972	Close-boarded fences including oak pale fences
Part 6:1972	Wooden palisade fences
Part 7:1972	Wooden post and rail fences
Part 8:1978	Mild steel (low carbon steel) continuous bar fences
Part 9:1979	Mild steel (low carbon steel) fences with round or square verticals, and flat posts and horizontals
Part 10:1972	Anti-intruder chain link fences
Part 11:1972	Woven wood fences
Part 12:1979	Steel palisade fences
Part 13:1978	Chain link fences for tennis court surrounds
BS 2632:1980	Specification for mains operated electric fence controllers
BS 3470:1975	Field gates and posts
BS 4008:1973	Cattle grids on private roads
BS 4072:1974	Wood preservation by CCA
BS 4102:1971	Steel wire for fences
BS 5589:1978	Code of practice for preservation of timber
BS 6167:1981	Specification for battery operated fence controllers not suitable for connection to the supply mains

BSI Registered Firms

Since 1984, there has been a scheme for fencing contractors under the British Standards Institute Registered Firms of Assessed Capability. To qualify, firms must undertake materials control procedures and keeping of records, and all fence erectors must be adequately trained. The scheme is implemented by the Quality Assurance Group of the Fencing Contractors Association (address of FCA is given on page 137).

This scheme allows specifiers of fencing to select a contractor operating a documented and independently assessed quality system. This is mainly of interest to organisations requiring large amounts of fencing work, and the scheme has the backing of the Department of Transport, the Property Services Agency, British Rail, the Royal Institution of British Architects and the Central Electricity Generating Board.

Manufacturers and Suppliers

Further details of products mentioned in the text can be obtained from the addresses listed below. This is not a complete list of all manufacturers and suppliers of fencing materials, and these firms are not recommended in preference to any others.

Fencing materials, accessories and tools are obtainable from agricultural merchants and specialist fencing suppliers. The Yellow Pages Telephone Directories list local fencing materials, manufacturers and services, and the agricultural press and agricultural advertisements in local papers will also give sources of supply. For particular items for high tensile and electric fencing, contact some of the specialist firms listed below.

Many fencing firms exhibit at county and national agricultural shows, and this is a good way of inspecting products and getting further advice.

Armstrong Addison and Co Ltd
   PO Box 24 North Dock Roker Sunderland
   SR6 0PP   0783 56012
   - creosoted and tanalised fencing and gates

The BRC Engineering Co
   Stafford ST17 4NN   0785 57777
   - Weldfence and Weldmesh wire fencing

Balfour-Westlar Ltd
   Manorside Badsey Evesham Worcestershire
   WR11 5LW   0386 832778

   Braincroft, Crieff Perthshire PH7 4JZ
                              0764 70140

   Devonshire Road Estate, Millom, Cumbria
                              0657 4572
   - specialist manufacturers and suppliers of
     high tensile fencing Hurricane high tensile
     netting special sizes made to order

Bramley and Wellesley Ltd
   Gloucester Trading Estate, Hucclecote,
   Gloucestershire GL3 4XD   0452 69613
   - Flexinet temporary electric fencing

Brian Hall Ltd
   Ashby-de-la-Zouch, Leicestershire
   LE6 5LG   0530 415151
   - tractor-mounted post drivers

British Gates and Timber Ltd
   Biddenden, Nr Ashford, Kent
   TN27 8DD   0580 291555
   - gates and fittings the 'Rambler' stile

Bryce Electric Fencing
   Morebattle, Kelso Scotland
   TD5 8AE   057 34 314
   - permanent electric fencing components

Bulldog Tools
   Clarington Forge Wigan, Lancashire
   WN1 3DD
   - garden, agricultural and contractors tools

Burton McCall Industrial Ltd
   Samuel Street, Leicester
   LE1 1RU   0533 538781
   - distributors of Felco wire cutters

CeKa
   34 Slough Road, Datchet, Berkshire
   - fencing pliers

Chatsworth Forestry
   Calton Lees, Beeley, Matlock, Derbyshire
   DE4 2NX
   - suppliers and manufacturers of agricultural
     fencing

Clovis Lande Associates Ltd
   104 Branbridges Road, East Peckham,
   Tonbridge, Kent TN12 5HH   0622 872581
   - Nicofence windbreak material

Curnow
   Unit 14, Ddole Road Industrial Estate,
   Llandrindod Wells, Powys
   LD1 6DF   0597 4626
   - belts and holsters to carry fencing tools

Downland Sheep Services
   North Sydmonton Farm, North Sydmonton,
   Newbury, Berkshire
                              063 523 613
   - permanent and temporary electric fencing

Drivall Ltd
   Narrow Lane, Hurst Green, Halesowen,
   West Midlands B62 9PA   021 421 7007
   - specialist suppliers of fencing tools and
     materials including post drivers shuv-
     holers Hayes and Monkey wire strainers,
     tension gauges wire tying tools, straining
     boards, wire PEL electric fence systems

Estate Wire Ltd
   Birley Vale Close, Sheffield
   S12 2DB   0742 392601
   - Triple Life stock netting of Corzal wire

Fairmile Fencing,
   Lilleshall Engineering Ltd, St Georges,
   Telford, Shropshire
   TF2 9DB   0952 613120
   - security, protective and safety fencing

M J Farthing Ltd
   2 Summers Road, Farncombe, Godalming,
   Surrey GU7 3BB
   - pneumatic post driver for tractor or
     petrol engine and compressor

R J Fleming Developments
   1 Cosgrove Road, Old Stratford, Milton Keynes
   MK19 6AG   0908 563247
   - mechanical post hole augers

Forest Fencing Ltd
   Stanford Court, Stanford Bridge, Nr Worcester
   WR6 6SR   088 65 451
   - panel, paling and post and rail fencing, gates
     and fencing tools and accessories

Gallagher Agricultural Ltd
   Curriers Close, Canley, Coventry
   CV4 8AW   ·   0203 470141
   - permanent and temporary electric fencing
     systems, components and accessories,
     Insultimber

'Goodman Croggon Ltd
   Head Office, 234-236 Broomhill Road, Bristol
   BS4 5RG   0272 770721
   - wholesale distributors throughout England,
     Scotland and Wales of a wide range of
     fencing materials and tools

Hickson's Timber Products Ltd
   Castleford, West Yorkshire
   WF10 2JT   0977 556565
   - manufacturers of Tanalith timber preservative

Holmes (Wragby) Ltd,
   Wragby, Lincoln   0673 858304
   - post and rail, panel fencing, gates

Hunter-Wilson and Partners Ltd
   Kilkerran Station, Maybole, Ayrshire
   KA19 8LS   046 581 440
   - specialist suppliers of fencing tools,
     materials and accessories, including wire
     dispensers, ratchet winders and high tensile
     spring steel wire

ICI Linear Composites Ltd
   Hookstone Road, Harrogate, North Yorkshire
   HG2 8QN   0423 69021
   - manufacturers of Paraweb

Jacksons Fencing
   Stowting Common, Nr Ashford, Kent
   TN25 6BN   023 375 393

   New Rock, Chilcompton, Nr Bath, Somerset
   BA3 4JE   0761 232666

   Wrexham Road, Belgrave, Chester
   CH4 9ES   0244 674804

   Ramshawfield, Bardon Mill, Hexham
   Northumberland NE47 7EZ   049 84 555
   - suppliers of a wide range of fencing materials,
     tools and accessories, including stakes,
     post and rail, hurdles, gates, cattle grids,
     wire, stock netting, chain link, chestnut
     paling. Delivery service in England, Wales
     and Southern Scotland

Larch-Lap Ltd
   PO Box 17, Lichfield Street,
   Stourport-on-Severn, Worcestershire
   DY13 9ES   029 93 3232
   - panel fencing

Livestock Fencing Ltd
   PO Box 73, Gloucester
   GL3 4AF   0452 64573
   - temporary electric fencing

M & M Timber Co Ltd
   Hunt House Sawmills, Clows Top,
   Nr Kidderminster, Worcestershire
   DY14 9HY   029 922 611
   - Uniposts, round timber post and rail

MMG Erosion Control Systems
   Waterloo House, King's Lynn, Norfolk
   PE30 1PA   0553 4423
   - Enkamat and N33 synthetic fabrics

Malcolm Ogilvie and Co Ltd
   Constable Works, Dundee DD3 6NL
   - Wyretex synthetic fabric

A Massel and Co Ltd
   Woodlands, Hazel Grove, Hindhead, Surrey
   GU26 6BJ   042 873 5069
   - anchor discs, manual post-hole augers,
     wire dispensers, tie-guns

Metpost Ltd
   Mardy Road Cardiff
   CF3 8EQ   0222 777877
   - Metpost products for erecting fence posts

Netlon Ltd
   Kelly Street Blackburn
   BB2 4PJ   0254 62431
   - Tensar netting

Nortene
   David House, 41-46 High Street, South Norwood
   London SE25 6HJ   01 653 6544
   - plastic-covered chain link, plastic mesh
     and windbreak material

Opico Ltd
   South Road, Bourne, Lincolnshire
   PE10 9LG   0778 421111
   - tractor-mounted post hole augers

Preformed Line Products Ltd
   East Portway Andover Hampshire
   SP10 3LH   0264 66234
   - manufacturer of Preformed fence fittings
     (spiral fence connectors lashing rods),
     available from specialist fencing suppliers

Pullmaflex UK Ltd
   Heol Las Ammanford Dyfed
   SA18 3ED   0269 2301
   - specialist suppliers of tools and materials
     for strained wire fencing

Rentokil Ltd
Timber Preserving Division, Felcourt, East
Grinstead, Sussex RH19 2JY 0342 833022
- manufacturers of timber preservatives,
including the Celcure range, and SupaTimba

H Ridley and Sons
Chilbolton Down, Stockbridge, Hants
SO20 6BU   0264 810665
- Ridley Rappa for handling temporary
electric fencing, electric rabbit fencing

J & H Rosenheim and Co Ltd
Glenford Works, Quay Road, Rutherglen,
Glasgow G73 1RN   041 647 5358/9
- Gerrard fasteners

Rutland Electric Fencing Co
Pillings Road Industrial Estate, Oakham,
Leicestershire   0572 2558
- permanent and temporary electric
fencing systems and components

Sparkford Sawmills Ltd
Sparkford, Yeovil, Somerset
BA22 7LH   0963 40414
- wooden gates

Spear and Jackson
St Paul s Road, Wednesbury, West Midlands
WS10 9RA   021 556 1255
- garden agricultural and contractors tools

Steelway-Fensecure
Queensgate Works, Bilston Road, Wolverhampton
West Midlands WV2 2NJ   0902 51733
- security and safety fencing, rails and gates

Sudbury Garden Products
8 Fore Street, Taunton, Somerset
0823 54615
- Chaperone rabbit and deer repellent

Thistle Distributors Ltd
Roddinglaw Works, Roddinglaw, Edinburgh
EH12 9DB   031 333 1804
- Durapost synthetic posts

Timberlink Ltd
Adderley Road, Market Drayton, Shropshire
TF9 3AJ
- sawn and roundwood fencing

Twil Group Marketing Ltd
PO Box 119, Shepcote Lane, Sheffield
S9 1TY   0742 443388
- Sentinel range of wire fencing products

Verus Instruments Ltd
Ash House, Church Lane, Bledlow Ridge,
High Wycombe, Bucks   HP14 4AZ
- timber moisture meters

Organisations

Conservation and Amenity

Botanical Society of the British Isles
c/o Department of Botany, British Museum
(Natural History), Cromwell Rd, London SW7

British Ecological Society
Burlington House, Piccadilly. London W1V 0LQ

British Herpetological Society
c/o Zoological Society of London,
Regents Park, London NW1 4RY

British Trust for Conservation Volunteers
Headquarters: 36 St Mary's Street.
Wallingford, Oxfordshire
OX10 0EU   0491 39766

North East: Springwell Conservation Centre
Springwell Road. Wrekenton, Gateshead,
Tyne & Wear NE9 7AD   091 482 0111

North West: 40 Cannon Street, Preston.
Lancs PR1 3NT   0772 50286

Yorkshire and Humberside: Conservation
Volunteers Training Centre Balby Road
Balby. Doncaster DH4 0RH 0302 859522

East Midlands: Conservation Volunteers
Training Centre. Old Village School,
Chestnut Grove. Burton Joyce. Nottingham
                                0602 313316

West Midlands: Conservation Centre,
Firsby Road. Quinton, Birmingham
                                021-471 2558

Wales: The Conservation Centre,
Forest Farm Road, Whitchurch, Cardiff
                                0222 626660

East Anglia: Bayfordbury Estate, Hertford,
Herts SG13 8LD   0992 53067

Thames and Chilterns: 36 St Mary's Street,
Wallingford, Oxfordshire
OX10 0EU   0491 39766

South West: The Old Estate Yard.
Newton St Loe. Bath, Avon   02217 2856

London: 2 Mandela Street, Camden Town.
London NW1   01-388 3946

South: Hatchlands. East Clandon, Guildford,
Surrey GU4 7RT   0483 223294

Northern Ireland: The Pavilion, Cherryvale
Park, Ravenhill Road, Belfast BT6 0BZ
                                0232 645169

British Trust for Ornithology
Beech Grove, Tring, Hertfordshire
HP23 5NR   044 282 3401

Civic Trust
17 Carlton House Terrace, London
SW1Y 5AW   01-930 0914

Conservation Society
12a Guildford Street. Chertsey, Surrey
JT16 9BQ   093 286 0975

Council for Environmental Conservation (CoEnCo)
Zoological Gardens, Regents Park, London
NW1   01-722 7111

Council for Environmental Education
School of Education, University of Reading
London Road. Reading
RG1 5AQ   0734 875324

Council for National Parks
4 Hobart Place, London
SW1W 0HY   01-235 0901

Council for the Protection of Rural England
4 Hobart Place, London
SW1W 0HY   01-235 9481

Council for the Protection of Rural Wales
31 High Street, Welshpool Powys
SY21 7JP   0938 2525

Countryside Commission
John Dower House. Crescent Place,
Cheltenham. Gloucestershire
GL50 3RA   0242 521381

Countryside Commission for Scotland
Battleby Redgorton. Perthshire
PH1 3EW   0738 27921

Dartington Institute
Central Office. Shinners Bridge, Dartington
Totnes. Devon PQ9 6JE   0803 862271

Field Studies Council
62 Wilson Street, London
EC2A 2BU   01-247 4651

Friends of the Earth
377 City Road, London
EC1V 1NA   01-837 0731

The Game Conservancy
Burgate Manor Fordingbridge, Hampshire
SP6 1EF   0425 52381

Institute of Terrestrial Ecology
66 Hills Road, Cambridge
CB2 1LA   0223 69745

Landscape Institute
12 Carlton House Terrace, London
SW1Y 5AH   01-839 4044

Mammal Society of the British Isles
Harvest House, 62 London Road. Reading
Berkshire   0734 861345

Ministry of Development, Government of
Northern Ireland: Conservation Branch
Parliament Buildings. Stormont,
Belfast BT4 3SS

National Association for Environmental Education
    Mr P D Neal, General Secretary, 20 Knighton
    Drive, Four Oaks, Sutton Coldfield,
    West Midlands B74 4QP

The National Trust
    36 Queen Anne's Gate, London SW1H 9AS
                                    01-222 9251

National Trust for Scotland
    5 Charlotte Square Edingburgh
    EH2 4DU   031-225 5922

Nature Conservancy Council (Great Britain
headquarters and headquarters for England)
    Northminster House, Peterborough
    PE1 1UA   0733 40345

Nature Conservancy Council (headquarters for
Scotland)
    12 Hope Terrace, Edinburgh
    EH9 2AS   031-447 4784

Nature Conservancy Council (headquarters for
Wales)
    Plas Penrhos, Penrhos Road, Bangor,
    Gwynedd
    LL57 2LQ   0248 355141

The Open Spaces Society
    25a Bell Street, Henley on Thames, Oxon
    RG9 2BA   0491 573535

The Ramblers' Association
    1/5 Wandsworth Road, London
    SW8 2LJ   01-582 6826

Royal Society for Nature Conservation
    The Green, Nettleham, Lincoln
    LN2 2NR   0522 752326

Royal Society for the Protection of Birds
    The Lodge, Sandy, Bedfordshire
    SG19 2DL   0767 80551

Scottish Conservation Projects Trust
    70 Main Street, Doune, Perthshire
    FK16 6BW   0786 841479

Scottish Rights of Way Society
    28 Rutland Square, Edinburgh EH1 2BW

Scottish Wildlife Trust
    25 Johnston Terrace, Edinburgh
    EH1 2NH   031-226 4602

Town and Country Planning Association
    17 Carlton House Terrace, London
    SW1Y 5AS   01-930 8903

The Tree Council
    Agriculture House, Knightsbridge, London
    SW1X 7NJ   01-235 8854

Woodland Trust
    Westgate, Grantham, Lincolnshire
                                    0476 74297

World Wildlife Fund
    Panda House, 11-13 Ockford Road, Godalming,
    Surrey GU7 1QU   048 68 20551

Agriculture, Forestry and Fencing

The Arboricultural Association
    Ampfield House, Romsey, Hants
                                    0794 68717

Agricultural Training Board
    32-34 Beckenham Road, Beckenham, Kent
    BR3 4PB   01-650 4890

British Deer Farmers Association
    Hon Secretary M. Crawford, Cluanie,
    Teanassie, By Beauly, Inverness-shire

British Goat Society
    Lion House, Rougham, near Bury St Edmunds,
    Suffolk IP30 9LJ   0359 70351

British Wood Preserving Association
    Premier House, 150 Southampton Row,
    London WC1B 5AL   01-837 8217

Cement and Concrete Association
    Wexham Springs, Slough,
    SL3 6PL   02816 2727

Country Landowners' Association
    16 Belgrave Square, London
    SW1X 8PQ   01-235 0511

Department of Agriculture and Fisheries for
Scotland
    Chesser House, 500 Gorgie Road, Edinburgh
    EG11 3AW   031-443 4020

Department of Agriculture - Northern Ireland
    Dundonald House, Upper Newtownards Road
    Belfast BT4 3SB   0232 650111

Farmers' Union of Wales
    Llys Amaeth Queen's Square, Aberystwyth
                                    0970 612755

Farming and Wildlife Advisory Group
    The Lodge, Sandy, Bedfordshire
    SG19 2DL   0767 80551

Fencing Contractors' Association
    St John's House, 23 St John's Road, Watford
    WD1 1PY   0923 27236

Forestry Commission
    213 Corstorphine Road, Edinburgh
    EH12 7AT   031-334 0303

Forestry Safety Council
    213 Corstorphine Road, Edinburgh
    EH12 7AT

Forestry Training Council
  Room 413, 231 Corstorphine Road, Edinburgh
  EH12 7AT   031-334 8083

Grassland Research Institute
  Hurley, Maidenhead, Berks.
  SL6 5LR   062 882 3631

Hide and Allied Trades Improvement Society
  34B St Mary Street, Bridgwater, Somerset
  TA6 3LY   0278 455026

Hill Farming Research Organisation
  Bush Estate, Penicuik, Midlothian
  EH26 0PY   031-445 3401

Ministry of Agriculture, Fisheries and Food
  Whitehall Place, London
  SW1A 2HH   01-233 3000

Ministry of Agriculture, Fisheries and Food
(Publications)
  Lion House, Willowburn Trading Estate,
  Alnwick, Northumberland
  NE66 2PF

National Farmers' Union
  Agriculture House, 25-31 Knightsbridge,
  London SW1X 7NJ   01-235 5077

National Farmers' Union of Scotland
  17 Grosvenor Crescent, Edinburgh,
  EH12 5EN   031-337 4333

National Federation of Young Farmers' Clubs
  YFC Centre, National Agricultural Centre,
  Kenilworth CV8 2LG   0203 56131

Royal Agricultural Society of England
  National Agricultural Centre, Stoneleigh,
  Kenilworth CV8 2LG   0203 555100

Royal Society for the Prevention of Accidents
  Agricultural Adviser, Cannon House,
  The Priory, Queensway, Birmingham
  B4 6BS   021-233 2461

The Scottish Landowners' Federation
  18 Abercromby Place, Edinburgh
  EH3 6TY   031-556 4466

Timber Research and Development Association
  Stocking Lane, Hughendon Valley,
  High Wycombe HP14 4ND   024 024 3091

Welsh Office Agriculture Department
  Crown Offices Cathays Park, Cardiff
  CF1 3NQ   0222 825111

Bibliography

This list includes works referred to in the text, and others relevant to the subject of fencing.

Agate, Elizabeth (1983) — Footpaths British Trust for Conservation Volunteers

Agricultural Training Board — Erecting Temporary Sheep Fencing (Post and netting) Trainee Guide S.1.B.13

Erecting Temporary Sheep Fencing (Electric netting) Trainee Guide S.1.B.14

Adult Cattle - Electric Fencing Trainee Guide MPB.2.B.4

Aldridge, Trevor M (1982) — Boundaries, Walls and Fences Oyez Longman A legal guide

Armstrong, R H Banks, C H and Gill, M P (1981) — A Guide to Electric Fencing Hill Farming Research Organisation,

Brooks, A (1975) — Hedging British Trust for Conservation Volunteers

Brooks, A (1979) — Coastlands British Trust for Conservation Volunteers

Countryside Commission for Scotland — Battleby Display Centre Information Sheets and Catalogue CCS Information Sheets on strained wire, post and rail panel fencing, gates and stiles

Forestry Safety Council (1978) — Fencing Forestry Industry Safety Guide Leaflet FSC 32

Gaisford, Michael — Wide scope for better fencing Article in Farmers Weekly 4th November 1977

Ministry of Agriculture, Fisheries and Food — Wire fences for farms Leaflet 711 (1981)

Gates for farms Leaflet 712 (1982)

Post and rail and other farm fences Leaflet 713 (1981)

Standard Costs Parts 1 and 2

Monmouthshire County Council (1974) — Fences in the Countryside - a design guide

New Zealand Ministry of Agriculture, Fisheries and Food — AgLink: Farm Production and Practice - Fencing Detailed leaflets on all aspects of strained wire and electric fencing. Available mail order from AgLink, MAFF, Private Bag, Wellington, New Zealand.

Pepper, H W, Rowe, J J and Tee, L A (1985) — Individual Tree Protection Forestry Commission Arboricultural Leaflet 10

Pepper, H W and Tee, L A (revised 1985) — Forest Fencing Forestry Commission Record 80

Pringle, R T — Farm fencing - a review Article in Agricultural Engineer, Spring 1984

Rowe, Judith J (1976) — Badger Gates Forestry Commission leaflet 68

Sandys-Winsch, Godfrey (1984) — Animal Law Shaw and Sons

The Scottish Agricultural Colleges (1979) — Erecting High Tensile Fencing Publication no 46 Available from The East of Scotland College of Agriculture, West Mains Road, Edinburgh.

Manufacturers' literature

The following manufacturers produce literature which contains useful information on the subject of fencing, as well as describing their products. Their addresses are pages 133-135. Some of the current leaflets and booklets are listed below.

British Gates and Timber Ltd — Gates and Fittings

Bryce Electric Fencing — Warning - Bryce permanent electric fence

Drivall Ltd — Hayes Wire Strainers The new Drivall range

Gallagher Agricultural Ltd — Power Fencing Manual

Goodman Croggon — Catalogue

Hunter Wilson and Partners Ltd — Recommended Accessories and Tools

Jacksons Fencing — The Good Fencing Guide

TWIL Group Marketing Ltd — Sentinel Fencing Advisory Service

Periodicals

Articles on fencing occur from time to time in the agricultural press. A free publication called 'Fencing News, the journal of the fencing industry, is mailed to manufacturers, contractors and specifiers of fencing. It is published six times a year by Grendon Publications Ltd. Details from 19 Lincoln Croft, Shenstone, Lichfield, Staffs WS12 0ND.

Index